DELEUZE AND GUATTARI

Theory, Culture & Society

Theory, Culture & Society caters for the resurgence of interest in culture within contemporary social science and the humanities. Building on the heritage of classical social theory, the book series examines ways in which this tradition has been reshaped by a new generation of theorists. It will also publish theoretically informed analyses of everyday life, popular culture, and new intellectual movements.

EDITOR: Mike Featherstone, *Nottingham Trent University*

SERIES EDITORIAL BOARD
Roy Boyne, *University of Durham*
Mike Hepworth, *University of Aberdeen*
Scott Lash, *Lancaster University*
Roland Robertson, *University of Pittsburgh*
Bryan S. Turner, *Deakin University*

THE TCS CENTRE
The Theory, Culture & Society book series, the journals *Theory, Culture & Society* and *Body & Society*, and related conference, seminar and postgraduate programmes operate from the TCS Centre at Nottingham Trent University. For further details of the TCS Centre's activities please contact:

Centre Administrator, The TCS Centre, Room 175, Faculty of Humanities, Nottingham Trent University, Clifton Lane, Nottingham NG11 8NS, UK.
e-mail: tcs@ntu.ac.uk

Recent volumes include:

The Time of the Tribes
The Decline of Individualism in Mass Society
Michel Maffesoli

Risk, Environment and Modernity
Towards a New Ecology
edited by Scott Lash, Bronislaw Szerszynski and Brian Wynne

For Weber
Essays on the Sociology of Fate
Bryan S. Turner

Cyberspace/Cyberbodies/Cyberpunk
Cultures of Technological Embodiment
edited by Mike Featherstone and Roger Burrows

Spatial Formations
Nigel Thrift

The Social Construction of Nature
Klaus Eder

Pierre Bourdieu and Cultural Theory
Critical Investigations
Bridget Fowler

DELEUZE AND GUATTARI

An Introduction to the Politics of Desire

Philip Goodchild

SAGE Publications
London • Thousand Oaks • New Delhi

First published 1996

Published in association with *Theory, Culture & Society*,
Nottingham Trent University

 SAGE Publications Ltd
6 Bonhill Street
London EC2A 4PU

SAGE Publications Inc
2455 Teller Road
Thousand Oaks, California 91320

SAGE Publications India Pvt Ltd
32, M-Block Market
Greater Kailash – I
New Delhi 110 048

British Library Cataloguing in Publication data

A catalogue record for this book is available
from the British Library

ISBN 0 8039 7600 3
ISBN 0 8039 7601 1 (pbk)

Library of Congress catalog card number 96-070411

Typeset by Photoprint, Torquay, Devon
Printed in Great Britain by The Cromwell Press Ltd,
Broughton Gifford, Melksham, Wiltshire

Contents

Preface

I hesitate before signing my name to this work. This is not because of some general critique of the role of an author (Foucault, 1986b), nor because of my shame and embarrassment at the book's clear inadequacies. It is rather because in this book I report what I have heard, rather than what I have read or thought. This book is therefore written in several different voices, although it is not always clear which one is speaking. Those who hallucinate unindividuated voices may report the speech they hear as indirect discourse: 'It was said that . . .' One stumbles over questions of the truth, value, authenticity, or authority of such a discourse. For whenever I attempted to write in my own voice – from the position of a majoritarian subject, a self-appointed 'authority' on Deleuze and Guattari, speaking to a majoritarian readership – the meaning and force of their thought evaporated in my representations. The scholarly apparatus of references to the primary texts, along with other rhetorical strategies, may endow this book with an aura of authority and authenticity, but take care not to be fooled. I imagine this book becoming a disembodied voice haunting those who read and study the combined work of Gilles Deleuze and Félix Guattari – if you let it, if you read it, if it has any power. It places less emphasis on summarizing and repeating what Deleuze and Guattari have written than on enunciating the implicit presuppositions that whisper on the margins of their texts; page references merely locate the whispers. How would one evaluate such a discourse? What use would one make of it?

Certainly, I have busied myself with the selection and ordering of this discourse. The aim was to produce a book that functions as a transformer – converting the high potentials and intensities of Deleuze and Guattari's work into a safe and manageable form where they might begin to be of use to many who would otherwise find them inaccessible. It focuses mainly on their cooperative publications – the two volumes of *Capitalism and Schizophrenia*: *Anti-Oedipus* (first published in French in 1972; cited here as translation published in 1984) and *A Thousand Plateaus* (first published 1980; translation 1988), as well as *What is Philosophy?* (first published 1991; translation 1994). The book aims to relay Deleuze and Guattari's social and philosophical thought to an English-speaking readership who might lack many of the conceptual landmarks and points of reference that Deleuze and Guattari orientate themselves on before putting such points to flight. Most of the intensity of their thought has been annihilated here by a flawed mode of expression, so as to accentuate a few motifs that recur as refrains – for this I make no apologies, but merely refer readers back to the primary texts. The potential of Deleuze and Guattari's thought should be evaluated by their own texts, not mine – but one must take care that it is their own thought that is evaluated rather than one of the many caricatures or simulacra that abound. This book intends to be self-effacing, therefore, but only on condition that it makes a productive return to the primary texts possible.

Several different voices speak in this text – and each reader will find some more accessible than others. In order to show the forces and philosophical strategies at work behind the main collaborative texts, attention has been paid to Deleuze's early philosophical work and development. The reader will be introduced to the underlying problems that motivate Deleuze's thought, and the reasons why certain theoretical strategies are adopted – this is undertaken in *Part I: Knowledge*. In order to indicate some of the consequences for social and cultural theory of the main collaborative texts, some attention has been paid to Guattari's later works, while also drawing out that which is implicit in the combined work – this is mainly undertaken in *Part III: Liberation of Desire*. *Part II: Power* includes an exposition of the differing discussions of the workings of power in society from *Anti-Oedipus* and *A Thousand Plateaus*, and contrasts the theoretical moves made by Deleuze and Guattari with those of their contemporaries. In addition, the text is interrupted at various points by voices that take off from Deleuze and Guattari's thought, along lines of flight, by considering several problems of a philosophical nature. These shed some light on different aspects of the text, but also gain a consistency when considered together.

Since Deleuze and Guattari's other works are taken to be the best commentaries on *Capitalism and Schizophrenia*, little discussion of the secondary literature, and the debates on how Deleuze and Guattari's thought is to be interpreted and evaluated, has been included. This is because interpretation and evaluation are not modes of thought adopted by Deleuze and Guattari. All too often, their statements and concepts have been translated into and represented within a heterogeneous mode of discourse by eminent readers who presume that such a process constitutes 'comprehension'; the resulting shadows and simulacra are then admonished for their clear theoretical and moral inadequacies. This is all well and good, but the conscientious student of Deleuze and Guattari should not assume that such an activity constitutes a proper critical assessment of the theoretical content of their texts. The sense and function of Deleuze and Guattari's thought only emerges when considered in relation to the problems and processes that are at work in it; it is such an explicitly philosophical reading that has been attempted here. Another frequent practice in secondary literature is to follow one or more lines of experimentation within Deleuze and Guattari's thought, but fail to fold these lines back upon each other, to let lines affect and augment each other, understanding and changing each other from their separate perspectives: to fail to give the rhizome consistency, emphasizing difference without repetition. This is a failure of humour: one may understand the literal sense of the texts, but fail to produce a virtual, abstract, and imperceptible sense. Of greater significance than what Deleuze and Guattari say is what they actually do on the 'outside' of their own thought.

This book emerged from chance encounters with Scott Lash in the local supermarket. I am grateful to him for his initiative and encouragement. The work was funded by a research grant from the Department of Religious Studies and Social Ethics at the University College of St Martin, Lancaster. I am particularly grateful for two publisher's readers' reports that forced me to shed just a little of my complacency and think a bit harder, as well as for support from Chris and Robert Rojek. David Herbert contributed long lunch-time conversations. Dan Welch and Drew Hemment explored some of the same problems. Mariam Fraser contributed in many ways throughout the time of writing.

Introduction: Knowledge, Power, Desire

Deleuze and Guattari's 'philosophy of desire', as expressed in their co-authored works, especially *Anti-Oedipus* and *A Thousand Plateaus*, has often been associated with a spirit of irreverence, indulgence, gaiety, transgression, liberation, and destruction of the past. One was given permission to throw out all the old models, structures, traditions, values, and practices that human thought had struggled for so long to acquire; one was given freedom to play and experiment with thought as far as one's fancy and imagination was able to lead one. The labours of critique and pretensions to privileged insight of the militant social theorist were abandoned at the same time as the values and traditions of the conservative intellectual. Play became the sole agent of an adolescent, postmodern revolution. Fortunately, this misapprehension of the import of Deleuze and Guattari's work was self-defeating: players have no need to remember the founders of games – they can invent new rules and moves, or go and play elsewhere; Deleuze and Guattari are easily forgotten. The field is then cleared for more conscientious readings.

The works of Gilles Deleuze (1925–95), professor of philosophy at Université de Paris VIII, are not a light read. His works on the history of philosophy, being commentaries on Hume, Bergson, Nietzsche, Kant, Spinoza, Leibniz, and Foucault, are distinguished by their sobriety, economy of expression, and depth of insight. His aesthetic commentaries, on Proust, Sacher-Masoch, Kafka, Francis Bacon, and the cinema, as well as many shorter essays, are distinguished by the philosophical rigour and discipline they apply to their subject. In addition to these, the main works of Deleuze's own philosophy are *Difference and Repetition* (first published 1968) and *The Logic of Sense* (first published 1969), as well as the cooperative work with Guattari. One finds little evidence of free play here; indeed, Deleuze has said that he has never had any time for the 'end of philosophy', or the 'overcoming of metaphysics', the radical slogans of his generation (Deleuze and Guattari, 1994: 14). Deleuze lived a quiet and retiring life as a prolific author, and often suffered from ill health. Many years of a serious respiratory illness, including a tracheotomy and being 'chained up like a dog' to oxygen cylinders, led to his leaping from the window of his Paris apartment in November 1995.

The life and work of Félix Guattari (1930–92) was largely characterized by serious practical and political engagement: he trained in psychoanalysis for seven years under Jacques Lacan; he worked in a psychiatric establishment, La Borde Clinique, from 1953 until his heart attack in 1992, developing a collective analysis by both patients and staff of the power-relations at work in society as a whole, and forming and participating in a number of left-wing and ecological groups which were critical of the mainstream leftist movement. These two figures – a Parisian professor of philosophy, working in the fields of aesthetics and the history of philosophy, and a psychotherapist and political activist – were not celebrants of postmodern playfulness. Both were scornful of the notion of 'postmodernity'. At the root of Guattari's critique of postmodernism is the hope that society can still be transformed by collective action (Guattari, 1989a).

This book will argue that at the heart of Deleuze and Guattari's combined thought lies an exploration of the possibilities of human relation, and their role in the reconstruction of subjectivity, society, and environment. This problem circumvents the sterile dialectical conflicts between individual and society, freedom and authority, personal gain and the common good, nature and artifice. The liberation that Deleuze and Guattari's thought brings is less a liberation from social expectations than a liberation to enter into social relations. The obstacle that prevents social relations from developing is always the interest of some third party in the relation: conventions, values, expectations, economic structures, and political entities, whether real or imaginary, provide a script for social agents who merely play out the roles. For example, enemy soldiers confronting each other across a battlefield act out the contest that they are required to fight by distant political and economic entities, supported by nationalist, racist, or tribalist sentiments; their social relation is limited to an exchange of bullets, instead broadening out to become an exchange of jokes, songs, cigarettes, and memories. Revolution is not a matter of tearing up the script, forgetting or destroying external political and economic institutions, as well as internal conventions and expectations, for one is then left with no relation at all. Instead, revolution occurs through making additions to the script, bringing in unexpected amendments by borrowing strategies from elsewhere. The soldier who brandishes a pack of cards instead of a gun indicates possibilities for a different development of the plot. Deleuze and Guattari's writing is itself of a similar nature: instead of directly throwing aside theoretical norms, it offers a whole range of digressions and alternatives that carry thought elsewhere, shattering the coherence of hegemonic discourses. Liberation occurs through addition.

A second image of Deleuze and Guattari's theoretical endeavour is nomadism. There are no longer any true or false ideas, there are just ideas. There is no longer any ultimate goal or direction, but merely a wandering along a multiplicity of lines of flight that lead away from centres of power. Arborescent models of structured thought and activity are replaced by an exploratory rhizome. Any move of thought or social relation is desirable, so long as it does not lead back into an old or new convention, obligation, or institution. This image of thought is closely related to the cultural milieu of Integrated Global Capitalism (as Guattari prefers to call it in his later works), for one of the most frequent operations of capital is to create temporary relations between workers and sites of production that irrevocably separate workers from their previous environment. Everything becomes mobile: images, consumer products, and people are cut off from their conditions of production and circulate around the globe, resting in juxtaposition with others of entirely different origins, before attaining an ultimate egalitarian status in the garbage dump, old age or oblivion. Deleuze and Guattari call this kind of movement *deterritorialization*. Their thought differs from the operations of capital insofar as it makes deterritorialization an end in itself instead of merely a means for the increase of capital.

Such an image of their thought has two major problems. Firstly, ultimate deterritorialization clearly produces complete garbage, the scrambling of all possibilities of meaning, use, and value. Secondly, it is inconsistent with itself: this image of thought holds up movement, change, chance, difference, flight, and nomadism as unchanging values. Perhaps it is better to be a paranoid slave than a schizophrenic nomad. If, however, one re-produces such an image in its own terms, then nomadism relativizes itself, wanders away from itself, allowing something else to be produced. Such a new image of thought is constructed in practice.

This book will also argue that this second image of Deleuze and Guattari's thought is little more than a mask, and, at best, a strategic move that can be superseded. Deterritorialization and nomadism are not ends in themselves for Deleuze and Guattari; instead, they wish to intensify social relations. They desire to construct a social space where immanent relations can be produced. Such immanent relations, instead of acting out roles given to them by some real or imaginary third party in the role of a transcendent scriptwriter, are capable of shaping, affecting, and changing any mediating factors just as easily as these can shape the relations, as if the script could also affect the scriptwriter. The social space does not pre-exist the relations that are formed in it; indeed, the space is only constructed by drawing the lines that form immanent relations.

Deleuze and Guattari can only make this social space available by actively constructing immanent relations themselves. Such immanent relations have at least three inseparable elements. Firstly, an intensification of relation is an increase in its number of dimensions, connections, and parts. As many connections as possible have to be established: production is no longer enclosed within a factory, but gains its strength from the surrounding milieu in whatever way it can, whether it draws on the environment, weather, meanings, or emotions that surround it. Everything is brought together; in this way, Deleuze and Guattari's thought resembles a garbage tip. *Multiplicity*, embracing heterogeneous terms, is the first element of the immanent relation. Yet intensity will not be produced by a group of sterile objects lying alongside each other. Secondly, they need to interact and affect each other – they need to acquire *consistency*. Something must happen, and something must be produced. This involves extracting terms from their social and cultural contexts that render them sterile and inactive, and assembling them into a constructive *machine* that is capable of producing something. Then, insofar as production does not repeat predetermined processes, the machine is singular and its product is entirely new. This product can then react back upon and affect its conditions of production, becoming a component of further machines. Hence immanent, machinic relations are created, produced by their own process at the same time as emitting a product. Creation is the second element of immanent relations. Thirdly, such processes must have a tendency to come into existence, a force of actualization that drives them. *Desire*, a concept deterritorialized from adult sexuality while not losing its erotic character, becomes applicable in any context or relation: it is a spontaneous emergence that generates relationship through a synthesis of multiplicities, the third element of the immanent relation. Desire is the machinic relation itself, in respect of both its power of coming into existence and the specific multiplicity to which it gives a consistency.

Multiplicity, creation, and desire are the principal elements of the social unconscious for Deleuze and Guattari; they are understood in terms of concepts such as 'deterritorialization' (travelling in foreign areas), 'intensity' (vibrancy and vitality), 'machine' (productive assemblage of components), 'consistency' (hanging out together), 'singularity' (unique and remarkable, or limit of a process), 'actuality' (concrete presence), 'virtuality' (real potential that is imperceptible in itself), and 'immanence' (presence alongside, ability to be affected). The three principal concepts are inseparable, and can only be grasped intuitively all together. These elements of a social unconscious do not have any kind of metaphysical pre-existence, as if they were reservoirs of potential energy to which one could gain access; they have to be multiplied, created, desired. Hence critical and destructive aspects of theory, aimed primarily at unblocking potential, are of little use by themselves. Deleuze and Guattari's 'revolution of desire' is not simply a matter of removing obstacles to human freedom, and celebrating the anarchy that results. Furthermore, these elements do not have a metaphysical ubiquity, as if they were present in all events and social situations. Interpretive aspects of theory, designed to extract the best meanings from social events and cultural products, are also of little use in themselves. Hence the 'revolution of desire' is not merely a matter of emphasizing differences, changes, and wanderings within understandings of society.

Deleuze and Guattari aim to make multiplicity, creation, and desire present in society. The theorist becomes an athlete of desire, aiming to include as much multiplicity and creation as possible in the work; the theoretical work then becomes a product capable of lying alongside other products, affecting them, interacting with them, leading off on new trails. Theory relates to society in and through desire. This accounts for the strange status of knowledge in Deleuze and Guattari's work. They do not seek an encyclopedic knowledge of the processes present in all situations and events, from a universal, dispassionate perspective, according to which one could take practical decisions leading to chosen ends. Nor do they seek a critical knowledge of social processes from a moral and superior perspective, so that a programme of transformation towards a better society can be ventured. Knowledge is no longer a question of being able to repeat the main points of as many books as possible in a library, nor is it a question of being able to criticize their weaknesses and failings; knowledge is more like the capacity to direct oneself, through encounters with others, towards the most interesting and profound books in that library. Only through this knowledge can one awaken desire.

Given that desire is a plane of immanent relations, then it is shaped by the actual relations, conventions, and meanings that exist in society. Similarly, all knowledge is shaped by the social formations in which it is given. The set of immanent relations that compose a given social formation actually determine the kinds of things of which one can be conscious at any particular moment. For this reason, desire is the social unconscious: it constructs and conditions consciousness, so that images are merely products of the social relations in which one is immersed. This insight leads to an encounter between a transcendental philosophy, concerned with the conditions of production of thought, a social theory, concerned with the immanent relations that compose society, and a politics of desire, concerned with the transformation of society through a transformation of its social unconscious. The politics of desire is the sole purpose of Deleuze and Guattari's thought; the social unconscious is its sole field of inquiry.

If desire naturally seeks multiplicity and creation, the problem then arises of how social formations come about that prevent desire's own autoproduction. Deleuze and Guattari separate instinct, need, want, and interest, which are produced with the appearance of having a fixed status and metaphysical pre-existence in certain social arrangements, from desire. The former are real, but they are a product of a certain machinic social arrangement; desire, by contrast, is the arrangement itself. There is no reason to suppose that needs and interests will bear any resemblance to desire. Consequently, unconscious desire can be produced in such a way that it acts against interests and conscious wishes. There are innumerable powers that operate in society to prevent desire, multiplicity, and creation from coming into existence; yet these operate less as a blockage against the realization of a potential, than by interposing themselves so that other relations come into play. Desire is 'repressed' by another desire when its immanence and consistency is disrupted. A power-formation is composed of immanent relations, but constructed in such a way as to preserve a part of itself, in the same way that a genetic code is preserved through a species, so that it prevents new encounters and relations that would transform its essence. The fixed component of a social formation is never physical, for all physical bodies come and go. Instead, it exists on the level of meaning: it could be a genetic code, a convention, a value, an ideal, a tradition, a custom, an institution, a language, or a religion, for example. Power operates through the construction of a certain kind of meaning that organizes social relations, shaping desire, the unconscious, and ultimately consciousness. Indeed, if one dismantles an actual social formation, the meanings still remain as a grid through which one interprets reality, and through which new relations will be formed. God is overthrown, but humanity is put in his place; a Tsar is replaced by a Stalin.

The politics of desire aims to break down the dichotomy between desire and interest, so that people can begin to desire, think, and act in their own interests, and become interested in their own desires. It acts directly on the unconscious, but can only do so by acting directly on its own social context and its own kinds of meanings at the same time. Theory becomes an attempt to 'think otherwise', to explore new kinds of thoughts and relations, new kinds of subjectivity and society. It aims to construct a collective social space where desire is liberated, and can spread by contagion through the creation of immanent relations between heterogeneous multiplicities. The three themes of knowledge, power, and desire, which recur implicitly throughout Deleuze and Guattari's work, constitute not independent dimensions or spheres of activity, but three inseparable strategic fronts, each giving access to and augmenting the others. Knowledge is concerned with kinds of multiplicities and relations that exist in society; power is concerned with strategies for production and transformation of relations; desire is concerned with the driving force behind creation and relation. This book explores how changes in each domain affect the others, as well as reacting back upon themselves. It proceeds by examining how knowledge, power, and desire operate in Deleuze and Guattari's texts.

Problem 1: What is philosophy?

Close the door, make sure no one's listening, put your ear close to the page: I'm going to tell you a secret. It's not for publication. But should it fall into the wrong hands, should your own hands be the wrong hands, this will be of little consequence – the secret will remain transparent, inaudible, imperceptible. For the question of philosophy can only be posed as a confidence between friends (Deleuze and Guattari, 1994: 2).[1] Philosophy evades public discourse; it is not the exchange or struggle between opinions that might provide pleasant or aggressive dinner conversations at Mr Rorty's (1994: 144). Instead, it has more affinity with gestures enacted through words. In any case, philosophy does not reveal its inner essence to a passive audience, whether friendly or hostile. It only acquires a meaning when one uses it to make something else. Philosophy is knowledge through pure concepts (*connaissance par purs concepts*) (1994: 7). But you will know nothing through them unless you have first created them – that is, constructed them in an intuition specific to them (1994: 7). Whenever it is known, philosophy is always new: its temporality is that of a future approaching the present with generosity or grace, or that of a past whose repetition one awaits (Deleuze, 1989: 141; 1990b: 162–8). One cannot accept philosophy as a gift from the past, polishing, preserving, or purifying the old concepts in a historical tradition. Old concepts may once more come to life, but only if one gives each one a specific intuition by using it against the present. Concepts only come into being when repeated, at an absolute level of deterritorialization . . .

The question 'What is philosophy?' poses the problem of a distinction between philosophy and its rivals. For example, philosophy is concerned with the conditions of production of knowledge. Recently, the human sciences, and especially sociology, have claimed to supplant it by giving a more adequate description of such conditions of production (1994: 10). While philosophy took refuge in universals or the eternal authority of pure reason, history, sociology, epistemology, psychoanalysis, linguistics, and cultural studies have sought to locate philosophy as a mode of cultural production. With the advent of structuralism, followed by deconstruction and discourse analysis, boundaries between these disciplines faded leaving a generalized 'theory' of culture and society, replacing philosophy by at first undermining, and later simply forbidding, its appeal to universal, ideal, and eternal foundations. Consequently, theory, lacking its own foundations, seeks to propagate itself through approximating universals of communication by allying itself with computer science, marketing, journalism, design, and advertising – borrowing from these not merely a field for analysis as the dominant modes of cultural production, but also its own mode of production. As is typical of Integrated Global Capitalism, the fragmentation and proliferation of sites of analysis and engagement is accompanied by the globalization of dominant theories, where the proper names of fashionable theorists have a function equivalent to that of successful brand names or media superstars. That Deleuze and Guattari's names are still used in this way is a matter of some amusement and little consequence.

The question of philosophy can be posed from the perspective of a cultural–historical determinism. A hermeneutics of suspicion can then undermine all attempts to ground the relationship between philosophy and a real world or eternal idea lying outside of thought. Under such conditions, however, it is doubtful whether philosophy is present at all: the concept is translated into a superstructural effect of an underlying economic, linguistic, social, historical, or cultural base. But this involves a most shallow form of metaphysical presupposition: however much the hegemony of the signifier, or discourse, or simulation may be explicitly denied or deconstructed, the translation of all thought into such arenas involves a performative metaphysics, metaphysics in action, and any disavowal merely results in a performative contradiction. Two presumptions are evident here. The first is that a philosophical concept is completely determined by a particular cultural field in which it is embedded. This shows a naivety in regard to the multiple determination of all thought and action from different levels (which can be well illustrated by the coexistence of genetic, biochemical, environmental, social, personal, and spiritual causes of the thought manifested in mental illness), as well as the problem of how such multiple determinations can be synthesized in a single event. The second presumption is that a substantive notion such as the signifier, discourse, or simulation can have a totalizing embrace of an actual event without excess or remainder.

The question of philosophy can also be posed in a purely philosophical way, as between friends – this destroys the last vestiges of metaphysical pretension (Goodchild, 1996: 14–15). Methodological suspicion is replaced by methodological friendship: instead of tearing away the veils from Truth in order to show that ultimately she has no essence apart from her veils (cf. Derrida, 1979), one adopts the signs she emits in order to fabricate something else, even if this is a further patchwork of veils and signs. Deleuze and Guattari pose the question of philosophy through the power of their friendship. If philosophy is produced, it is by virtue of that friendship and in the space of that friendship; if it is to be repeated, it will be through the creation of further friendships.

What is the significance of the friend in philosophy? At the origins of philosophy, in the writings of Plato, the philosopher claims to be the friend of wisdom, or perhaps its jealous lover, striving for it potentially rather than actually possessing it (1994: 4). This places the friend in a position of rivalry with other claimants. But how would one distinguish the true from the false claimants, those who participate in the ambience of wisdom, and those who merely simulate its aura? How can one distinguish the true philosopher, the creator of concepts, from his or her double? Not only is philosophy challenged by exterior rivals, but it also generates its own illusions or doubles so as to hide behind its own smokescreen: it may be taken as a contemplation of essential truths, as a reflection on practices or states of consciousness, or as a communication of opinions in order to create consensus (1994: 6). The question of philosophy therefore expresses a will to discriminate the true friend from the rival.

This way of posing the question of philosophy is remarkable for its apparent reinstatement of Platonism, over two decades subsequent to Deleuze's exposition of his philosophy as the 'reversal of Platonism' (Deleuze, 1990b: 253). The Platonic philosopher could be distinguished from his rival sophists by the degree to which he participated in the Idea which he contemplated. Platonic love is necessary to see beyond the object of one's desire to the pure form of beauty – in the *Phaedrus* Socrates is distinguished as the true lover from the other suitors of Phaedrus, in spite of his ugliness and apart from the beauty of his rhetoric, through his inner moral beauty that consisted in wishing to educate the boy into the love of moral beauty (Plato, 1973). This self-referential or reflexive structure, where beauty is only ever given as repeated or recollected, defines the eternity of the Idea of beauty in the ironic myths of eternal repetition (Deleuze, 1990b: 254–5). Nevertheless, Deleuze indicated that the vital question in Platonism is less that of distinguishing between the good and the poor copy, than that of distinguishing between the good pretenders, who are friends founded on sim- ilarity, and false pretenders, who are simulacra who possess no resemblance. Plato founded philosophy in the domain of representation by calling attention to resemblance as the means through which the eternal repetition of the Idea might become known. Philosophy is here concerned with elaborating conditions of truth – measured through the resemblance of the copy or representation either to the recollected Idea, or, as modified by Aristotle, to the empirically examined object. Deleuze had found such a philosophy of representation, modelled on Platonic recognition of the truth, inadequate for a number of reasons (Deleuze, 1994: 129–67). Primarily, such a concentration on the supposed relationship between thought and the truth deals solely with the possible as an ideal, ignoring the real conditions and forces that produce thought as well as the real thoughts that do in fact occur. Secondarily, because the fundamental problem of modern philosophy (which Deleuze attributes to Foucault, Whitehead, and Bergson) is not that of attaining the eternal, but 'how is it possible that anything new might come into the world?' (Deleuze, 1992: 166).

Deleuze therefore effected a reversal of Platonism. The simulacrum, as con- trasted with the copy, produces resemblance merely as a surface effect of unknown forces: it operates by implying huge depths and dimensions that the observer cannot master, and includes a differential point of view within itself (Deleuze, 1990b: 256). Following Nietzsche, the reactive 'will to truth' of the philosophy of representation is replaced by the active condition of the will to power as a 'will to beauty' (Heidegger, 1979), where thought is evaluated by purely aesthetic criteria.[2]

Should one believe that Deleuze and Guattari became reactionary in their old age, proclaiming the purity of philosophy against its rivals and simulacra? Can one observe a renewed Platonism in their work, a Platonism of true simulacra (Mattéi, 1983) or a Neoplatonism of the outpouring and emanations of desire (Caputo, 1993)? This would be to ignore almost everything they ever wrote (a not infrequent occurrence). It would also be to misunderstand the significance of the friend in philosophy. For, even in the *Phaedrus*, Platonic friendship was intensely erotic, and philosophy was already threatening to become erosophy. The immor- tal genius of this Platonic dialogue is present in its use of irony, where every atom of the conversation is saturated with innuendo and relevance to the relationship between Socrates and Phaedrus. A lover is rarely interested in the explicit content of a conversation, but jealously scours every statement and gesture for signs of affection or indifference, of fidelity or betrayal (Deleuze, 1986). Such signs are produced in the juxtaposition of divergent series: the contents of the conversation are juxtaposed with the lived experience of the relationship. Deleuze reversed Platonism, not by rejecting it, ignoring it, or deconstructing it, but by elevating the play of signs as phantasms or erotic simulacra above participation in the ideal. The jealous lover of wisdom looks beyond explicit meanings for signs of affection or betrayal. Philosophy may therefore be distinguished from its rivals by the positive affective charge associated with it – upon which Nietzsche focuses his entire philosophy as 'pathos of distance'. Of course, positive affective charges occur wherever there is creation; in the case of philosophy, the arrival of the philosophical concept is announced by the affective levels it activates (Spinoza, 1989: 201–9).

Finally, however, friendship has a further significance in philosophy. For philosophical friends are united neither by a love of the Truth as a universal Idea, nor by a love of each other as individuated persons. For in this philosophy of simulacra, everything happens in between. Philosophy has no higher aim than friendship itself – a utopia or pure milieu of immanence, a society of friends, even if this means calling to a new people and a new earth (1994: 87, 100–1). Philosophy can be distinguished from its rivals by the extent to which it reunites rather than fragments, constructing a new earth as the plane of immanence of desire. When friendship reaches its immanent form, then the desiring-revolution has begun.

Notes

1. Hereafter, unnamed date references always refer to co-authored works by Deleuze and Guattari.

2. In the realm of simulacra, philosophy is caught in the wrenching duality of aesthetics: on the one hand, it designates a theory of sensibility as a form of possible experience; on the other hand, it designates the theory of art as the reflection of real experience (Deleuze, 1990b: 260). For these two divergent series to be tied together, the conditions of experience in general must become those of real experience, while the structures of the work of art become techniques of experimentation (Deleuze, 1990b: 260–1). Only in the active work of creation do these divergent series become tied together and affect each other, not through the mediation of some totalizing idea, but by being drawn upon in a real event of creation. A sort of internal resonance is produced between these basic series, and this resonance induces a forced movement (Deleuze, 1990b: 261).

PART I

KNOWLEDGE

1

The Emergence of Desire

People like to say that Deleuze and Guattari have a 'philosophy of desire'. One may understand this in several different ways. Firstly, it can be taken as a theory of society, culture, and nature, in which everything is produced by a form of concealed sexual desire – where others focus upon language, structure, history, economic production, or power-relations at the foundation of human society and culture, Deleuze and Guattari simply choose desire. Secondly, it can be assumed that manifestations of sexual desire constitute the field of their investigations; they merely choose to address themselves to desire. A third assumption is that desire is a precondition of knowledge for them, so that they can only learn about society and culture insofar as they are driven by their passions to be involved in them – sexuality then forms the basis for epistemology. Finally it can be assumed that the expression of sexual desire, enhanced by a discourse concerning it, is the key to a social and cultural liberation from oppressive power-formations.

In fact, all these notions are somewhat crude caricatures. The concept of 'desire' only appears as a main focus of Deleuze and Guattari's thought in the publications between 1972 and 1977.[1] It functions neither as a universal principle governing the whole of existence, nor as an underlying ground determining the nature of all existence – instead, desire lies outside or alongside existence. To understand the precise and esoteric meaning of 'desire' for Deleuze and Guattari, and the importance it carries, it is necessary to trace the emergence of the concept in Deleuze's earlier work on the history of philosophy. Instead of subsuming desire under conceptions of an objective ground, a specific field of inquiry, a transcendental presupposition, or a sexual practice, it is necessary to observe how desire posits itself as its own, autonomous concept. In Deleuze's early readings of philosophers, he developed irrecuperable concepts of 'intensive difference', 'becoming', 'force', or 'exteriority' that escape previously existing systems of thought – especially the Hegelian dialectic – and combine to produce a philosophy of desire as spontaneous, chaotic, and irreducible emergence. Such concepts only take on their own consistency and force, however, when they are no longer represented in dialectical contrast with their polar opposites.[2] For an irreducible concept of difference to survive attempts at dialectical or deconstructive recuperation, it must cross a threshold where it begins to posit and think itself. The philosophy of desire emerges through the differentiation of several layers of difference: differences that shape and associate ideas; differences that express feelings and forces; differences that synthesize forces into actual bodies; and differences that are implicated in an entity's emergence and reproduction of itself. The integrity of desire is only attained when each of these layers of thought, emotion, body, and ontology interacts with the others.

This chapter will trace the emergence of these conceptions of difference through Deleuze's work on Hume, Bergson, Nietzsche, and Spinoza, respectively. We are not concerned with the accuracy of Deleuze's readings, nor with whether he agrees with the thinkers described; the aim is to trace the development and meaning of categories to describe the social uncon-scious, through which the social unconscious grasps life, that will form the basis of Deleuze and Guattari's mature thought. It is a question of observing the creation of the concepts, and setting them out as a vocabulary, through which Deleuze and Guattari's thought will become comprehensible. This chapter simulates a philosophical investigation.

Problem 2: Crack open words . . .

'How about placing language in a state of boom, close to a state of bust?' Deleuze stuttered. 'This is the only way to introduce desire into various fields' (Boundas and Olkowski, 1994: 25). It seems that a writer, faced with the modulations of intensity of philosophical thought, has two possibilities: either to report the modulation as a content of language, as Nietzsche so frequently reported his own affective states (for example, Nietzsche, 1968: 420), or to place the modulation in the style or mode of expression, as Nietzsche did in the dithyrambic style he gave Zarathustra (Nietzsche, 1961). Deleuze found a third possibility: the performative.

> This is what happens when the stuttering no longer affects preexisting words, but, rather, itself ushers in the words that it affects; in this case, the words do not exist independently of the stutter, which selects and links them together. It is no longer the individual who stutters in his speech, it is the writer who *stutters in the language system (langue)*: he causes language as such to stutter. (Boundas and Olkowski, 1994: 23)

At the limits of language, words keep silent in the intervals where stuttering punctuates language. 'It is not surprising that, strictly speaking, difference should be "inexplicable". Difference is explicated, but in systems in which it tends to be cancelled; this means only that difference is essentially implicated, that its being is implication' (Deleuze, 1994: 228). Philosophy is a minor or foreign language that speaks in the intervals. Crack open words, crack open things (Deleuze, 1991b: 115). Crack open 'desire' . . .

Hume

Deleuze studied philosophy at the Sorbonne from 1944 to 1948 where he was trained in the history of philosophy. The curriculum at that time was largely influenced by the 'three H's': Hegel, Husserl, and Heidegger. These transcendental philosophies explore the conditioning of human thought and consciousness – by locating it in the dialectical progress of history, by considering the interpretations of phenomena produced by an intentional subject, or by considering the kind of meaning of existence which was fundamentally presupposed in any understanding or knowledge, respectively. Deleuze's first book, *Empiricism and Subjectivity* (1991a), first published in 1953 when he was aged 28, was remarkable for choosing as its subject the Scottish empiricist philosopher David Hume. Hume was one of the main predecessors of the Anglo-American approach to philosophy that is closely linked to the methods of the natural sciences; his thought appeared to be triply naive from the Continental perspectives of dialectical history, phenomenology, and fundamental ontology. Firstly, Hume's empiricist philosophy was aimed at discovering the conditions under which legitimate beliefs might be produced; it was unable to account for the historical progress in understanding that changes human subjectivity through reflection upon its previous states of consciousness. Secondly, it made use of supposedly 'raw' elements of impressions from the senses, without examining the way in which their meaning is already shaped by the interests and intentions of the human subject. Thirdly, it assumed a sceptical model of human reason in terms of subjective association and habit that entirely obscured the fundamental philosophical problem of the nature of knowledge and models of human reason themselves.

Deleuze, however, used Hume to escape from these dominant traditions of Continental philosophy.[3] For each of these philosophies presupposes that we already live in a meaningful world, and that we can only begin to build knowledge within the context of a pre-given meaning, whether this meaning is produced by history, subjectivity, or fundamental ontology – or, in the terms given by later developments in the Continental tradition, structure, language, society, communication, or culture. Deleuze used various arguments in his works on Hume, Bergson, Nietzsche, and Spinoza to suggest that each of these options already presupposes too much. History, subjectivity, and the meaning of Being are products in consciousness; to take any particular form of these as the starting point for interpretation and understanding fails to attain the underlying level of the processes by which such forms of consciousness are produced. Deleuze's entire philosophical project was directed towards a level prior to particular forms of consciousness – it therefore concerns something which might be termed the 'unconscious'. Deleuze wished to understand the processes of life that exist prior to consciousness, and upon which meanings in consciousness are formed (Deleuze, 1983: 103–4). While accepting the historical and cultural formation of consciousness, he turned the Continental tradition against itself by rejecting the Hegelian assumption that any particular 'meaning' is active in this process of formation, and can consequently be used as the basis from which to interpret other kinds of subjective meaning. In Deleuze's thought, the unconscious processes that produce meaning will be of a different nature from the meanings produced – the unconscious is a place of production, not expression (1984: 109); meaning is purely a surface effect. This approach also has a political import: certain forms of consciousness are perpetuated by appealing to established interpretations and meanings embedded in culture; such a culture can be transformed, therefore, by attaining a level of communication unmediated by established meanings.

Deleuze's reading of Hume attempted to explore this level of the construction of knowledge, meaning, and subjectivity in one and the same process. How is thought produced and regulated? What becomes thinkable through the use of certain concepts? It also differed markedly from those readings prevalent in Anglo-American philosophy: Hume's epistemology is regarded by Deleuze as inseparable from his social theory. Hume's main problem was the constitution of human nature, by which a human being can become a conscious subject. Deleuze used Hume to investigate the constitution of meaning, prior to all interpretation. Hume was concerned with the production of the kind of meaning which is not directly given in experience: he replaced the model of knowledge with that of belief (Deleuze, 1991a: ix). Reason, then, works through the inference of probabilities: we may believe that the sun will rise tomorrow, but we cannot know that it will. Hume took as basic the data of sense-impressions, and these are spoken about as though they were entirely separate, independent, and atomistic. Now, the essence or meaning of individual, phenomenal impressions was of no significance for Hume; what is relevant is the way in which these can be associated in the human mind. Questions of meaning, essence, and existence are displaced in favour of extrinsic principles of association. Human nature is able to associate diverse sense-impressions through principles of resemblance, contiguity, and causality: a single idea may then stand in for a variety of sense-impressions, although such general ideas are not any different in nature from the sense-impressions received in the mind (Deleuze, 1991a: 24). We have beliefs based upon previous repetitions: we believe that the sun will rise tomorrow because of previous experience; here, a multitude of sensations is synthesized into a single expectation. Associations of this kind are based on resemblance, contiguity, and causality – these being regarded as rules or principles of human nature. Although such principles determine the form which beliefs may take, they do not tell us which beliefs or associations we actually choose to form. Another input is required – in addition to these principles, the human mind is also subject to a variety of passions. We only form a belief for a specific, practical purpose, determined by a need, interest, or passion (Deleuze, 1991a: 120). Human nature is composed of both the rules governing its reasoning and the passions motivating that reasoning. Each subject will be produced from this nature as a specific set of beliefs and expectations. As such, the knowledge of human nature is entirely practical: it is a morality, concerned with governing or directing the passions. Philosophy is the theory of what we do, not what we are (Deleuze, 1991a: 133).

Hume constructed a parallel between the way in which sense-data are associated in individual minds, and the way in which people associate together in society (Deleuze, 1991a: 32). Hume believed that people are not naturally selfish; they are also passionately sympathetic to those who are closest to them (Deleuze, 1991a: 38). The partiality of such human passions leads to a conflict of interests, and it is the function of culture to reduce this conflict for the mutual benefit of all concerned. Culture extends natural sympathies: in the same way that the associating powers of reason extend our knowledge beyond the evidence of the senses into the realm of belief by moving from habit to expectation, they can also be used to extend our passions by moving from evident customs to social bodies and institutions, of which we are members and in which we take an interest. Such institutions are founded upon the powers of reason to invent and believe; culture is therefore the extension of positive natural sympathies and passions through reason to form institutions. From this perspective, society is founded upon useful conventions, habits, or customs that satisfy various needs (Deleuze, 1991a: 45). In this regard, the two main components in the formation of society are private property, delimiting an area of interest, and values, forming the focus for conversation as opposed to conflict (Deleuze, 1991a: 41–2). Institutions, therefore, objectify collective interest. Consequently, the image of society that emerges is one not founded upon law, contract, or domination, but founded on the imaginative extension and integration of sympathetic passions. Where knowledge organizes beliefs under the constraints of needs, passions, and interests, institutions organize actions and passions under the constraints of reason. The two domains are not quite parallel or isomorphic, but are in reciprocal presupposition and mutual interaction.[4] This essence of society is entirely positive, based upon belief and invention. Similarly, an image of positive social relations underlies the whole of Deleuze and Guattari's thought.

Nevertheless, negative and critical aspects do emerge within such a model. In the first place, some passion is required to maintain a belief in institutions, for a natural tendency of passion is to disinvest its extended form and to return to its local sphere of interest. Culture must produce an institution that maintains a passionate belief in the common good: the State or government takes on this role of the common good as an object of belief, requiring the highest loyalty; it reinforces and revitalizes belief in its existence through the mechanism of exercising sanctions such as punishment, taxes, and military service (Deleuze, 1991a: 50–1). Where other institutions are merely means towards the satisfaction of passions, the State produces the fictive construction of the 'common good' as an end worth serving. The State then assumes the authority to discipline those who do not serve the common good, and has a critical role in repressing unintegrated passions.

Reason also has a critical function: there is a need to deal with beliefs which are 'illegitimate' in the sense that they do not correspond to experience. These may be superstitions, arising from associations that take data to be essentially or permanently related which are in fact only accidentally related, as in astrology. Reason, therefore, does not only have an extensive role in inventing beliefs and institutions; it also has a corrective role in testing such beliefs against experience, or such institutions for their utility. Reason is both extensive and corrective, inventive and critical. In both cases, however, it is the same kind of reason at work – one which is based on habit. Deleuze discovered a paradox in this dual role for reason: a rule based on an imaginative construct is required as a corrective principle by which other rules can be assessed. How, then, will the corrective principle be tested? Hume's philosophy is essentially sceptical: there is no possibility of any certainty, truth, or knowledge. The only useful reason is practical – reason imaginatively constructs beliefs and institutions for the purpose of fulfilling the passions directing it.

Since corrective principles are habitual, imaginative constructs, reason is capable of generating its own illusions: if a fictional construct can be extended to the whole of experience, it can no longer be corrected. For example, from the mind's capacity to construct ordered associations, one can construct an image of God as the transcendental unity of associations, the source of all meaning and order, according to a teleological argument. Similarly, from the diversity of passions, one constructs a polytheistic belief in various forces that transcend experience. Likewise, from the continuity of experience, one constructs a belief in the world as a totality (Deleuze, 1991a: 73–4). These transcendental fictions can then be used as corrective principles by which to judge experience; they remain immune to corrective reason themselves because, although they belong to pure fantasy, they are extended to encompass the whole of experience as ultimate criteria. We should also expect to find analogous fictions at the moral level of passions and institutions. The State, however, remains a conventional institution; it can be critically assessed according to whether its sanctions embody the common good, or whether governors use their authority to satisfy their own passions (Deleuze, 1991a: 51). The 'common good' as apparent source of all conventions and values, however, which Deleuze and Guattari will later call the 'socius', is an incorrigible fiction because it is the complete body of all social meaning. In effect, the transcendental fiction could be any kind of idea or social body having a totalizing function; Deleuze's work on Hume anticipates a clear denunciation of any kind of totalizing perspective or relation of production at the level of both theory and practice. At the level of theory, Deleuze and Guattari had an empiricist scepticism towards any kind of totalizing metanarrative or metaphysics. At the level of practice, they sought a revolution that escapes from any totalizing socius such as the 'earth', the State or Capital, and the social relations governed by these.[5]

Deleuze followed Hume in choosing the priority of practical over theoretical reason; this is a political choice that cannot be validated by theoretical reason. For where Hume avoided transcendentals by choosing to relate human nature to the field of given experience, Immanuel Kant reversed this order of priorities by relating given experience to the transcendental subject necessitated by the unity of apperception, with its a priori categories and judgements (Deleuze, 1991a: 111).[6] Deleuze did not regard Kant's move as an error of theoretical judgement. His objection to Kant was primarily political: he regarded Kant's idea of a transcendental and legislative subject as a historical construct derived from the institution of the State, for it is here that conventions of unity, transcendence, and legislation emerge. The human subject interiorizes a court of Pure Reason, or conventions and values abstracted from their institutional setting (1984: 217–22; 1988: 119–34). The human subject is fashioned in the image of a totalizing and repressive State because it embodies a socius, and is no longer subject to critique and correction. This opposition to Kant must also be taken to apply to the entire post-Kantian tradition of philosophy insofar as it claims to judge or interpret experience from the perspective of a pre-given subjectivity, meaning, history, economic relation, or any other kind of idea or body. Along with Foucault, Deleuze remained sceptical about any kind of 'human science' or social and cultural theory which emerges within such a tradition of thought, because it constructs its own object of investigation through its own discursive practice (Deleuze, 1988d: 19).

Deleuze's return to empiricism may seem naive insofar as it appears to privilege Hume's atomizing of experience in order to develop synthetic associationism on this ground. Yet Deleuze did not follow any of the routes which Anglo-American thought has taken since Hume;[7] like Kant, he moved away from a naive notion of raw experience. Deleuze was not content with a simple dualism between experience and the ideas that represent it, nor between sense-impressions and their organization into beliefs. Prior to the active and imaginative work of the conscious human subject that builds on experience, he sought a passive or unconscious field, outside of words and things, through which data are constituted as immediately given in the mind. He found the solution already in Hume. Firstly, the flux of sense-impressions only becomes discernible when it manifests a difference; the fundamental category of empiricism is difference (Deleuze, 1991a: 87). The smallest possible difference is not a quantitative change, neither mathematical nor physical – insofar at it enters thought, it is an idea. The 'atom' of sense-experience, therefore, is a difference which exists in the mind. Consequently, it does not exist in some extended field, such as space or time (or history, language, society, etc.), but space and time are constituted by the association of such atoms. Of course, not all ideas give the quality of spatial extension, but all atoms give the quality of time in which they occur. The smallest possible experience is therefore a difference or moment in the experienced passage of time (Deleuze, 1991a: 91–2). So Deleuze's empiricism is tied not to a naive, atomistic conception of matter or experience, but to time as the basis of both meaning and experience. (Time, here, is not regarded as an empty linear sequence of nows, but is actually constituted in subjective experience by the way in which moments are associated.) Secondly, such atoms appear in a group or a collection: association is possible only on the basis of a habit or repetition. The root of the subject is a synthesis of moments of time, which joins past and present atoms of experience to form an expectation of the future. This synthesis of time in the form of habit or convention is the simplest possible unit of experience and belief. Within Hume's epistemology, Deleuze discovered a practical ontology of difference and repetition.

Exploring further, Deleuze then sought the conditions that enable such syntheses of time. Here he found a double spontaneity in an organism associating data: firstly, ideas are not associated by any internal resemblance, but only by their proximity in the mind, or the small differences between them – these relations are given spontaneously by the imagination; secondly, these relations in the imagination are determined by the disposition of the contemplating mind, which itself is dependent upon the passions (Deleuze, 1991a: 96–7). Hence the two sources of syntheses are imagination and passion – the relations they construct are external to ideas, and do not depend upon them at all. Deleuze did not need to attribute any other qualities except time to the atoms of ideas, because the practical relations which are formed between these ideas are entirely independent of their terms. There is no need for any presupposition of the essence of such ideas, or the meaning of their existence; Deleuze's empiricism bypasses all essentialist or interpretive knowledge to be concerned solely with a practical and utilitarian knowledge of relations. The principle that governs his empiricism is 'relations are exterior to their terms' (Deleuze, 1991a: 101). The 'atomistic' moment of experience can be divided into three arbitrarily related differences: a flux of the sensible; the invention of a synthesis by the contemplating mind as a result of repetition; and the difference between this flux and synthesis. This system of perception will be called a 'signal–sign' system, or an 'intensity'. The 'atom' of experience therefore is not modelled on some kind of miniature billiard ball – it is an intensity, a determination of pure time, which, like a musical note, has no qualities except vivacity and a certain tendency for resonance (Deleuze, 1991a: 132). Lacking qualities, it is 'unconscious', a basis for all conscious thought. (In practice, of course, it is always possible to reconstitute a sensation, an idea, and a perceiver from intensities. Through repetition, these may be associated to compose objects, signifieds, and subjects. Indeed, it is not easy to write without making use of phrases that designate objects, signify abstract relations, or manifest subjectivity. These constitute a double from which philosophy must continually extract itself.)

While the atom of experience is an intensity, the association of such intensities only takes place through an expectation of their repetition. Such an expectation stands in for the variety of intensities, although it is also an idea with an intensity itself, having a certain tendency for resonance and vividness. Expectations, once fixed, become habits or conventions; they are unconscious presuppositions that form the basis of beliefs and institutions. Furthermore, these unconscious presuppositions may occasionally be designated by being associated with arbitrary and external marks or events; the designated habit becomes encoded. Deleuze and Guattari will later analyse the unconscious presuppositions present in society in terms of codes (1984: 139–53). Codes have a social function in the sense that they can be recognized by various people through observing habits; they form the basis for a kind of communication and common culture. Learning to use codes does not require any complex procedure of interpretation or deciphering, for the relation between a code and its object is entirely arbitrary. Instead, learning about a culture or institution requires initiation into its use of codes, an expertise which can only be acquired through habit and practice – one becomes accustomed to a set of conventions.

Many characteristics of Deleuze's mature thought were derived from his study of Hume. He made reason purely practical, based on its utility in satisfying desires that come from outside reason; he explored a philosophy of immanence, whereby the human subject is constituted on the plane of the given as a result, rather than a presupposition, and the given is encountered in a field of purely exterior relations; all ideas and social relations of this practical reason are external to the terms or subjects which they associate; society is regarded as positive and inventive, building institutions from the micropolitical level upwards in terms of codes and repetitions; and there is an intersection between intra-psychic and social relations, so that institutions and conventions are constructed on the basis of reason's capacity for belief and invention, and codes are formed in order to satisfy the passions that arise in society. A significant corollary of this final point is that theory cannot be undertaken in abstraction or isolation: a theory will always be an expression of a certain disposition of the passions, and therefore will be constructed for the sole purpose of expressing the institutional arrangement through which passions operate, whether social or psychological. Instead of retreating into a set of ahistorical fictions, Deleuze placed 'culture' at the foundation of all theory and philosophy, where this 'culture' is defined entirely in terms of relations between passions, or the field of desire. This link between culture and philosophy signals the importance of Deleuze's thought for social and cultural theory.

Problem 3: On truth and illusion

Our laws are not generally known; they are kept secret by the small group of nobles who rule us. We are convinced that these ancient laws are scrupulously administered; nevertheless it is an extremely painful thing to be ruled by laws that one does not know ... perhaps these laws that we are trying to unravel do not exist at all. There is a small party who are actually of this opinion and who try to show that, if any law exists, it can only be this: The law is whatever the nobles do. (Kafka, 1988: 437–8)

Who are our nobles today?

A notion of truth is essential for practical living. Yet truth is not something self-evident: the truth-value of any particular proposition is independent of the content of the proposition in all cases except for tautologies and self-contradictions. Apart from such purely analytic propositions (and who is to judge that a proposition is truly analytic?), a proposition does not disclose its relationship to the state of affairs that it designates. If knowledge is attached to a notion of truth, then philosophy must make appeal to some transcendent term that will guarantee the conditions under which truth is produced, so that the gap between thought and being is bridged; philosophy has not restricted itself in the metaphysical foundations it has invented to guarantee truth. The problem remains, however, of the truth of such foundations – leading to an infinite regression; the problem also remains of whether thought does, or indeed can, conform to being. Mathematics and logic do not encounter any problem here, since they entirely construct their own field of investigation. Likewise, science is capable of sufficiently managing the behaviour of the objective world as to allow conformity between theory and observation, enabling the replication of results in both the closed environment of the laboratory and the sheltered environment of the technological artefact. Both its material of investigation and its theoretical discourse are managed successfully enough for some of the secrets of the universe to disclose natural laws. The human sciences may attempt to model themselves on the physical sciences, but they have a more difficult task: much human thought and behaviour is conditioned by a wide variety of mutually dependent variables which cannot be easily individuated and isolated. While facts and information may be relatively uncontroversial, the processes by which such facts are generated do not disclose themselves so easily.

There exists a popular caricature of post-Nietzschean French thought that one may occasionally encounter among those who do not study it: the French, we are told, believe that there is no truth, and are either unaware of the self-contradiction inherent in such a belief, or are unconcerned by it since there is no truth anyway. Those who do study French thought, however, have little interest in such an issue. For the problem raised by Nietzsche was not that of the existence of truth, nor that of the existence of a will to truth, but that of the motivation for the 'will to truth' (Deleuze, 1983: 95; Nietzsche, 1973: 15). By removing all consideration of content from the law, Kafka's story reveals what it is like to live under the law; analogously, by removing all content from truth, Nietzsche exposed what it is like to live in search of truth. The reason for such a Nietzschean inquiry is this: how we live, in search of the laws of nature, justice, or truth, is of much greater significance than the nature of such laws, justice, or truth. More significant than the epistemological question of the existence of truth are the ethical and political problems of what one does in the search for truth.

A proposition may be split into two components: its content, referring to objects, persons, and meanings, having a certain truth-value; and its mode of expression, the style in which it is written or spoken, having a certain moral value. By formalizing their modes of expression, logic, mathematics, and science discipline thought so as to concentrate upon the truth-value alone; the question of the moral status of such a formalization, and its consequent impact upon nature and society, exceeds scientific discourse. Apart from any particular context where its effects are observed, it is not clear that such a formalization does have any moral status. For the mode of expression is merely a style, a syntax – a regularity in selecting and composing the elements of discourse. The moral question, however, is concerned less with that which can be disciplined and expressed through a particular formalization than with that which escapes formalization, remaining unrepresented and inarticulable. The powers that act in thought, without speaking or being spoken about, may not easily be evaluated or resisted; the powers that are acted upon, without speaking or being spoken about, may not easily be defended.

Propositions refer to a content that is independent of them. If I assert that the sun will rise tomorrow, you may understand that the occurrence of this event is entirely independent of my assertion. Those components of discourse that Foucault called 'statements', by contrast, construct their own objects, concepts, and subjective sites of enunciation at the time in which they are spoken (Deleuze,

1988d: 8, 18). Statements are merely concerned with the organization of the mode of expression through certain repetitions and regularities. Nevertheless, it is possible to generate a wide variety of entities through the regularizing function of statements. In Kafka's story, the regularity of the statements of the nobles is sufficient to generate the notion of a secret law that is being faithfully administered, even though the contents of the law are never stated or ultimately deducible. The statements function as asignifying signs, since their content is never revealed.

Similarly, the regularization of the asignifying signs of perception may construct a wide variety of entities. There are four different ways of regularizing such signs, and each such strategy of regulation constitutes a visibility, a way of seeing, since it is immanent within perception itself. By associating different perceptions of light, one may form an indicative sign of the sun as the common source, generating the sun as an object. By selecting the growth of crops to be associated with the sun, one may form an abstractive sign of a correlation between the sun and growth, generating the idea of the sun as a cause of growth. Taking this correlation, an effect of association, as a cause by simply regarding it as a constant, one constructs an imperative sign that the sun shines for the purpose of making the crops grow, obeying its own inner imperative or natural law. Finally, by associating several purposive actions in the universe, one constructs a hermeneutic sign of a metaphysical being or imaginary divine legislator who decrees that the sun should shine to make the crops grow (cf. Deleuze, 1993: 173–4). Consequently, the truth of my belief that the sun will rise tomorrow is dependent on divine providence in postponing the apocalypse for at least one more day. Such processes of associating asignifying signs are capable of populating a world with objects, logical relations, moral purposes, and metaphysical beings. It makes little difference whether the ultimate metaphysical source of causality and purpose is the natural world, the legislative subject, or God. Furthermore, it makes little difference whether such moral purposes are right or whether such metaphysical beings truly exist.

Nothing can be decided through such an analysis about the truth of the existence of certain objects, ideas, moral values, or metaphysical entities. In order to distinguish true opinions on such matters from superstition, regulation of habits of association may be invoked, such as a more thorough contemplation, or self-critical reflection, or communication to achieve consensus (1994: 6). Each of these processes, however, tests an opinion by means of another opinion, giving no solid grounding for the truth. Under such conditions, which opinions will dominate?

There exist certain ideas, capable of self-regulation, that may reveal themselves as instances of the absolute where thought encounters reality. The history of Western philosophy is riddled with these: the One, the All, the Whole, the Platonic Idea, Aristotle's Pure Act, Anselm's Cause of Itself, the Cartesian, Kantian, and Husserlian Subjects, Hegelian Spirit, and Heideggerean Being are just a few; more recently, History, the Signifier, Capital, Production, Desire, Probability, Information, Communication and Culture have become predominant occupiers of such a role. Their self-regulatory structures are composed of three simple elements. Firstly, there is a capacity to be differentiated from themselves after the manner of the distinction between expression and content in a proposition: one distinguishes between the one and its unity; between the all and its universality; between a thought and thinking it; between an existing thing and its existence; between historical events and historical processes; between beings and Being; between a signifier and its signification; between use-value and exchange-value. Secondly, one uses the second determination to reflexively qualify the first, drawing attention to the unity of the one, the universality of the all, the thinking of a thought, the existence of an existent, the historicity of history, the Being of beings, the signification of a signifier, the value of utility. This stage threatens to be repeated in infinite regression. Nevertheless, such a regression can be grasped all at once in a moment of metaphysical revelation: the reflexive notion enfolds reality within itself by selecting as a material of reality that which conforms to its own determination (see 1994: 38–41). Absolute reality reveals itself to philosophical intuition as the One that unites itself, the All that embraces itself, a thinking substance that thinks itself, a cause of itself that causes itself, a history that narrates itself, a Being that unveils its own truth, a transcendental Signifier, or Capital that assesses the value of money. Through such processes of self-regulation, a notion absolves itself of further critical testing and relations with other notions, while offering itself as a criterion of truth through which all other opinions can be evaluated. It constitutes itself as an absolute and propagates itself. A plurality of absolutes leaves one with four choices: either pledging allegiance to one absolute to the exclusion of others; or renouncing all manifestations of the absolute; or trying to synthesize the absolutes in a higher unity; or exploring the processes through which absolutes are constructed.

One might suspect that such absolutes are illusions of reason. They attain predominance in the discourse of theology and philosophy, where thought is detached from the practical exercise through which it is integrated with specific problems and bodies, in order to attain a transcendental exercise where it operates on itself alone. Nevertheless, their influence extends far beyond their origins, for some corrective criteria must be invoked whenever one poses questions of truth and value in accordance with a 'will to truth'. If one is not a philosopher, not creating one's own concepts, one's thought will be regulated by those of someone else – the shape of thought finds its topological folds and openings in the concepts that it can use. Here we must again distinguish between what people say and what they do: it is not necessary to speak of metaphysics for one's speech to be permeated by metaphysical presupposition.

It has never been necessary to make appeal to such metaphysical absolutes or 'grand narratives'. For performative statements do not need to be grounded in ultimate opinions; their effect is felt if people act in accordance with them. A statement can only be evaluated in accordance with the implicit presuppositions, immanent acts, or incorporeal transformations it expresses, introducing new configurations of bodies (1988: 83). A discourse of statements is inseparable from the institutions through which its social presuppositions are enacted. A statement produces its own objects, subjects, and significations as 'fictions'; so long as its presuppositions are believed and enacted in a non-discursive realm, then it accomplishes its task. The question of truth loses its relevance and meaning when the institutional practice that interacts with discourse does not pretend to produce any isomorphism or correspondence between the realm of words and the realm of things.

> As long as we stick to things and words we can believe that we are speaking of what we see, and that we see what we are speaking of, and that the two are linked: in this way we remain on the level of an empirical exercise. But as soon as we open up words and things, as soon as we discover statements and visibilities, words and sight are raised to a higher exercise that is a priori . . . .
> (Deleuze, 1988d: 65)

Those who are pronounced criminal, insane, diseased, or dead will be treated differently by society without recourse to an inquiry into the essence of their criminality, insanity, disease, or mortality: a discourse and a set of practices may be associated through regularity, without any elaborate rationalizations. Consequently, all statements express social presuppositions, but such presuppositions cannot be stated in and for themselves: 'Our laws are not generally known; they are kept secret by a small group of nobles who rule us.' Our social presuppositions are generated and maintained by a set of imperceptible, mute, and blind powers.

> No doubt power, if we consider it in the abstract, neither sees nor speaks. It is a mole that only knows its way round its network of tunnels, its multiple hole: it 'acts on the basis of innumerable points'; it 'comes from below'. But precisely because it does not itself speak and see, it makes us see and speak. (Deleuze, 1988d: 92)

Bergson

Deleuze's work on Hume left a dichotomy in human nature between convention and passion. Passions stand outside the mind rather like transcendental ideas; the formation of such illusions is inevitable. The Kantian problem of the way in which conventions or beliefs are given in the mind has not been fully solved, for while the formal shape of a convention is given by imaginative associations on the basis of habit, the passionate force that gives a vividness to ideas, turning them into belief, has not been accounted for. Deleuze suggested that Hume had anticipated Bergson: habit is not merely an impartial expectation, but a dynamism that attempts to determine the future through repetition (Deleuze, 1991a: 92). In order to understand this 'force' of the past, Deleuze turned to the work of Bergson in order to make a transcendental deduction of passion.

We have noted that the atom of experience, the intensity, expresses itself in extension as a difference in time: it is a change, movement, or 'coming-into-being'. When Bergson considered perception, he found no essential difference in nature between a movement of physical stimulus and the corresponding movement or change that is produced in the brain; the brain, being material, does not add anything essentially different to movement. The activity of the brain does not consist in adding consciousness to matter, but rather in blocking a response to certain stimuli. The brain gives a kind of autonomy through its selectivity, allowing one not to react to every stimulus. This interval between stimulus and response allows the mind to select only that which is of interest (Deleuze, 1988a: 24). Now, Bergson explained the meaning of this interval in terms of the lived experience of time: for any change, one has to wait for it to take place (Deleuze, 1988a: 32). If one stirs sugar into a cup of tea, one has to wait for it to dissolve. To coin another example: if one attends a public execution, one has to wait for the guillotine to drop. Each change has a duration in which it exists; this duration is experienced as a quality composed of all the elements of the event. An execution, for example, may include: the criminal, the crowd, the executioner, the priest, the weather, the smell, the crime, one's relation to the criminal, the anger of the crowd, expectations of the moment of death – entirely heterogeneous terms can be synthesized into a single experience of waiting. Bergson therefore extracted duration as a transcendental idea corresponding to all changes; duration is the empty field in which all intensities will be experienced.

Deleuze effectively used Bergson as an alternative to Kant in order to make a transcendental deduction of the conditions of experience. Instead of extracting a universal subject with its interpretive categories as conditions of possible experience, Bergson extracted duration as a condition of real experience – the lived duration of someone who is present. This process differs from the Kantian deduction in two ways: instead of categories such as unity, totality, necessity, etc., being added to perception in order to form intelligible experience, duration is already present in the given, and it is formed by subtracting the change from the given. Nothing is added to perception; something is merely taken away. Secondly, the experience of waiting has an intensity of its own, even if this merely signifies the absence of an intensity. It can therefore be considered as part of the immanent plane of intensities; it is an experience alongside other experiences.[8] This transcendental and incorrigible idea of the imagination, duration, is therefore something produced within real experience, rather than being added to it, even though it can be extended to the whole of experience. The Bergsonian turn to duration is superior to the Kantian transcendental deduction, for Deleuze, since it does not presuppose any arbitrary transcendentals that are added to experience. Once this immanent deduction has been made, we can turn Hume's problem around and relate experience to duration, instead of relating the human subject to experience.

Duration has rather different properties from the transcendentals of the Kantian subject. Reason can now be subjected to a proper transcendental critique defined by the immanence of its criteria (1984: 75). The result is a critique of the majority of concepts in use in the European tradition of thought as a whole, including its social theory. For if we build our concepts on the basis of an imaginative extension of associations, such generalizations ignore the differences in kind that lie at the heart of experience. For example, our power of synthesis may lead us to posit the general concept of unity, or the One, upon which all number is based. Corrective reason observes that this does not correspond to the diversity of experience, and passes to its opposite, the multiple, through a movement of negation. This movement of negation from the one to the multiple is abstract: it does not express the real differences in kind that are encountered in experience. Consciousness synthesizes diverse experiences, so it is necessary to move to the third stage of the dialectic, the synthesis of the one and the multiple. Throughout this dialectical process of reasoning, characteristic of Hegelian and Marxist traditions of critical theory, one remains at the same level of generality – one does not return to real experience to find the intensity or real difference expressed there (Deleuze, 1988a: 43–7).[9] In Bergsonism, by contrast, knowledge never concerns possible experience, but real, lived, experience, engaging the whole of the subject in his or her passions.

In Deleuze's thought, philosophy can be considered as an art of working with unconscious presuppositions, and social theory as exploring social presuppositions. Bergson's method of intuition gave Deleuze a way of distinguishing between true and false presuppositions: those which are constructed within the mind and added to experience, like Kant's categories, are codes and conventions that do not correspond to the underlying ground of experience. True social presuppositions are always immanent in experience, and can be uncovered by subtracting intensities and changes from experience. Although general concepts may appear to govern thought, one never finds these in experience – these need to be added by the imagination, and will remain fictions. Duration, by contrast, is found in real experience because one always has to wait for experience to happen.

Deleuze explored Bergson's analysis of experience further. Duration is not an empty quality, like some abstract notion of empty space or a continuous line imposed upon experience. Duration always involves a certain quality of expectation; we therefore only find a variety of lived durations. The synthesis of expectation involves further factors. For time is not composed of discrete moments, points, or atoms; time passes by flowing – one moment does not disappear without another one appearing. Duration, in the living present, is a contraction of successive moments of time. Secondly, a recollection of the past is necessary to make possible a synthesis of present and past experience in an expectation; yet this recollection is not the expectation itself. The past has to recur, or become present in a recollection – in a certain sense, it also endures. Here we have two different kinds of duration: the contraction of time in its passage, and the virtual coexistence of the past with the present. Memory is a second passive synthesis of time, composed of moments of contraction, where previous experiences are grasped as synthetic wholes.

The precise quality of our experienced duration, therefore, is shaped by the present movement of perception or stimulus, as well as being shaped by the recollection that occurs in the interval. Consciousness is not only influenced by what happens in the present; we experience from the perspective of our own memory. Since the immanent plane upon which our reason acts and associates is the plane of our own memory, the kinds of 'knowledge' produced in the forms of habits, beliefs, values, conventions, and codes are not objective and impersonal, but relate entirely to our own memory. Memory functions as a field for the recording and preservation of all habits and conventions we develop; in addition to being a habit itself, it is the transcendental principle that associates and synthesizes habits. Yet memory, although composed of a multiplicity of differing, associated terms, is not divided into separate events; it synthesizes conventions into a single intensity of experience. As Freud discovered, an affective charge is produced by the internal resonance of two divergent series, one infantile or past and one post-pubescent or present (Deleuze, 1990b: 261). The multiplicity is grasped as whole, with a single quality. The memory from which we survey other movements, therefore, has its own expressive, experiential quality. This quality can then mark the limits of our experience; different qualities relate to different memories and experiences. Memory marks out a kind of territory or region of the unconscious: for example, we know a town by all that we see and experience there, but memory gives to the experience of the town an enduring quality through which the atmosphere of the town is grasped as a whole. Memory is synthetic, expressive, affective, phantasmatic, and territorial, concerned with wholes. Moreover, the contents of memory concern publicly accessible and shared events in the form of conventions, beliefs, and values. Although changes may be interpreted by individuals in slightly differing ways, depending upon their past experiences, the memories of those who inhabit a common space or society are relatively similar: they share a common culture.

Deleuze pointed out that in Bergson's later work he came to the conclusion that things in space are not merely discontinuous points, but also endure, since time passes for matter as well as for thought (Deleuze, 1988a: 48). Consequently, duration gives not merely a psychology of perception, but an ontology – everything has a duration, and we always perceive or synthesize one duration from the perspective of another duration. At first sight, it seems strange to attribute 'memory', the second aspect of duration, to inanimate matter. Yet when one considers the continuous and purposive way in which change takes place through the action of a force, one has to infer physical qualities such as momentum as a kind of memory of a body. Duration, as the contraction of successive moments of time, is also the material expression of a force as well as being a mental expectation. Then memory will combine both aspects of duration, both mental and material, for the contents of memory are contracted moments of the present, as well as coexisting in the past; they are forces, or impulses, distributed among a set of conventions. Memory is therefore a principle of action just as much as it is a principle of awareness; it is evident in the habitual and regular functioning of nature. Memory is a drive for repetition. In terms of human nature, the dichotomy between imagination and passion is overcome: memory is the source of both passion and association. Passions are no longer to be considered as universal drives and instincts; they are effectively constructed through previous experiences – such experiences are grasped as synthetic wholes, and passion becomes a power of transference, a desire to repeat the quality of the whole. Moreover, much of our past experience is held in common: passions are constructed ecologically and socially by the totality of past experience.[10]

Life is therefore composed of a multiplicity of differing kinds of durations or *territories*. Such territories are communicable: we do not perceive another territory directly, but we can come to some sort of knowledge of it by extracting a set of movements from another territory and reterritorializing them on our own duration, expanding that duration in the process. One can then observe that a second level of socialization, or initiation into a culture, involves sharing the passions and affective qualities of others, as well as competence in codes and conventions. When knowledge is taken as a Bergsonian experience of durations as territories, having affective and expressive qualities, then it includes as much subjectivity as objectivity. It leads to what one might call a Weberian 're-enchantment of the world' (Guattari, 1992: 108). The fundamental division is no longer that between the subjective and the objective, the mental and the material, artifice and nature, but between spontaneity and receptivity: the power to affect and the power to be affected (Deleuze, 1988d: 71). Both of these are aspects of duration or force.

For Deleuze, Bergson's thought generated its own incorrigible illusion. For since durations are able to relate to each other, a further, impersonal and extra-individual duration may be posited that grasps the movement from one duration to another; it is the time in which such interactions take place. If we extend this process of encompassing durations, we come to a monism of time, in which a single duration grasps the whole of being. This memory is also a force: Bergson invented the notion of the *élan vital* as the creative, driving force of all life, in a kind of monism of desire (Deleuze, 1988a: 94). Indeed, this theoretical illusion is then doubled by a practical illusion: it would appear that the socius has its own collective passion that acts through individuals as though they were members of its body. People become mere agents of the common 'passions' of society, as though society had its own passions and forces. This complete social conditioning is unconscious; for while individuals act on the basis of their own memories and passions, these passions have been formed by the conventions and experiences of nature and society as a whole throughout the history of evolution. Individuals are condemned to a repetition of socially constructed instincts (Deleuze, 1988a: 109). For Bergson, however, freedom from such a complete cultural determinism is rare, but possible, and comes in the form of creativity. For individuals act on the basis of their own memories and passions; to interrupt this, a second, inter-cerebral interval must appear between intelligence and society as a gap between territories (Deleuze, 1988a: 109). In this gap between the pressure of society and the intelligence of the individual, Bergson located creative emotion: an emotion prior to all representation. For Bergson, some rare individuals are able to sense the *élan vital* itself directly as an emotion, a creative force that crosses all levels of duration and embodies the whole of life in a moment. These are artists and mystics, and their revolutionary and creative force derives from acting out the force of the whole of life instead of that of a limited society (Deleuze, 1988a: 111–12).

Deleuze, however, did not accept Bergson's underlying monism. For him, the relation between memories or territories is not itself territorial, nor able to be synthesized into the Whole or One of mysticism. Such a duration exceeds real experience. In his thought, artists are able to connect to something outside of all territories, but this outside is no longer a synthetic whole – it will be plural, different, and chaotic. The artist – and also the philosopher – will be capable of real creation, escaping the dominant powers of society that create repetitive desires. This creative emotion from Bergson stands as a precursor of Deleuzean desire.

Nietzsche

Bergson's philosophy gave a harmonious yet highly deterministic understanding of the nature of society: relations between people have a duration,
and so also have a collective memory that acts as a force expressed in social
relations. There is no limit to synthesis in a monistic philosophy: while
individuals may at times enter into conflict, the impulses that they express
ultimately derive from a common root. Deleuze, however, turned to Nietzsche's thought in order to explore relations of force, both physical and social,
where forces may effectively act upon each other for better or worse, apart
from any harmonious synthesis. Deleuze's account of Nietzsche breaks up
Bergson's monism by exploring a typology of forces and their possible
syntheses. Forces are the real terms that give rise to thought or action;
whether physical or social, they act upon other forces by giving them senses
and values; they seek to enforce obedience in the form of agreement
(Deleuze, 1983: 1). As opposed to violence, which is an action upon specific
bodies or objects, a relation between forces is strategic or tactical: to incite,
to induce, to seduce, to make easy or difficult, to enlarge or limit, and to
make more or less probable are pertinent examples (Deleuze, 1988d: 70).
This kind of synthesis is the direct action of force upon force; it does not
invoke a further continuous duration in which synthesis takes place. Relations between forces can now become quite discontinuous: relations between
people are not necessarily synthesized by codes or territories, but may rely
upon a purely external impulse that comes from 'outside' the terms it relates
(see Deleuze, 1977). From this perspective, a knowing subject is merely a
site at which forces engage with each other. Social and cultural pluralism
becomes conceivable once more.

Nietzsche maintained a distinction between the level of conditioned
products that are able to come into consciousness, and the level of underlying, unconscious forces that act and condition life (Deleuze, 1983: 41,
73–5). Instead of being safely synthesized in some virtual realm of the
memory, these conditioning forces meet up in the real lives of bodies, where
they conflict with each other. Forces always act upon other forces, according
to a 'will to power': they attempt to gain power over each other. It is
important to emphasize that in Deleuze's reading the 'will to power' is not
a conscious desire of a person for power, but something that only acts at the
transcendental level of conditioning forces; moreover, it is not a force itself,
but a principle of the synthesis of forces, a way in which forces act upon
each other. A force will always attempt to synthesize other forces in such a
way that it attempts to gain power over them, that is to say, impose its own
sense and values (Deleuze, 1983: 49–52).

Deleuze's reading of Nietzsche brings a devaluation of conscious, conditioned meanings and representations in favour of an elevation of the
'body' (Deleuze, 1983: 39–42). Here, the body is no longer defined in terms
of how it appears to consciousness, but is defined genetically in terms of the
forces that give rise to it. Indeed, the body is regarded as an assemblage of

forces, a site where forces act upon each other, rather than a phenomenon located in space and time (Deleuze, 1983: 40). While Deleuze explicitly directed his reading of Nietzsche against Hegelian idealism, his true enemy is the entire tradition of philosophy that attempts to interpret life in terms of meanings produced within consciousness. Instead, all life can only be understood in terms of relations of force expressed through bodies.

The method of interpretation which Nietzsche adopted to examine life is called 'genealogy': for Deleuze, this is not a case of looking for ancestral forebears or concealed historical origins that would continue to determine the essence and meaning of a phenomenon; instead, genealogy has a synchronic, topological, or geographical orientation. Phenomena are regarded as symptoms of forces: the nature of a body is deciphered by what it does, the forces that are acting through it, along with their senses and values. Genealogical interpretation is an action of an interpreting force, weighing senses and values: a phenomenon is endowed with a sense, or 'interpreted', by the force that acts through it at any particular time – 'sense' is a direction imparted by a force. The aim, here, is less to find a 'true' interpretation than to make sense, to give a direction. This interpreting force, however, also presupposes a certain scale of values – it makes an evaluation of the values presupposed by the forces acting on a phenomenon. In the same way that memory produces a convention and an impulse, force gives a sense and value; one can plot continuities between concepts in Deleuze's work, even when their names and contexts are changed. Genealogical interpretation can only act from a particular perspective, with its own sense and values. It is already politically engaged.

Unlike Nietzsche, however, problems of value no longer hold any importance in Deleuze's own philosophy: this is because our evaluations are completely determined by our mode of existence, our way of being, or style of life – the value of values results directly from the assemblage of conditioning forces at work in a body (Deleuze, 1983: 1). For Deleuze, a genealogical interpretation attempts to diagnose the mode of existence expressed in a phenomenon through the senses and values that it produces. This genealogical interpretation, of course, also expresses the mode of existence of the interpreter; it is a way of acting upon a phenomenon, and endowing it with one's own senses and values. Such interpretations are the way in which one set of forces acts upon another.

Nietzsche's own use of genealogy was much more historically oriented; in some cases, it accords with Deleuze's Bergsonism insofar as the concealed essence of a phenomenon is often given by the past events that have happened to it, so that a concealed force continues to operate upon a phenomenon as a kind of transcendental memory. Hence Nietzsche traced the meaning of a phenomenon such as punishment to its original function as compensation for a debt in terms of the pleasure derived from inflicting pain; the moral meaning is a later addition (Nietzsche, 1956). An essence is therefore something built up over time – a history. Deleuze reoriented Nietzsche's thought in a synchronic direction more appropriate for a structuralist generation, in order to allow for new arrangements of forces to seize a phenomenon and reinterpret it. Unlike structuralism, however, meaning is defined for Deleuze's Nietzsche not in terms of differential relations between arbitrary signifiers, but in terms of differential relations between forces. The whole of life must be considered in terms of actions and passions, and so is essentially composed of social relations. While these forces are transcendental conditioning factors and hence unknowable, they can be distinguished genealogically according to a typology of sense and value.

Deleuze distinguished between two senses of forces in Nietzsche: active and reactive forces (Deleuze, 1983: 42–4). The natural tendency of any force is to act upon other forces until it has exhausted itself, so that another force can come to act in its place. Many forces will also be passive, or acted upon, while themselves acting upon others. The results of such engagements are bodily events of change and becomings. Yet consciousness brings with it the possibility of a different kind of force. Any act can be represented in consciousness, but the representation will be a third term in addition to the active force and passive force. Any action is a change or a becoming, but consciousness is only able to hold knowledge by extracting a stable state or a being. Active forces, therefore, never come into consciousness. A third term is required that can react upon the active force so as to separate it from its true nature and power, and produce a representation of it (Deleuze, 1983: 74). Deleuze cited Nietzsche's example from the *Genealogy of Morals*: eagles naturally tend to carry off lambs, but if the sheep ask why they carry off lambs, they separate their idea of an eagle from its natural action, as though an eagle were something different in itself from a power to carry off lambs (Deleuze, 1983: 123). An eagle becomes a representation, and the sheep's collective consciousness is based on a reactive force. In human terms, someone can be restrained from expressing their active force by means of 'conscience': the active force is replaced by a representation. In the human case, the reactive force of conscience can be successful in separating an active force from what it can do; one restrains oneself from acting on impulse. A reactive force differs from an active force, therefore, in aiming to prevent action, rather than produce it; it has no initiative of its own. The sole aim of a reactive force is revenge. The way it operates upon active forces, however, is not by direct opposition or trial of strength, in the form of conflict or oppression, nor simply by preventing it from acting or emerging into consciousness, in the form of repression, but by inverting the sense and value of the active force so as to ally the active strength to its own purposes, which we may perhaps call 'seduction'.

Deleuze connected 'conscience' with 'consciousness' in Nietzsche's thought. He interpreted the genealogical principle of our human way of thinking as being entirely based upon revenge, insofar as we produce knowledge as a static being separated from the action of becoming (Deleuze, 1983: 64). Not only is our 'knowledge' essentially false, incapable of representing the transcendental reality of active forces, but it also aims to prevent forces from acting, so that we only deal in inverted and flattened representations. Life is replaced by an image. Deleuze's Nietzsche evaluated consciousness as expressing a 'negative will to power': it is exhausted insofar as it is unable to create its own senses and values; its sole task is to resist the action of other forces. The notion of 'power' at work here is something rather different from the strength of a force, or its ability to overcome other forces. Power is qualitatively divided into separate types: a positive power to act in the form of creating senses and values; and a negative power to react in the form of resisting or diverting the power of other forces. For Nietzsche, those who have the most power are those who direct the lives of others: although great commanders have a certain amount of power expressed in enforcing their will upon others, philosophers can have the greatest power in history as the creators of meanings, values, and goals which people adopt to direct their own lives. Ultimately, for Nietzsche, even the philosophers have not been able to question the value of their values, and so create truly new values. Much philosophy has been an attempt to defend established values. Nietzsche's evaluation of the human condition is that it essentially expresses a negative will to power, for this is the principle that generates human consciousness (Deleuze, 1983: 34–5). He therefore awaited something beyond the human, to be achieved by his own revaluation of all values. This will lead to a mode of consciousness and knowledge beyond human nature.

Culture, for Deleuze's Nietzsche, is founded upon the senses and values given by dominant forces: it is a training and selection so that people will learn to accept dominant senses and values (Deleuze, 1983: 133). It is initially the inculcation of habit; this habit is reinforced by a memory of punishments received during training, so that eventually this memory becomes a conscience, exerting the internalized pain of guilt. While culture itself expresses a set of reactive forces, preventing spontaneous human activity, it is based upon the action of inculcation that involves the infliction of pain. Culture becomes a kind of memory of the will, a faculty of making promises, so that members of a culture share a commitment to a common future goal. At this stage, people relate to others by inflicting pain, so that all are integrated into the collective wills and goals of culture; culture becomes the apparent source of all senses and values (Deleuze, 1983: 133–5). It becomes the quasi-cause of social events, although it is in fact merely a representation. In Deleuze's reading, culture serves the active and positive purpose of creating responsible individuals who are capable of making promises, so directing themselves towards future goals on the basis of the past, without attempting to preserve a particular set of codes and conventions; but this process of culture becomes side-tracked within history because most cultures refuse to allow their own senses and values to be questioned – they become a set of incorrigible fictions (Deleuze, 1983: 138–41). Where conscience is merely a faculty for remembering promises, history records the senses and values of the promises themselves, and propagates them, diverting culture to preserve reactive forces of preservation. Historical change becomes possible through reflecting upon the past achievements of consciousness. Consequently, in the development of culture, force is replaced by its phenomenal product. Human consciousness within culture is then used as a technique of domination through remembering and preserving the senses and values of past forces.

The human condition is therefore dominated by a negative will to power (Deleuze, 1983: 166). Reactive forces may seduce active ones, but when they encounter each other, the need for preservation leads to resistance and conflict. In fact, there is no real meeting or synthesis; the forces merely oppose each other. Such encounters are worked out in practice through either the cruelty of inculturation, or the clash of competing cultures, senses, and values. Although active forces may still exist, in humanity these are related to other forces through the medium of representation. They are resisted and separated from their own force; they are made to become reactive. Human life in general expresses this conflict between opposing forces, so that every one acts in order to limit the powers of others. The only will to power which we can know is negative. The senses and values which are given to us by our conditioning will oppose other senses and values from elsewhere, each demanding our full allegiance. The resulting 'cultural relativism' of differing meanings and values can only lead to violence, as forces try to work out their opposition in physical terms. The dominant cultural senses and values will be those which have the most power, in both physical and social terms, as the capacity to extend their own senses and values over others; indeed, one of the most effective ways of ensuring such obedience is to introduce such values into the consciences of others. The human condition is dominated by a dialectical history that is only able to synthesize forces through opposition and conflict.

Deleuze found in Nietzsche the clue to a different kind of mode of existence, beyond historical humanity. The 'overman' does not express a different kind of force; he is not merely a victory of active forces over reactive ones. In essence, the overman expresses a different quality of the will to power, a different way of synthesizing forces apart from those based upon memory or consciousness. By relating the overman to a quality of synthesis, rather than to any particular force, Deleuze radically subverted the distasteful political implications of Nietzsche's position. For Deleuze, there will no longer need to be any supreme force or great commander who subjects all other wills to his own; indeed, Deleuze found a different way of relating wills apart from violence and conflict. For this reason, his reading of Nietzsche differs significantly from many of Nietzsche's own expressed opinions, and is politically much more interesting: instead of favouring a self-affirmative aristocracy, Deleuze always favoured the lowest.[11] '

Deleuze's revaluation of Nietzsche's thought passed through several stages. Firstly, Deleuze thought according to the de-substantialized terms of relations and syntheses, rather than forces, drawing upon Nietzsche's critique of metaphysics. Secondly, these relations are no longer to be mediated by the interpretations and evaluations produced within consciousness; a force or relation is in itself an act of interpretation and evaluation. Thirdly, the sense and value of a force or relation is given by the way in which its component forces are synthesized, and not merely by the 'strongest' component. Where Nietzsche mainly observed violence and conflict, Deleuze anticipated a different kind of synthesis.[12] The 'will to power', in Deleuze's reading, is the transcendental term that mediates or synthesizes relations (Deleuze, 1983: 50). Now, most syntheses are negative in the sense that they ultimately will their own annihilation: a negative will to power is a will to nothingness. Relations of conflict always aim at their own dissolution in victory for one party, or some higher synthesis where a new force replaces the previous ones. In practice, however, this moment of annihilation is perpetually postponed: reactive forces are not able to triumph alone, but only by opposing and seducing active forces. Deleuze then interpreted Nietzsche's doctrine of the eternal return within this specific context: neither the phenomenon, body, nor force returns, but only the synthesis or will to power (Deleuze, 1983: 48, 68). At the level of force, the thought that one might live one's life over and over again provides an ethical test: one is forced to evaluate one's own present mode of existence by one's own scale of values. One gains a genealogical reflexivity, so that one applies forces back upon themselves to interpret and evaluate themselves. Only two kinds of forces can survive such a test: those that wholly affirm themselves and those that react against themselves, producing an infinite chain of seductions and displacements. The ethical test of the eternal return of forces was not sufficient for Deleuze, therefore, and he had to apply the eternal return at the level of the will to power. Here, a negative will to power negates itself immediately and directly, leaving only an affirmative will. The eternal return makes an ontological selection so that only active forces return (Deleuze, 1983: 72).

A different kind of synthesis emerges: once a relation takes the form of affirmation, then forces begin to affirm each other. This affirmation is a desire for mutual interaction, relation, and synthesis: it is *desire* (Deleuze, 1987: 92). Where Nietzsche had applied the eternal return at the ethical level of forces, resulting in an infinitely self-affirmative force called the 'overman', Deleuze applied it at the ontological level of relations, resulting in an affirmative mode of acting, relating, and existing which he calls desire. Forces want to act and to be acted upon, they want to give themselves and change their nature; they look for syntheses which will be able to produce something new (Deleuze, 1989: 141). The relation of desire is an affirmation of difference and only manifests itself in creation or production. It is self-positing, a power of coming into existence that eternally recurs upon itself, giving the territories or forces it relates consistency, and producing a new entity through synthesizing heterogeneous territories. This desiring-production is a transcendental yet immanent term that only refers to a certain kind of quality of synthesis: each force acts upon the other to transform it. In terms of territories, each force deterritorializes the other.

For Deleuze, genealogical interpretation and the eternal return are not 'true': they do not restore us to a simple knowledge of the real world. Instead, they are critical techniques for selecting a certain kind of knowledge which is worth knowing, a certain kind of force or power which is worthy of action, and a certain kind of desire which is worth loving. This interpretation, evaluation, and passion are self-authenticating insofar as they are productive, creative, and affirmative. Now, although Deleuze's reading of Nietzsche is maintained at the rigorous and abstract level of concepts, such concepts only designate certain kinds of relations between people. They produce a kind of social theory which only takes on meaning when one begins to live in this way. Deleuze used Nietzsche's thought as a critique of the terms which are worth thinking about in social theory. The kind of knowledge which he selects is a knowledge of 'concepts', where concepts designate qualities of relation between people. After the selective test of the eternal return, concepts will only designate affirmative relations, that is, different modes of desire. Deleuze ultimately selected desire, rather than knowledge or power, as that which is most worth thinking about in social theory.

Problem 4: On judgement and justice

A verdict falls on one side or another: innocent or guilty. For a verdict to be socially valid, it must be communicable and representable. If the judgement is simply a question of establishing a matter of fact from incontrovertible evidence – did he commit the deed, or was it someone else? – then this binary representation seems appropriate. If, however, it is a question of induction from circumstantial evidence, and problems of the motivations and sanity of the defendant come into play, then the distinction between innocence and guilt is less clear-cut. One might appeal to an expert witness, an 'authority' who pronounces his or her opinion on the matter – and who is entrusted with the power to decide what is normal in such cases. Judgement relies on a magical ability to read the soul, to predict a past that can never be known; it assumes that there has been no deviation from the norm. Judgement enframes the defendant within an order of generality: the thoughts and forces that led to the deed are always unrepresentable by right. In this respect, prisons are full of those whose cases have not been heard – in the sense not only that they have not been allowed to give account for themselves and explain their reasons before the court, but also that their cases are inaudible in principle. Judgement is rarely just.

To judge is always to imprison, whether one condemns or acquits. One assigns a fixed essence to that which is by nature merely a simulation of itself, a dynamism, a becoming. Moreover, judgement always appeals to the infinite and the absolute: it is necessary to represent the whole of time and space, the whole of experience, or acquire an infinite power of reading the soul, in order to judge how the specific case should be represented; it is also necessary to compare the case against an absolute standard. The infinite ground of judgement is attained by repeating the same absolute standard in every case, as though it pre-exists every application. The ground itself must have a reflexive, self-positing structure: only justice is just (Deleuze, 1994: 62). This structure of turn and return that grounds the ground is the Platonic structure of myth (Deleuze, 1994: 60–1): the ground is never presented for itself. It is always absent, lost in a primeval past before time began, ironically withdrawn into itself, leaving one merely with the problem of whether a case truly resembles the absolute standard (Deleuze, 1994: 63–4). Justice is founded on infinite regression. In this respect, one can never have done with judgement: there is an infinite excess of the absolute over the case. Before God, all are guilty – and each conscience witnesses to an infinite debt before God (Deleuze, 1993: 158). Apparent acquittal becomes equivalent to an indefinite reprieve: the true judge is beyond experience and conception (Deleuze, 1993: 159). The only hope of restoring the infinite judge to experience is to imitate him, participating in his judgements: one judges others by appealing to the infinite. It makes little difference that in modern thought God has been displaced, for man takes his place as the absolute against which guilt is judged. Even the essence of man is infinite and withdrawn. One asks 'What is man?', and responds with axiomatic solutions in the form of rights. Like King Oedipus, modern man judges and punishes himself (Deleuze, 1993: 162); Kantian philosophy is the heir of Oedipus (Deleuze, 1994: 87).

Judgement therefore subverts the course of justice. Instead of being judged from the position of the one who has been wronged, one is judged from the perspective of a precedent: an absolute standard, existing from eternity. Judgement is unjust because it lacks measure: the verdict is never commensurate with the deed because it exists in a different order – the order of incorporeal speech-acts, not deeds. Judgement therefore depends on two dissimulations: the order of deeds, along with motivations and impulses, is assimilated to the order of facts, representing the unlimited in terms of the finite; and the order of facts is represented in relation to an infinite order of ideas of justice. The mythical order of absolute justice is affirmed only when people begin to act as if it were true, judging others accordingly.

A Heraclitean conception of finite justice can be opposed to this Platonic conception of infinite justice: 'It should be understood that war is the common condition, that strife is justice, and that all things come to pass through the compulsion of strife' (Wheelright, 1959: fragment no. 26). In a Nietzschean system of cruelty, debt is no longer inscribed in an eternal law book that condemns to eternal servitude beneath its apparent gentleness, but is inscribed directly on the body in an exchange between forces (Deleuze, 1993: 160). In contrast to a judgement that appeals to a past order of time, the exchange of action and reaction in the present makes finite reparation. Existence in the present, the strife between a multiplicity of forces, is innocent (Deleuze, 1984: 22). Indeed, rejecting this common law of the present, and making appeal to participate in divine standards, is hubris – injustice itself (Wheelwright, 1959: fragment no. 88).

From a moral perspective, grounded in an infinite ideal of justice, this present strife appears to be a general condition of war. But war is merely the effect of a will to destruction in the name of that which is just (Deleuze, 1993: 166). When animals fight, ferocity is usually gauged in relation to a limit that is anticipated yet avoided: the last threat before physical violence is provoked, or the last blow before serious damage is inflicted. In the absence of morality, there is a different order of evaluation. Similarly, babies are incapable of comprehending morality, and one cannot relate to a baby according to a moral order: there is merely an order of actions and passions (Deleuze, 1993: 167). The liberation of emotional and ethical conduct from subordination to moral ideals and obligations allows a greater degree of sincerity in relations: one acts in accordance with feelings – such as anger, shame, betrayal, or jealousy – instead of holding them within. Conduct is gauged by an internal balance of tendencies and impulses that seek to resolve themselves in action, rather than being turned back against themselves by some moral ideal. Once expression has taken place, mutual understanding and forgiveness can follow.

Deleuze distinguished between 'combat against' and 'combat between' (Deleuze, 1993: 165). 'Combat against' is always against a judgement and its representatives, whether one maintains a grievance against a finite judgement (1988: 122) or battles against the infinite form of judgement as such: its target is an incorporeal speech-act, a statement, or else a whole regime of signs. 'Combat between', by contrast, determines the composition of forces in a combatant. The struggle between force and force is neither violence (a conflict between bodies) nor resistance: a force takes hold of another force, giving it an additional sense and value, enriching that which it takes hold of, while also enriching itself (Deleuze, 1993: 166). There is a coupling of forces: the capacities of the 'defeated' force remain, but they are now deterritorialized, directed to a different site of application, producing different ends, while the 'victorious' force is also changed and enhanced by the encounter.

Nietzschean justice involves the meeting of inequalities. Marks inscribed on a body are unequal to the codes and intensities that represent them. The force or drive is an effect of this inequality: it is the intensity of the mark, a synthesis of the perception of excitation (Deleuze, 1994: 97). Moreover, the force that seizes another appeals not to a cyclical myth that infinitely withdraws into itself, but to a finite layer of the past that it constitutes through its action (Deleuze, 1994: 106). The principle that governs forces, whether considered as a 'pleasure principle' or a 'reality principle', is not infinite, but local and finite, specific to the body in question (Deleuze, 1994: 108): the ground is replaced by a local territory. There is no appeal to an unattainable myth or dream here; instead, one gains access to the principles that shape forces through intoxication or insomnia (Deleuze, 1993: 162–3). In Spinoza's ethics, soul and body are inseparable: one evaluates with one's body, its territories and erogenous zones – one merely loves or hates.

There is also a third, esoteric kind of justice that restores the infinite form: justification, a justice of the future. This is the justice of the eternal return: justice is repeated, but always differs in its repetition. Here justice, instead of being subjected to an ideal or infinite obligation, or being filled by the present play of forces, becomes essentially symbolic, spiritual, and intersubjective (Deleuze, 1994: 106). For there is an inequality between each local and finite territory in the Bergsonian memory and the action that is produced on its basis. Repetition of the memory in action is just as impossible as saying precisely what one wants. In this respect, Heraclitean justice falters because one can never attain the appropriate measure of response – an action never balances an affect. Learning to react, to counter-attack, or express repressed emotions never restores a true justice to the situation. Justice – as found in micropolitical relations – becomes deeply problematic, always withdrawing from itself, disguising and displacing itself in its expressions. This problematizing of justice, far from preventing ethical conduct, is the very condition under which ethical conduct becomes possible. One no longer knows how to act, the deed is too great to be performed. Attempting to live the Heraclitean justice of the present, in such a context, is the condition for becoming-equal to the just act; but because one's conduct is regarded as problematic, one awaits a future outcome that is beyond accomplishment. This faith in the future (Deleuze, 1994: 90) is a divine game that results from the affirmation of all chance: the rules of the game, the principles of justice and moral ideals, are in play at every stage, along with conduct (Deleuze, 1994: 116). One does not know which force will arrive from outside to determine the sense and values of thought and action. If faith, the affirmation of all chance, necessarily produces a winning combination, it is because it allows a chaotic force of the future to work. The outcome will be an entirely new creation, a surprise event, an autonomous product (Deleuze, 1994: 90). The repetition of a force of the future in the present is a conduct that excludes all ideals, obligations, and emotions at the same time as it excludes the wants and interests of the agent.

That which is created is always consistency: a new bond between persons, a new social plane in which to dwell. Inequality, the general condition of life, is not equalized but outweighed: the infinite weight of the future produces a shift to a new threshold of deterritorialization where prior inequalities gain a new sense and value as the conditions of existence. Injustice itself becomes just.

Spinoza

Desire is a purely affirmative synthesis between differing modes of existence. Deleuze discovered, implied within Nietzsche's thought, the possibility of living according to an 'affirmative will to power', a synthetic principle that affirms differences. There is no longer any need to appeal to a higher unity that joins differing conventions or impulses. Nietzsche's own philosophical writings, however, largely explore a negative will to power; for a fully affirmative philosophy, Deleuze turned to the work of Spinoza. One must be cautious when handling Deleuze's reading of Spinoza. Spinoza's philosophy was founded on the concept of a monistic philosophical substance, together with the lucidity and certainty of rational processes of deduction, both of which seem untenable in our historicist and sceptical age. Deleuze read Spinoza through Nietzschean eyes: he only explored those aspects that pass the test of the eternal return. 'Substance', instead of being modelled on inert matter, becomes a power of production and a sensibility (see Hardt, 1993: 71–3). He transformed the meaning of Spinoza's thought, while remaining entirely faithful to the texts, by discovering a plane of immanence in Spinoza's thought that has an analogous role to the selective function of the eternal return, but which can subsequently replace it.

The problem of synthesis works as follows: any relation of territories, impulses, or forces requires a 'body' in which such forces act upon each other. When such forces are in conflict, synthesized according to a negative will to power, then in a certain sense there is no full relation between them. A master imposes his own conventions, values, and drives onto a servant without bothering to ask about those held by the servant. The principle of synthesis remains exterior to the relation itself; one can draw a sharp distinction between the 'body', or the empirical episode in which the relation is worked out, and the transcendental level of the 'will to power' which determines that one set of conventions and impulses remains detached and unaffected by the other. The episode does not affect the conventions and drives of the master; it has no determining role on the relation itself. By contrast, when posing the test of the eternal return, Deleuze seeks a kind of relation that will determine and affect itself – the episode will react back on the transcendental condition. A distinction between the transcendental and the empirical cannot survive the test of the eternal return: for the transcendental conditions the empirical, but the empirical then returns and conditions the transcendental. The two terms exchange places, and ultimately become indiscernible. Indeed, concepts such as 'will to power' and 'eternal return' will not survive their own selective tests; the test will negate itself.[13]

One cannot say that nothing at all has changed, however. When forces meet and interact, the relation that they construct affects their own nature and changes them in the process. Deleuze and Guattari will later call this a process of becoming or double deterritorialization: one force acts on another by lending it a fragment of its 'code', offering some of its conventions and habits. It imposes senses and values on the other force. The latter then responds by acting on the former, imposing its own senses and values. Through this exchange of fragments of code, the overall memory or territory belonging to each force is expanded, possibly in a way that overrides former codes and conventions (1988: 306–7). Each force is transformed in its essence: it is deterritorialized. The two processes gain a 'consistency'. The emergence of *Homo sapiens* as a tool-making animal takes place through double deterritorialization: a hand is a front paw that has been deterritorialized from the earth and reterritorialized on a branch or tool; a stick, in turn, is a deterritorialized branch (1994: 67). Deleuze is fond of citing the example of the orchid that 'captures' or constructs a complementary part of the genetic code of a wasp: it forms itself to look like a female wasp, so that male wasps will come to it and redistribute its pollen in a mutually beneficial symbiotic relationship. A process of double deterritorialization is also present in the way Deleuze allows Spinoza's and Nietzsche's thought to encounter and transform each other in the context of Deleuze's own thought. The essential component of such relations of becoming is that differing modes should mutually act upon each other and transform each other.

Deleuze discovered becoming as the prototype of an immanent relation. Such relations of becoming involve nothing outside of the territories, impulses, or forces that encounter or act upon each other. More accurately, the shape and progress taken by such relations is entirely determined by the modes related; yet the question of whether or not such a relation will take place comes from outside. The existence of affirmative syntheses depends on whether or not territories tend to relate and act upon each other; it depends on desire. If desire is still a transcendental term, it concerns the fact that something happens, rather than what happens. This understanding of the role of desire emerges through Deleuze's consideration of Spinoza's thought.

Spinoza had distinguished between inadequate and adequate ideas. Whenever we encounter something that affects us, we form an idea of that relation by associating it with our perception of what we encounter; hence we learn from experience what is good and bad to eat. Consequently, it is possible to plan life so that the maximum of beneficial encounters are obtained, and the minimum of harmful ones. Yet such ideas are unreliable and imperfect: we may believe that we are eating a good meal, without knowing that someone has poisoned it. A second kind of idea occurs when we encounter something that agrees with our essence, or is composed of the same parts. For when it affects us, our own essence expresses itself in our minds: we feel what we perceive. We have a 'common notion' of the relation that we encounter and feel expressed in our own minds; we can form an adequate idea. Hence we gain self-knowledge by encountering others like ourselves.[14] Deleuze, however, had no such ideas of fixed essences, and was much more interested in the synthesis of differences; yet the way in which he transformed Spinoza's common notions so that they still produce knowledge is quite remarkable.

Spinoza had two ways of considering a body. Firstly, a body is conceived in terms of the relations between its parts in extension. These parts are also composed of further parts. One tends to think in terms of the component organs and cells of a body, yet Spinoza has something strange to say: bodies are only distinguished in extension by degrees of 'speed and slowness, movement and rest', and not with respect to substance (Spinoza, 1989: 49); they can only be known through the changes that happen to them. Deleuze understood this principle in terms of composition of a body: each part will be distinguished according to certain thresholds – it depends on whether a part arrives in time, neither too early nor too late for it to be included (1988: 257). Deleuze will therefore think of such parts as becomings, the crossing of thresholds that change the essence of a thing. Insofar as such becomings form a constant body, we may think of them as habits or conventions. They are potentialities, or tendencies to act in a certain way. Deleuze cites the example of a tick, an insect with only three capacities: to climb upwards towards the light into the branches of trees; to smell a passing mammal and fall upon it; and to seek the warmest area of the mammal in order to suck its blood (Deleuze, 1988b: 124). If there is no tree available, or if no mammal arrives on time, the tick will die. Such potentials or habits are called 'affects'.

Secondly, a body may be considered in intensity, all at once, in terms of the modification that it is undergoing. Here an affect is a feeling: it is either the sadness that results from the diminishment of one's power of acting, or the joy which results from adding to oneself the powers of another. Such affects can be distinguished again according to whether the relation is synthesized in the past, or projected towards the future. Apprehended as already past, even if it is still happening, the affect is an emotion or pathos, an instantaneous apprehension of a multiplicity of different terms (1988: 32). The affect shows a second aspect: it is an expressive quality, or territory. Projected towards the future, the affect is a sympathy, a desire for relation, the 'drive in person' (1988: 259). The affect, therefore, is also an erotic desire.

With these Bergsonian considerations in mind, the meaning of Spinoza's common notions can be transformed. If one encounters another body, however unlike one's own, and enters a relation of becoming, then this movement of becoming is held in common, even if it is experienced in different ways. The relation can be considered as a new potential or habit, even if it only happens once: it is the capacity to enter into a certain kind of relation with the other body.[15] The relation is also felt and experienced as a quality, in intensity. These two ways of expressing the same relation of becoming are adequate to each other: one feels that which is expressed in the relation. One learns what one's body can do. One gains a knowledge of the relation; but this knowledge is neither a convention nor an impulse, for it is effectively realized in the relation. The most significant knowledge is that the relation occurs at all: one reaches the level of a third kind of synthesis – the level of desire.

Deleuze read Spinoza's common substance as a 'power of existing'; for him, the power itself does not exist in itself, but only insofar as it is realized (Deleuze, 1990a: 85–95). The dichotomy between essence and existence is removed; the 'power of existing' is therefore an ontological desire to come into existence. Desire is not immanent to the plane of existence; desire is the immanent plane of existence. 'To be' is to be coming into a relation, to be a becoming, to produce a new affect, relation, or modification between terms that are themselves modifications. Desire only exists when it produces an affect; yet it then turns back upon itself and conditions itself. Like Spinoza's substance, desire is a cause of itself; yet unlike the usual interpretation of Spinoza's substance, desire only exists in the relations and modifications it produces. There is a kind of vicious circle of desire by which desire overdetermines itself: events, relations, or becomings on the plane of immanence produce desire when they encounter each other and produce a new relation; desire then produces the new relation on the plane.

Deleuze, therefore, extracted an ontology of desire from Spinoza: to 'be' is to desire, to become, to relate, and to produce. He also constructed an epistemology of desire. Yet we may distinguish different kinds of knowledge. Everything that exists is a becoming, but to comprehend a becoming one has to form a relation with it. Now, insofar as one simply perceives a becoming as an intensity, a code, or a territory, one does not allow it to affect one's own underlying mode of existence or body of affects: something fixed is extracted from the becoming. Codes remain unchanged, and territories encompass the becoming within a greater whole. Perhaps the nervous system is affected, but the contemplating mind remains aloof; the becoming is encoded or reterritorialized. This action will itself be a 'movement of slowness', a becoming, but in Nietzschean terms, it is a becoming-reactive, expressing a negative will to power that aims to annihilate the relation. This is a modality of desire, but one that operates when desire does not have sufficient power to enter into a full relation. By contrast, there is a form of knowledge where knowledge itself is a becoming or condition of itself. Desire becomes knowledge of itself, as well as cause of itself (Deleuze, 1990a: 113–28). This awareness of desire, in which desire becomes an ontological affect, or how one feels about life as a whole, is also the liberation of desire: desire is enabled to communicate and intensify itself. Such relations do not happen in abstraction; they only happen when the relation is expressed in the production of something new. In philosophy, Deleuze replaced Spinoza's common notions with the creation of concepts. For when a concept is created, its conditioning and its meaning are adequate to each other: it says what it is, and is what it says.[16]

Finally, Deleuze borrowed a third element from Spinoza's practical philosophy. Spinoza does not seek knowledge for its own sake, nor for the sake of planning and controlling life. Spinoza found an active joy immanent in knowledge; to gain adequate knowledge in the form of common notions is to be affected by the common substance, or life itself. Knowledge therefore produces a desire for more knowledge; ontology naturally transforms itself into ethics. For Deleuze, something similar occurs; yet desire is not a highest value, or something that must be sought. One gains access to desire through encountering becomings expressed in other modes of existence; desire is produced when becomings are connected together. For Deleuze, there is a joy immanent in desire; but desire only exists in the relations of production that it creates. Desire produces itself, spreading by contagion; but this contagion is the real production of mutually affective and transformative social relations. To produce and know desire, therefore, is to express a politics of desire: the production of desire is inseparable from the creation of new modes of social existence.

The 'liberation of desire' preached by Deleuze should be understood according to this Nietzschean and Spinozist basis; in essence, it has very little to do with Marx, Freud, or Reich, and much less to do with the 'sexual revolution'. Sexual desire, as is well known, can produce any number of pathological social and psychic processes; at times, Deleuze even advocated the civilizing effects of culture to keep desire in check (1988: 165, 227–31). Deleuze's use of a positive selection aims to separate desire from its own death-instinct and all relations of violence, producing an entirely positive and creative mode of existence. Deleuze did not advocate a return to primitive savagery, but the construction of a culture of desire alongside conventional culture. Yet one must be careful not to over-emphasize the ontological aspects of desire; desire is encountered not in theoretical abstraction as a timeless essence, but only in the real relations that exist between people. The knowledge of desire only arises from an immanent engagement with the social field.

Conclusion

Deleuze sought knowledge of a kind of relation that is not mediated by transcendent presuppositions. The only kind of immanent relation is a spontaneous attraction between heterogeneous terms resulting in the incorporation of each other into their modes of existence. The modification of each term affects the other, and observes a parallel movement to its own change in the other. The relation gains a kind of consistency and autonomy. Yet to have knowledge of such relations requires that one lives them and produces them. This kind of relation is exemplified paradigmatically in sexual attraction – hence Deleuze calls it 'desire'. Nevertheless, desire is a deterritorialized concept in that it does not derive its entire meaning from the territory in which it is first located, in this case, sexual relations. Desire is a 'sexuality' which extends beyond gender relations, because it can relate entirely heterogeneous terms and territories, a multiplicity of sexes. Deleuze and Guattari will use three kinds of knowledge to examine three different kinds of syntheses: codes, territories, and becomings. While the latter expresses desire, the former two are regarded as products from within a plane of immanence.

Deleuze and Guattari have no interest in creating a truly universal theory of society. The knowledge which they attain is not universal or impersonal, but derives from their own modes of existence, and expresses their own capacities, memories, and desires. Hence they do not write about all kinds of cultural products, but only about those which they love. They do not write about all kinds of power-formations, but only about those which they wish to destroy. The revolution of desire does not primarily aim to create a society of liberty, equality, and justice, but a society of multiplicity, desire and creativity. Deleuze and Guattari's social theory, therefore, is concerned with a knowledge of desire, by desire, for desire. This desire is only encountered, however, in the real relations which exist upon an immanent plane. One therefore accomplishes little by talking about 'desire' in the abstract; much more is to be gained by developing strategies for the liberation and creation of desire. Deleuze and Guattari's thought only expresses their involvement in such strategies for creating a liberated and immanent society.

Their 'theory' derives from an entirely different genetic element from most human knowledge; it is difficult to over-emphasize the significance of this revolution. Although they may use some of the same words, ideas, and concepts, these are always 'deterritorialized' – their meanings are changing, following lines of flight. Even in France, Deleuze and Guattari write in a kind of foreign language, and belong to a foreign culture (Deleuze, 1993: 9). Any reading of their thought that misses such differences fails entirely to engage with the conversion of 'knowledge' that they have effected, and with what is actually happening in their texts.

Notes

1. *Anti-Oedipus* (1984), *Kafka* (1986), and *Dialogues* (Deleuze, 1987) are the main texts.

2. Frequently in secondary literature on Deleuze, people attempt to compare Deleuzean and Hegelian conceptions of difference in order to examine which can be thought without the other. For example, Todd G. May asks whether difference is internal or external to the system (May, 1993: 7). By raising such a problem one already recuperates difference by presupposing a system in relation to which difference will be assessed. Much secondary literature wrestles with problems that have no place in Deleuzean thought. It is of no consequence how difference is assessed; what matters in Deleuzean thought is how difference differentiates itself from itself (Deleuze, 1994: 28).

3. An excellent philosophical exposition and vindication of Deleuze's return to empiricism has been conducted by Bruce Baugh (Baugh, 1993).

4. This interaction between knowledge and institutions anticipates the relation between statements and visibilities that Deleuze will explore in Foucault's work (Deleuze, 1988d).

5. See below Chapter 4, 'Capitalism and Schizophrenia'.

6. Deleuze argues that where Kant invokes the idea of the subject, Hume constructs a purposive view of human nature (Deleuze, 1991a: 111–21).

7. Although there are many points of comparison to be made with Alfred Whitehead, whom Deleuze only cites in his later writings (see Alliez, 1993: 67–74).

8. Deleuze will later call duration the unproductive 'body without organs'.

9. Michael Hardt reads Deleuze's Bergsonism in opposition to Hegel (see Hardt, 1993: 1–19).

10. Guattari calls this an 'ecology of the virtual' (Guattari, 1992: 127).

11. This audacious reversal of Nietzsche has attracted criticism as reinstating 'all that Nietzsche fought against' (Caputo, 1993: 50). But questions remain as to the consistency of Nietzsche's texts. By rethinking, rather than representing, Nietzsche's thought, Deleuze is perhaps more authentically Nietzschean than those who remain disempowered by Nietzsche's nihilistic vision.

12. See Deleuze's distinction between 'combat contre' and 'combat entre' (Deleuze, 1993: 165).

13. This is hinted at by Deleuze and Guattari (1988: 6).

14. See Spinoza (1989: Book II) for a fuller explanation of this kind of knowledge. Also, Deleuze (1990a: 273–89).

15. Indeed, Spinoza says that such a power of existing is the essence of the body (Spinoza, 1989: 91).

16. See the discussions of 'univocity' (Deleuze, 1990b: 179–80), and the relative and absolute sides of the concept (Deleuze, 1994: 21).

2

The Abstract Machine

Problem 5: On knowing the social unconscious

Knowledge of the social unconscious presents several problems. Firstly, what kinds of unconscious processes and presuppositions are there? How can one have a knowledge of that which is in principle unconscious? What kinds of unconscious processes are theoretically knowable? Deleuze and Guattari's solution is to use a plane of immanence as a selective ontology: only exterior relations such as intensities, codes, territories, and becomings are appropriate for a philosophy of desire. These relations are the unconscious syntheses that operate in practice on the surface of thought, between the conscious and unconscious; their derivation was outlined in the previous chapter.

Secondly, following Nietzsche, thought renounces its claim to a privileged relation to truth so as to allow truth to become a creation of thought (1994: 54). This problematizes knowledge: how can one have a knowledge that does not claim to be true or false? How can one assert testable propositions about certain social events and processes? Deleuze and Guattari renounce any belief in their propositions. For propositions relate independent variables on a plane of extensive coordinates through reference (1994: 22) Every fact refers to a certain time and place, a history and geography in which it is actualized. The truth-value of any social scientific proposition is then measured by the degree to which it occupies a given space or population. Statistical surveys are useful tools for measuring the truth-values of such propositions. The characteristics omitted from such an account of society include 'movement' in the broadest sense: the social processes involved in the production of a certain socio-economic arrangement, such as secularization, globalization, commodification, and retraditionalization, for example, cannot be tested so easily. Moreover, when social processes cease to be independent variables related through a hypothetical function (for example, does globalization produce an increase in nationalism and fundamentalism?), but become mutually dependent variables that effect each other's essence (for example, does fundamentalism also change the nature of globalization?), then movement becomes 'infinite' variation – not necessarily a large movement, but unlimited variation, folding and refolding a set of movements back into each other in an infinite, fractalized becoming, where meaning is continually changing (1994: 37). The plane of immanence selects infinite variations.

In Deleuze's empiricism relations are external to their terms. This means that knowledge of society is a theoretical construct given by the mind of the observer. All knowledge takes on the character of 'fantasy' or 'fiction', which may at best only approximately model the real relations existing in society. What is significant for Deleuze and Guattari, however, is the way in which such a fiction is constructed. Imagination is not purely spontaneous, but operates in the service of needs, interests, forces, and desires. Immanence has a second import: the theorist is not some impartial observer surveying the plane of social relations, but is immanent within the plane, a mode of existence like all the others. The mode of existence of the theorist is produced within the network of social relations in which he or she lives. The fictions produced by the theorist are therefore symptoms of this network of intensities, codes, territories, and becomings – one does not speak on one's own account, nor represent the thoughts and activities of others, but speech is produced by a 'collective assemblage of enunciation'. The relation between theory and society that interests Deleuze and Guattari, therefore, is not one of representational modelling or reference, but the genetic relation by which society produces theory. The question of the truth of any body of theory is of much less importance than the political and sexual interests that it expresses. This is a very different conception from the Enlightenment ideal of knowledge, according to which one is expected to know how society works before one is able to express practical and political interests in order to attain desired goals. For Deleuze and Guattari, the practical engagement with society already exists at the unconscious levels of power and desire, and theory is merely a conscious symptom or product of unconscious interests. Where a fiction of society appears in theoretical representation, real social relations are already expressed in the social unconscious that positions the theorist.

Renouncing the position of mastery gained by the critical intellectual and allowing oneself to be positioned by an existing network of social relations may lead to a converse problem – theory may merely speak on behalf of existing power relations. Theory suffers from its own historical and cultural determinism. Indeed, one of the most effective ways of discrediting the claims to relevance of any theory is to situate it within a particular historical and cultural milieu, so that one may learn from the historical and cultural processes evidenced within the theory, but not from the theory itself. This, however, is merely an excuse for a failure to engage with its concepts, and begs the question as to whether a theory was involved in propagating or resisting a particular historical and cultural milieu.

Deleuze and Guattari's thought was deeply engaged in the struggles of its own period from the 1960s and 1970s in Paris, drawing on theories from structuralism, Marxism, psychoanalysis, and Nietzscheanism to engage in the fight for a collective social, economic, psychosexual, ecological, and aesthetic revolution, with hopes of liberating minorities, the mentally ill, and prisoners. Since that time, there has been a significant shift in the strategies and distribution of power as well as in strategies of resistance, and a collective loss of faith in the possibilities offered by resistance. Deleuze and Guattari's discussions and opinions on these issues may have a little less relevance today – especially for those who despair of the possibility of change through collective social action. Yet one fails to engage with their thought, if one extracts opinions without exploring their concepts, constructing a world-view without exploring their philosophy.

Deleuze and Guattari resisted historical and cultural determinism by constructing a plane of immanence in a third sense. For the forces that operate in the social unconscious are movements or variations: to incite, to induce, to seduce, to make easy or difficult, to enlarge or limit, to make more or less probable (Deleuze, 1988d: 70). While the theorist is open to be affected by all these forces from outside, their influence can be tempered by the selective test of the eternal return: if the forces are folded back upon themselves, reflexively applied to themselves, then only self-affirmative forces will be capable of raising themselves to a power of infinite variation. The only lasting synthesis between forces will be one of reciprocal affection and mutual affirmation, a symbiotic relation where each contributes to the essence of the other. The plane through which Deleuze and Guattari relate to social and historical forces is a plane of consistency, a selective plane of thought where only relations of consistency are admitted – 'consistency' is a relation that holds heterogeneous terms together by their mutual action upon each other, implying a continuity produced through repetition (1988: 327–37). Although thinking may be a perilous act, engaging with forces of the void, of life and death, of reason and madness, folding the forces of the outside constructs a

safe haven where thought is again possible (Deleuze, 1988d: 95, 123). Philosophical thought constructs and expresses relations of consistency on such a
plane. Deleuze and Guattari's concepts are not determined by their historical and
cultural milieu; they merely have relations of consistency where thought encounters being in a zone of indiscernibility – this is 'geophilosophy' (1994: 85).

In this respect, Deleuze and Guattari's theory is possibly unique. It should
never be judged according to its apparent 'truth' or 'falsehood'. For the kind of
relations which Deleuze and Guattari talk about are created by them in the
service of their own desires and interests, while these desires are in turn
constructed on a plane of immanence. Their aim is not to describe the world, but
to change it, or, more precisely, to create a new world to overlay and replace the
present one, in the form of a new arrangement of desire. The only criterion by
which to judge Deleuze and Guattari's theory is an immanent one: it is a question
of whether one loves or hates it, of whether one can use its resources to build
something else. Deleuze and Guattari's social theory does not tell us about
society in general, nor about the society in which we live; it only tells us about
the social unconscious which Deleuze and Guattari have created, out of the
resources which lie to hand, and it provides a resource through which we may
create our own social meanings and relations.

The Plane of Immanence

What kind of social unconscious did Deleuze and Guattari create? The
unconscious specific to their thought will be its abstract machine, a set of
functioning components. One may track down the abstract machine specific
to their thought by observing the strategies at work in their thought. Deleuze
and Guattari have described the major components of philosophy, and by
implication their own thought in particular, as the laying out of a plane of
immanence, the creation of concepts, and the invention of conceptual
personae (1994: 77).

'The plane of immanence is not a concept that is or can be thought but
rather the image of thought, the image thought gives itself of what it means
to think, to make use of thought, to find one's bearings in thought' (1994:
37). Such an image of thought is constructed by thought, but, once
constructed, it is discovered as pre-existent or already presupposed – one has
already oriented oneself within such an image of thought in order to find the
image. All philosophical absolutes are like Platonic Ideas, showing the kind
of tension that is found between that which Plato did and that which Plato
taught (1994: 29): they must be created, but once created, they pre-exist in
their own anteriority or eternity. For example, Kant adopted legislation as an
image of thought, Nietzsche adopted evaluation, and Heidegger adopted
interpretation. Followers of each may claim to ask more critical, valuable, or
primordial questions than the others, but in practice there remains a
differend (Lyotard, 1989b) (more accurately, a differend of differends)
between them – the problems they raise relate to differing planes, so that
when one criticizes the other, they are no longer talking about the same
concepts. The empirical question of whether and when thought does indeed
conform to legislation, evaluation, or interpretation is of less significance
than whether thought can claim these activities by right: does legislation

legislate legislation as the image of thought? Does evaluation evaluate evaluation to be the most valuable image of thought?

The image of thought that Deleuze and Guattari adopted is one concerned with images of thought itself: philosophy becomes noology (see 1988: 374–80; 1994: 44; Goodchild, 1996: 35–7). Concepts and images of thought are assessed not by their content, but according to their mode of expression or the way in which they are thought. This strategy undermines all pretensions to transcendence. For although there exist certain self-positing absolutes in philosophy, such as the Idea, Being, the One, the Whole, or the Subject, Deleuze and Guattari were concerned with the mode of expression of such absolutes, rather than viewing all of life from the perspective of their content. Whose interests do they serve? What power-relations do they express? Are they affirmative of desire? This strategy is able to distinguish philosophy from its precursors in religious or wisdom traditions. A religious figure, and religious doctrine as a whole, may be structured as a mandala or spiral, reflexively pointing beyond itself toward the infinite: it is essentially paradigmatic, projective, hierarchical, and referential, heralding an absent transcendence that can only project a fallible image onto the plane (1994: 89). Now, philosophical absolutes may be treated as religious figures, as, for example, in Neoplatonism, which always seeks a One beyond the One (1994: 44). When they are simply presupposed by thought, however, they provide the plane of immanence within which thinking can take place, a One that is immanent in all things.

In noology, since the image of thought concerns thought itself, it is defined reflexively, and is capable of taking thought to a level of infinite variation. The first movement that characterizes Deleuze and Guattari's image of thought is a renunciation of projection in favour of connection (1994: 90). They decline the offer of a window onto the eternal. The content of thought is no longer presumed to have any reference, any relation to the truth (1994: 54). Philosophy is distinguished from sophism, wisdom, and opinion. For the content of thought is no longer presumed to be clear and distinct, transparent in relation to the truth toward which it points. Thought is composed of signs, but instead of following the projection of signs towards that which they signify, Deleuze and Guattari treated all signs as asignifying: there is always a declination of the sign away from its signified, towards a neighbouring sign (Deleuze, 1990b: 269). The relations between signs form an incorporeal plane of surface effects, but it is only on such a plane that formations of power and desire become transparent in the mode of expression. This image of thought as declination, when presupposed as a plane immanent within thought so that it becomes the mode of expression of Deleuze and Guattari's thought, selects the asignifying sign as its content or material of being. Thought addresses itself to matter, but the body that it chooses to think is merely an incorporeal surface effect, an asignifying sign. One can already see how expression and content are entirely relative (1988: 44), so that an arrangement of asignifying signs, the mode of expression of a body, can be taken as the content of Deleuze and Guattari's thought. When it comes to the problem of pure expression and pure content – the problem of mind, matter, and their relationship – then we are dealing with transcendental illusions: mind and matter only exist relative to each other in the fundamental unity of the plane.

Declination produces a critique of all transcendent presuppositions. Deleuze and Guattari's critique is strategic: they did not aim to show the error of presuppositions, but opposed the strategy by which these are elevated to an unquestionable and unaffectable status. Objective presuppositions might include unique, totalizing and unchanging concepts, such as 'God', the 'world', and the 'subject', or the 'one', the 'whole', 'objectivity', 'identity', and 'opposition', or the 'State', 'labour', 'exchange', and 'communication'. Deleuze and Guattari had no interest in questions of the existence of God or the subject, but only in criticizing the strategies by which such questions are raised. Subjective or inter-subjective presuppositions might include totalizing conditioning factors that govern the way we think, such as concepts of 'being', 'history', 'language', 'society', 'culture', 'economic production', 'discourse', 'power', 'desire', 'death-instinct', or 'gender difference'. Here again, Deleuze and Guattari questioned the strategy by which such empirical concepts are raised to the status of transcendentals. Moreover, one should be sensitive to the degree to which such factors, whether or not they are mentioned by philosophers or theorists, do indeed govern thought in practice. For Deleuze and Guattari, as we saw earlier, there exist differences that cannot be contained by any such encompassing concepts; there are desires and becomings which may even affect God (1984: 16). Deleuze and Guattari's critique is nomadic in style: it does not aim at simple destruction, but aims to bring all fixed identities and elevated transcendentals back down to earth, forcing them to flee across the desert. All terms will appear upon a single plane of thought where there are no longer any ultimate and unchanging distinctions, and any term can be affected by any other (1988: 69). Hence: 'God is a lobster, a double pincer or a double bind' – God becomes an animal or a strategy (1988: 40).

The second movement that characterizes Deleuze and Guattari's thought is violence exercised against itself (1994: 55). For having renounced the transcendent ordering and organization of thought, one is merely left with the possibility that there might be a composition of asignifying signs, an assemblage, where thought grasps the consistency of a set of relations all at once; there is no guarantee, however, that such a thought will indeed take place. Placing diverse terms together, or wandering nomadically along a rhizome, is no guarantee of consistency. Indeed, nothing could be less interesting than a free association of terms of equivalent value. Where previously in philosophy, thought could take itself as a passive contemplation of a pre-given object or idea (1994: 45–7), now nothing is given in advance. Thought begins from a state of inactivity, from a condition in which we are not yet thinking, and must be submitted to various forces and disciplines before it becomes capable of its own activity. Such forces arise from outside thought.

As Heidegger pointed out, what is most thought-provoking at present is the fact that we are not yet thinking (Heidegger, 1993: 370). Deleuze and Guattari borrow this image of thought (1994: 55), but instead of relating the problem solely to the history of philosophy, they open thought to the entire psychosocial field. If we are not yet thinking, then there is a certain configuration of power-relations that actively prevents thinking (which Deleuze and Guattari will call 'Oedipus'). Indeed, the discipline of the history of philosophy itself may repress thinking by requiring that one should read various classics and commentaries before daring to speak in one's own name (Deleuze, 1991b: 14). What is most worthy of thought, therefore, will be the way in which such configurations of power-relations do indeed repress thought. Thought becomes inseparable from its own micropolitical struggles in a particular social and cultural milieu. Some of Deleuze and Guattari's specific struggles will be explored in the middle section of this book.

Nevertheless, Deleuze and Guattari's engagement with their own micropolitical struggles requires no biographical accounts of lived experience, and little critical intellectual commentary on their social and cultural milieu. For in order to draw a diagram of power or to personalize desire, however deeply one is affected by these, it is sufficient merely to write about machines. Deleuze and Guattari populate their social unconscious with machines, for these will be the partial and transitional objects for both the investment and production of desire: each machine can be considered from three points of view, according to a longitude, latitude, and essence (1988: 257). Each machine has a composition, function, and potential.

When Heidegger considered the mode of being of an airliner on a runway, while questioning the essence of technology, he did not give an analysis of its material composition, for this would conceal what and how it is; instead, he grasped its mode of being as a whole as 'standing-reserve', ordered for transportation (Heidegger, 1993: 323). This is already to move to the domain of power, to observe how the machine affects us, how it is affected by us, and how the essence of technology affects us by concealing the mode of being of the airliner from us. Guattari's analysis of an airliner was somewhat more concrete, taking ontology beyond humanism by considering how machine speaks to machine prior to its effect on humanity: he chose the example of Concorde (Guattari, 1992: 73–4). From the point of view of composition, Concorde must be considered as the constellation of several universes of reference, each with its specific machinisms: a diagrammatic universe with its plans and theoretical feasibility; technological universes transposing this feasibility into material terms; industrial universes capable of effectively producing it; a collective imagination corresponding to a desire to make it happen; and political and economic universes hoping to extract the credit and profit from its operation. The one component lacking was economic, ruining the consistency of the whole project: its power of coming into existence was only sufficient for twelve examples circulating between London, Paris, and New York. Although the name 'Concorde' will have circulated through these various universes, and although the signs they used may refer to each other, it was not in virtue of such reference alone that the machine was built; rather, it was through each universe fulfilling its own independent function that the whole became possible. The constellation itself, named 'Concorde', was produced through the conjunction of asignifying signs.

This plane of composition identifies machinic heterogenesis, a productive interaction between diverse formations, as the meaning of contemporary ontology. Where a scientific ontology would only describe a machine in terms of its material and functional components defined by the independence of their variables, and where a historical ontology would describe a machine in terms of the intentions and ambitions of various human subjects, or the meaning of Being that they presuppose, Deleuze and Guattari leap to the domain where machines interact with machines, prior to artificial distinctions between nature and artifice, mind and matter. Various 'human' characteristics, such as rationalities, political economies, and desires, are already integrated as components of technological machines. Secondly, Concorde may be considered according to its function as a mode of transportation and deterritorialization. Although this is limited in the case of Concorde because of its comparative rarity, a possible outcome would be a reduction in time of transportation beneath a certain threshold where new kinds of business and personal relations become possible. In general, airliners act as agents of deterritorialization in a very literal sense, enabling vast migrations of tourists and ethnic populations, but also in a purely conceptual sense, insofar as this migration has a consequent effect on the forms of living that are possible. Technical machines are also components of human life, not merely in the literal sense of prostheses, but insofar as they constitute components of new forms of human life such as those forms of interaction between tourist and villager. Their effects on human life do not result from the exertion of some form of power or governmentality, although powers will be quick to exploit their potential; instead, it is an effect of deterritorialization, offering new possibilities for living, often to the extent that the old ones lose their viability and consistency. Following a Marxist inspiration, Deleuze and Guattari envisaged society being shaped by desire and production, the investment of desire in machines and machinic heterogenesis, prior to the stratification of desire into regimes of governmentality and power.

A machinic assemblage may therefore be considered according to its composition, in terms of the various groupings of signs as components, and according to its functions, the various affects it has or relations of deterritorialization into which it may enter. Indeed, since the plane of composition is not an extended plane, one cannot designate an individuated object according to certain space–time coordinates, in the way that we know that Concorde exists because we can point to specific instances of it. A machinic assemblage exists as an individuated but partial object (lacking a totalizable unity) according to the extent that it has affects, that it has a capacity to enter into machinic relations of deterritorialization and reterritorialization with other machinic assemblages – it makes a difference. Finally, a machinic assemblage may be considered according to its essence as a 'power of existing', a power of coming into being. Concorde was limited in its essence because of the lack of consistency between all its components: certainly, its speed affected its economic viability, particularly through the prestige conferred upon its customers; but it was not able to enter into a symbiotic relation with new forms of business activity that, dependent upon its speed, would guarantee its viability. It could make a difference, but that difference was not repeated. Each machinic assemblage can be considered according to an abstract machine that denotes its potential for coming into existence as a power of repetition. Each abstract machine is like a little refrain, a tune that gains its consistency through being repeated over and over again (1988: 343). Deleuze and Guattari's social unconscious, instead of being populated by concrete machinic assemblages (or machines that stand in reserve on concrete) having a certain actualization in space and time, is populated by abstract machines defined by their composition, function, and potential for existence.

What determines whether or not an abstract machine will gain consistency and come into existence? An obvious answer would be desire: if desire is invested in a machine, in the way that a child plays with a toy train, or a technological invention becomes caught up in someone's fantasy of economic success and fame, then it may focus sufficient creative energy to bring it into existence. Yet being caught up in someone else's fantasy is merely a ruse of power (Deleuze is cited by Žižek, 1994: 212). Deleuze and Guattari did not maintain any artificial boundaries between the psychic and the social, the personal and social unconscious, so that a fount of libidinal energy could be invested into material and social existence. The abstract machine is not an object for the investment of desire; indeed, the abstract machine is a desiring-machine, a machine that desires, a source of desire – its consistency and power of existing are desire. Instead of desire being regarded as a displacement of the familial romance between two sexes, each abstract machine is a sex, generating its own sexuality, its own non-human loves. This may seem like a metaphorical extension of sexuality beyond its normal range of application; Deleuze and Guattari deny this (1988: 69). After all, there is as much sexuality in the interactions of DNA molecules as there is between human sexes. Instead, their work is a deterritorialization of sexuality to the molecular level, seeing the kinds of interactions that operate here as functioning between all kinds of abstract machines.

For Deleuze and Guattari, therefore, philosophy does not involve a passive contemplation of society – not even of its social unconscious or its desires. A plane populated by abstract machines indicates a possibility of a social theory, but does not necessitate that one will actually begin thinking. Moreover, to invest one's desire into a certain theory of society, even one formulated in terms of abstract machines, is merely another ruse in gaining power over and managing the social field. Abstract machines, however, are resistant to representation, and do not allow themselves to be thought in this way: they lose all consistency and function, becoming gatherings of inert components when represented in thought.

What, then, will be the role of Deleuze and Guattari's philosophy? Is *Anti-Oedipus* compromised as a theory of desire insofar as it merely represents the machinic operations of desire once more? Does *Anti-Oedipus* present a non-authoritarian social imperative – 'liberate desire!' – through combining philosophy, politics, psychoanalysis, and avant-gardism, that is ultimately blocked by its own self-contradiction of becoming authoritarian and unproductive? It is certainly possible to read the text in such a way; but this does not constitute a proper engagement with Deleuze and Guattari's thought. Indeed, such a reading explores their thought as a body of pure theory, caught up within the regime of the signifier, entirely desexualized and disempowered. One need not doubt that such oedipalized and deconstructive readings are possible; but they will never succeed in capturing and comprehending the thought, laughter and desires of Deleuzoguattarians: 'In truth [*sic*], there are never contradictions, apparent or real, but only degrees of humor' (1984: 68). What kind of truth could never be contradicted? A truth that is implicated, and always annulled by its explication.

The most striking aspect of *Anti-Oedipus* is its style and humour: as a theory, it only gains significance through the ways in which it affects a reader, creating machinic relations and desires. As a theory, it does not refer to any particular machinic assemblage in history and culture, except through simulation that creates its own reality:

> It carries the real beyond its principle to the point where it is effectively produced by the desiring-machine. The point where the copy ceases to be a copy in order to become the Real and its artifice. To seize an intensive real as produced in the coextension of nature and history, to ransack the Roman Empire, the Mexican cities, the Greek gods, and the discovered continents so as to extract from them this always-surplus reality .... (1984: 87)

The book is merely a brute object, a matter of fact, a reality:

> contrary to a deeply rooted belief, the book is not an image of the world. It forms a rhizome with the world, there is an aparallel evolution of the book and the world; the book assures a deterritorialization of the world, but the world effects a reterritorialization of the book, which in turn deterritorializes itself in the world (if it is capable, if it can). (1988: 11)

Deleuze and Guattari did not choose to think about their own social and cultural milieu in order to give an intellectual critique. Instead, they wrote insofar as they were affected by this milieu, caught up in its machinations of power or liberated by its desiring-machines. The book becomes a production of thought generated by a collective assemblage of enunciation, a flow deriving from a writing-machine, a word-processor churning out page after page of permutations of paradigmatic and syntagmatic relations between signifiers. When the image of thought is that thought itself requires some violence exerted on it from outside that forces it to think, then the material of being it selects is the affect. The plane of immanence which thought inhabits is composed of signs and affects; thought wanders amid a plane of desire, diverted by signs and affects.

The Creation of Concepts

Deleuze and Guattari describe a third characteristic of their image of thought: our inability to think is not merely a fact of thought that will be overcome once we are forced to think; instead, it belongs to thought by right, indicating a fundamental incapacity at the core of thought. Even when thought does function, thought as such begins to exhibit 'snarls, squeals, stammers; it talks in tongues and screams, which leads it to create, or try to' (1994: 55). For Deleuze and Guattari's thought is blocked in an impasse: they are forced to think by the intolerable affects which they experience living in their social and cultural milieu; they cannot think in terms of representation about their social and cultural milieu; neither can they think purely in terms of abstract machines and consistency because these are imperceptible. This impasse indicates an incapacity that lies at the heart of their thought and will never be left behind. For this reason, a concept is never transparent, revealing its own meaning; nor is this transparency a state of error that could be removed if one does begin to think. Instead, a concept always has to be created in an intuition specific to it. Thought as such stutters because it must think, yet cannot think in a major language nor in the silences between words; yet stuttering at least produces something, generating an arrangement of asignifying signs in its own performance. Concepts only live in creation and performance.

This image of thought separates philosophy from reflection. For in philosophies of subjectivity such as those of Descartes, Kant, and Hegel, it is presupposed that thought is or can become transparent to itself, reflecting accurately upon itself. Such philosophy pretends to function by reflecting upon its own processes until it acquires a full knowledge of the categories or concepts that govern such thinking, when it will no longer be under illusions about itself or alienated from itself. What Kant and Hegel fail to notice is the extent to which they create or borrow the concepts that govern their thinking. For only a certain kind of subjectivity will be able to acquire knowledge of the universal categories and concepts that govern its thinking: the subject of enunciation (thinking subject) recoils into the subject of the statement (thought subject), so that it becomes subjected to its own laws (see 1988: 129–30). Once the subject is formed in such a way, it becomes stratified among dominant significations, where the significations of key concepts are fixed – reflection merely reconstitutes a higher dogma. For as structuralists such as Roland Barthes and Louis Althusser have shown, the signification of concepts is inseparable from a particular historical and cultural context and its ideological hegemony. It is presumed that thinking about thinking can become transparent; but this is the image of thought that has become impossible for Deleuze and Guattari because it excludes becoming, the autonomous act of thinking itself.

Deleuze and Guattari distinguished between two kinds of theory that result in different kinds of readings of society and history (1988: 361–74). The first is that of the 'majority': one is given a perspective, together with a set of categories and presuppositions, by the historical, social, cultural, and economic site which one occupies, a perspective expressing preconscious interests. One then uses such a site to construct a map of the socio-historical field, and may attempt to intervene and change the field according to the values and ideology produced by one's perspective. The significant point for Deleuze and Guattari was not the ideological status of such 'knowledge', which could be replaced by a pure, reflective 'science' conscious of its own class and economic interests, but that the underlying perspective is transcendent to the theoretical elaboration, and not directly affected by it. This social theory, whether it examines the socio-historical field upon an immanent plane or not, is called 'majoritarian' because of the mode of existence expressed by it. Majority is defined not by number, but by a constant mode of existence that transcends its conscious plane of theoretical analysis. From such a constant perspective, instances retain the same phenomenal characteristics and can be identified, coded, and reterritorialized. Dominant social presuppositions take on the mask of necessity through reflection: everyone knows them and can understand them. This constant perspective has a tendency to propagate itself, and so become the thought of the majority. For in order to discuss the same social and historical events, and for one's words to mean the same thing, it is necessary to adopt a compatible perspective, with its categories and presuppositions, so that the same names and codes can be used. Majoritarian theory therefore operates as a process of cultural reproduction: one has little choice but to accept the majoritarian perspective – perhaps that of a white, adult, rational, male, able-bodied, heterosexual speaker of a major European language, dweller in a town – even if one belongs to an entirely different social assemblage, merely in order to participate in majoritarian culture. (For example, the dominant international political agenda is largely set by organizations such as CNN and Reuters through a certain strategy of constructing 'impartial' knowledge; while the rationalities adopted by such networks express certain relations of forces, especially of the kind that Foucault named 'governmentality', the rise to dominance of such majoritarian presuppositions does not take place through the contest of forces so much as through frequency and redundancy of repetition, resulting from the machinic heterogenesis of an impersonal mass-media desiring-machine that lacks subject, object, and signification.) Once a majoritarian perspective is adopted, one's thought will then operate in the service of interests that are not one's own. This cultural predicament is not ideological: one does not have to believe in the adopted perspective in order to practise it; it is a predicament of desire, resulting from a desire for status and relation within majoritarian culture.

The other kind of theory is 'minoritarian': here again, one's perspective is determined by one's site in the social assemblage, together with its preconscious interests. This time, however, one's perspective is immanent in the theoretical field, for the signs and events one encounters may directly affect the unconscious assemblage of desire. One's own perspective becomes a part of the machine that is consumed as the process takes place. 'Minority' is defined not by a small number, therefore, but by the variation of the collective assemblage of enunciation (1988: 105–6, 469): one follows a line of flight or deterritorialization. The aim of this theory is to relate to other social assemblages not at the level of knowledge, but at the level of desire. It is not necessary for a politically active form of thought to take the form of 'theory' at all; indeed, Deleuze and Guattari refer almost exclusively to artists and writers as exemplars of the political programme they envisage, as opposed to activists or theorists. For the medium in which the experimentation is undertaken is not as significant as the abstract lines traced within this medium – such lines are produced by the machinic processes of desire. Fiction is a privileged medium of social and political thought, for Deleuze, since it is not bound up with any theoretical illusions: it is no longer a question of 'telling the truth' in order to bring people to a reflective consciousness of their real situation, for where minorities are colonized by majorities, the people (as a set of modes of existence) are still missing (insofar as the only consciousness available to the oppressed is that of the majority) and only fiction can invent a people (Deleuze, 1989: 216, 222). The important factor is not what it says, but how it works. Nevertheless, there are majoritarian and minoritarian forms of literature, one operating in the service of economic and cultural interests, the other operating in the service of the experimentations of desire. Deleuze favoured a certain kind of Anglo-American literature that explores the nomadic wanderings of desire, such as D.H. Lawrence, Henry Miller, Samuel Beckett, or Jack Kerouac, as well as a few European authors who show similar tendencies, such as Kleist, Proust, and Kafka (Deleuze, 1987).

Deleuze's philosophy, however, is in some respects closer to theory than to fiction. If minor thought is defined by variation of one's mode of existence, a pure form of minor fiction is one which takes this variation for its objective and desire. Deleuze is interested in those works of art which ask reflexive and theoretical questions: Deleuze and Guattari's literary theory is expressed through a reading of Kafka centred on Kafka's posing of the question 'What is a minor literature?'; Deleuze's book on painting is centred on the question 'What is the logic of sensation?' explored by Francis Bacon; and Deleuze's work on the cinema is centred on those directors who make thought the essence of cinema, and the question 'What is cinema?' the essence of their films. These theoretical questions focus their attention on the mode of expression. Similarly, Deleuze's entire philosophical oeuvre is an experimentation with the question 'What is philosophy?' (1994: 7). Once the majoritarian transparency of reflection is abandoned, these questions can only be resolved by experimentation throughout an oeuvre. A minor philosophy is considered in terms of its mode of expression as the creation of concepts. These theoretical questions do not look for a fixed essence, but aim to create a mode of existence at the same time as tracing its lines, processes, and becomings. The process affects the presuppositions and initial conditions. The initial state of the assemblage is therefore of less significance than the processes through which it passes, or the way in which it creates itself. One's initial social and existential territory may be changed by one's own artistic experimentation; thinking is a violence which one exercises first of all against oneself (Deleuze, 1991b: 140).

Here we come to the most definitive form of the theoretical impasse. For when we turn our attention solely towards the mode of expression, all content and meaning is evacuated. For example, Kafka wrote a story about Josephine the singer, a mouse who delivers concerts in front of all the other mice, having no sounds or words. All that remains is the pure event of the 'concert' as a social presupposition, and its effect on the mice; yet the mice agree that something has indeed happened and their lives have been changed (Kafka, 1988). The philosophical plane of immanence, composed only of exterior relations, abstract lines, and concepts, has precisely this nature: it is evacuated of all content, and therefore remains unthinkable and imperceptible. Deleuze and Guattari's concepts are entirely deterritorialized: they have no meaning, and only express a kind of nonsense – 'deterritorialized' means 'outlandish' (Deleuze, 1993: 93). 'Desire' is such a deterritorialized concept: it does not refer to an attraction or interaction between bodies, but designates a pure, social relation, a change in direction that could not have been anticipated. The events to which concepts refer only happen in the social unconscious; they always emerge from outside all social assemblages, forces, and interests, and effect different syntheses, relations, and attractions. It would appear that philosophy is saying nothing at all, whereas in fact everything is happening.

The vital characteristic of a minor philosophy, therefore, is that its concepts have crossed a threshold of absolute deterritorialization (cf. 1986: 16). Deleuze and Guattari illustrated the nature of their concepts with the example of that of 'another person' (*autrui*) (1994: 16–19). One major concept of another person is that of 'an other – a subject that presents itself as an object – that is special in relation to a self' (1994: 16). This concept is explained in terms of two components, an other and a self – it is reterritorialized on these abstract concepts that ultimately rely on dominant significations. Of course, it is also possible to invert the priority and explain the other and self in terms of alterity, relying on primordial significations of alterity such as obligation or response. But if a concept reaches a threshold of absolute deterritorialization, then dominant significations are no longer required. A minor concept of another person derives from another problem that concerns the mode of expression: 'what is the nature of the other person's position that the other subject comes to ''occupy'' only when it appears to me as a special object?' (1994: 16). Deleuze and Guattari find different components for the minor concept: 'Suddenly a frightened face looms up that looks at something out of field' (1994: 17). Another person is a face that expresses a possible world, the reality of which is confirmed by its language. Here again, the three components of face, possible world, and language can be reterritorialized on majoritarian significations of the other, such as the inscrutable Chinese face that expresses the mystery of the Orient through the strange intonations of the language that is spoken. But the components can be raised to a threshold of absolute deterritorialization by following a line of flight until they lose all signification: the possible world does not exist outside of the face that expresses it, the head only becomes a face insofar as a language is spoken, and language in turn is only distinguished from sound insofar as it speaks about a possible world. Each component of the concept shapes the others in mutual and reciprocal presupposition. There are no longer any transcendent, hidden, or fixed presuppositions, and the concept can be affected and change its meaning when it encounters other problems and other components.

Having crossed a threshold of absolute deterritorialization, concepts no longer refer back to their primordial significations: the concept of a 'possible world' no longer refers to China or anywhere else. Concepts, instead, designate pure events in thought (1994: 21). A second characteristic of a minor philosophy is that everything takes on a collective value (cf. 1986: 17): concepts are presuppositions that shape meaning, and the event of creation of a concept is a collective event in thought that changes presuppositions and meaning. Since every concept is a combination of components that did not exist before (1994: 75), the event of a concept is primarily the event of its creation, when it is dated, signed, and baptized (1994: 8). Yet a concept also designates an event as a 'haecceity', as something that happens: the 'animal-stalks-at-five-o'clock' (1988: 263). On the one hand, the time and place of the event could be regarded as extensive coordinates; but this begs the question of how the event is individuated, and which components are significant. In relation to thought, before the extensive coordination of space, time, and animal as independent variables on a plane of reference there must be an intensive ordination of a space, a time, an animal, and an action on a plane of consistency that grasps the happening all at once. Instead of designating a state of affairs that could be true or false, the concept ordains the sense of an event by thinking its components as inseparable, at an infinite speed: 'Five o'clock is this animal! This animal is this place!' (1988: 263). A concept is not referential but expressive; it expresses a created indiscernibility of meaning that could not be stated discursively.

A third characteristic of a minor philosophy is that everything is political. A major philosophy can be concerned with a pure philosophical realm of ideas, of Being, or of the a priori, the innate, or memory (1994: 68), where concepts, participating in the absolute, are absolved of a relation to the mundane world of human interaction which they govern. A minor philosophy is political, however, not in the sense that it speaks about politics, but in the sense that its concepts do not exist in a private and apolitical world but are shot through with the relations of power and desire that affect everyday life. Deleuze and Guattari's concepts express a politics of desire: they have a power of coming into being, an autopositing that resists dominant significations. Their mode of resistance is not that of conflict and opposition but that of mutual affirmation and creation: critique largely operates through 'passing by', through creating an alternative. Yet an alternative that offers a choice of a minor theory as opposed to a major theory will not be sufficient to liberate desire or overturn power, for those in power can continue to invest in dominant significations. The creation of concepts which find an endoconsistency between their relative components will accomplish little without these components also attaining an absolute condensation or coincidence in the concept (1994: 21). A concept gains its absolute status through self-reference or reflexivity (as opposed to reflection), where it acquires a power of self-positing. For this to occur, the event of creation of the concept and the event that the concept designates must enter into their own relation of consistency: the event of thinking and the event of thought, transcendental and empirical, the determination and the determinable, expression and content, reciprocally affect each other and become indiscernible. As Éric Alliez has remarked, the great concepts of Deleuze and Guattari are those which are concepts of the concept (Alliez, 1993: 100). For example, 'deterritorialization' is an absolute, self-positing concept because it deterritorializes itself in the moment in which it is created – it gives itself its own meaning. This is the only power of a minor philosophy. Yet under such conditions, although concepts are absolute, they are not eternal: their meaning can be changed through the exploration of new problems, new images of thought, and new conceptual personages.

A minor philosophy, asking the reflexive theoretical question, aims to make its own mode of existence into the deterritorialized plane of desire. It disinvests desire from its previous social assemblages, so that desire can begin to operate as a liberated and spontaneous plane. This revolution or liberation of desire is also the creation of desire, its condition of possibility. The plane of consistency is constructed at the same time as it comes to determine one's mode of existence. To repeat the theoretical impasse from a different direction: it is impossible to leap onto the plane, for the plane is not pre-existent but needs to be constructed. If one constructs a machinic assemblage by deterritorialization, it is abstract but dead. Deleuze and Guattari therefore borrow a solution from Kafka: one always proceeds indirectly, following the connections of relative deterritorialization and reterritorialization made by ordinary desires. It is impossible to theorize about the plane of desire, but one can effectively live it by acting out its desires. One's mode of existence now follows a line of escape or deterritorialization: it operates by dismantling the assemblages, moving from one place to another, passing through blockages, failures, crises, and impasses, so that all new relations are born from the abstract machine of desire and not from concrete machinic processes. Hence the work, *Anti-Oedipus*, cannot be regarded as a completed system of thought, but must be seen as an assemblage that only comes to make sense when one dismantles it, fleeing it in all directions. Here we reach a third, more abstract level: one's mode of existence belongs not to the empirical level of the functional machinic assemblages, nor to the transcendental level of the deterritorialized and dysfunctional lines, but to the plane where they meet. This is the level of abstract machines, the true plane of immanence, consistency, or desire. To live according to such abstract machines is to liberate desire.

Conceptual Personae

The Mechanosphere: *Homo sapiens*, that tool-making animal, becomes a slave of its own creations – each person becomes a cog in machinic processes that are largely beyond their control (1988: 456). Technical machines, military machines, industrial machines, economic machines, communication machines, fantasy machines, entertainment machines, media machines, computing machines, consumption machines, and governmental machines – each operates to produce an effect designed by a human, but to serve an end that no human has chosen. A saviour is born, a revolutionary: he will lead the battle against machinic domination so as to create a utopia of humanity, while a military–industrial complex builds a war-machine that will oppose his efforts (cf. 1988: 421, 466). The ultimate weapon (designed by whom? captured by whom?) is a time-machine: a destruction-machine returns to the past to prevent the birth of the saviour, while the saviour himself returns, not quite to become his own father, but at least to save his own birth, locked in a timeless struggle with his own double and adversary, the destruction-machine. The story of the *Terminator* films presents a very modern myth.

Which side do Deleuze and Guattari support: humanity or the machines? If robots so closely resemble humans, and humans aim to destroy robots, can one ultimately distinguish between the two? Perhaps this battle, like so many others, results from a false dichotomy: Deleuze and Guattari might support the mode of expression itself, where the struggle is replaced by an instance that affirms both humanity and the machines in their disjunction – the plot. In relation to our present, a robot appears from the future, is destroyed, and the silicon chip in its head is used to advance science to the point where it can build machines capable of dominating humans. The scientific advance is a possible future that invents itself, just as the revolutionary is a man who saves himself. The robot appears to our present as an other: the impassive face of Arnold Schwarzenegger expresses a possible world of machinic domination, a world that can be actualized by the language of the technical code stored inside his head. Yet just as this possible future can create itself, it can also destroy itself: in the second story, a replica robot controlled by humans returns to our time to destroy the original silicon chip and himself, unsuccessfully opposed by a formidable adversary created after science has crossed a further threshold of deterritorialization – the new robot has a metal body without organs, capable of melting, flowing, and resolidifying like money (see 1988: 411 for the relation between metallurgy, the body without organs, and money).

The plot depends on a purely cinematic device: the time-machine is produced by intercalating the series of images with subtitles indicating places and dates; a similar effect could be attained through use of the sound-track, or by making irrational cuts and discontinuities in the montage (Deleuze, 1989: 36). Indeed, the reason for Deleuze's interest in the cinema is that its technique of producing movement and time from irrational cuts in a series of photographic stills has much in common with the fourth characteristic of his image of thought: 'If thought searches, it is less in the manner of someone who possesses a method than that of a dog that seems to be making uncoordinated leaps' (1994: 55). Of course, one may well be justified in believing that time travel is physically impossible if speeds remain limited by the absolute speed of light, although one might accept some possibility of reverse causalities in physics and biology (1988: 431). But time travel is possible in the cinema insofar as all time is narrated and fundamentally false: there is only a before and after in the image; the present never exists except in bad films (Deleuze, 1989: 36). Similarly, time travel is possible in philosophy insofar as it has declined all reference to the truth of presence, so that thought may attain an infinite speed of variation. For the plane of consistency is topological: it may be folded and refolded so that points are given a proximity to each other, without one needing to travel any 'distance' through time. One can no longer say which component of a concept comes first: is the face, possible world, or language first in the concept of another person? Which movement of thought comes first on the plane: declination from the truth, violence exerted from without, stuttering, or uncoordinated leaping?

A montage of photographic stills can express an emergent or possible future that only exists insofar as it emerges. The essential requirement here is that a series of terms has crossed a threshold of absolute deterritorializa-tion. For example, a genetic code is caused materially by chemical inter-actions, but the sequence of amino acids in a nucleic sequence is entirely arbitrary. The reproductive power of the code allows a machine of expres-sion to be produced that is entirely indeterminate in relation to its material support. Similarly, the arbitrary relation between a phonetic or linguistic signifier and its signified allows a language to emerge as a set of codes and conventions that are largely autonomous in relation to their material of expression. The best example is music: implicit affects and sensations emerge in a neutral and autonomous matter – the pure form of time – through the mediation of rhythm, melody, and harmony. The swarming of possible and emergent modes of existence through the crossing of thresholds of absolute deterritorialization constitutes a materialist vitalism.

In philosophy, 'others' may create and posit themselves as possible futures – these are the material of being that corresponds to the image of thought as uncoordinated leaping. Empiricism, the philosophy that consists in associating signs and images, knows only events and others – and the others of philosophy are its conceptual personae (1994: 48). For once a concept posits itself, then it is no longer I who think, but another who thinks in me (Deleuze, 1984: viii). One should always pay particular attention to the modality of discourse. Modal logic relates propositions to their possible worlds: one should specify not only whether a proposition is true or false, or whether it predicates existence or non-existence, possibility or impossibility, necessity or contingency (see Kant, 1929: 113), but also in which possible world these are the case. Nevertheless, in modal logic, each possible world is that of the majority, even if no one exists there, for propositions are assumed to have a modality independently of where and when they are spoken, and the truth of their content is independent of their articulation. Nothing is indicated about the real forces that produce thought.

In a minor philosophy, the others who inhabit possible worlds no longer reproduce the formal discourse of the majority, but instead speak in foreign languages, even if they have to distort a major language until it becomes foreign. Indeed, the possible worlds no longer exist outside of the others who articulate them. For when statements are considered as speech-acts that perform events in discourse modifying social presuppositions (1988: 78), then the one who is speaking makes a difference as to whether the act can be accomplished. A speech-act refers back to a psychosocial type which functions as a subjacent third person: 'I decree mobilization as President of the Republic', 'I speak to you as father', and so on (1994: 64). In a minor philosophy, these psychosocial types no longer function as authoritative social roles in our world; instead, they are entirely deterritorialized – they are the people who do not yet exist, who will inhabit a world that is yet to come (1994: 109–10). 'Speaking as a schizophrenic, "desiring-production is at work everywhere, functioning smoothly at times, and at other times in fits and starts" ' (1984: 1). 'Speaking as a band of nomads, "a book has neither object nor subject; it is made of variously formed matters, and very different dates and speeds" ' (1988: 3). 'Speaking as a lobster, every stratum is a judgement of God; not only do plants and animals, orchids and wasps, sing or express the glory of God, but so do rocks and even rivers, every stratified thing on earth. Every articulation is double: the first concerns content, the second expression' (see 1988: 44). 'Speaking as a public garden or zoo, "possibilities of life or modes of existence can be invented only on a plane of immanence that develops the power of conceptual personae" ' (1994: 73). Deleuze and Guattari write with their tongues so firmly fixed in their cheeks that it is small wonder that they stutter and are difficult to understand. If one does not know who is speaking, or if one lacks sensitivity to the modality of the discourse, one may not notice all the events that take place. Indeed, this image of thought as proceeding by uncoordinated leaps generated by self-positing others separates philosophy from communication, for communication presupposes a common language.

Conceptual personae do not make thought transparent or communicable. Instead, the role of conceptual personae is to express thought's territories, as well as its movements of deterritorialization and reterritorialization, in order to deterritorialize the thinker and produce thought and desire (1994: 69). This relation between conceptual personae and territory indicates a return to content. In majoritarian discourse, content remains an inert and passive signified material for the activity of expression: one speaks of a chariot, but no chariot comes out of one's mouth (see Deleuze, 1990b: 134). Yet content can participate in subjectivity, and give a consistency to the ontological quality of expression, by means of a reversibility between content and expression that Guattari calls an 'existentializing function' (Guattari, 1992: 40). The other is a crystal or a seed of thought (1994: 69): its power of coming into being is dependent on whether it can crystallize in the given environment. It is such a crystalline structure that Deleuze finds as the essence of the time-image in the cinema. The seed is a virtual structure in an actual environment; for it to grow, the environment must be virtually crystallizable when an actual seed is implanted (Deleuze, 1989: 74). The other may reveal itself to thought insofar as it makes use of a crystalline structure, or emerges as a complexity in a dissipative structure (Prigogine and Stengers, 1985).

This leads us to the problem of the content of Deleuze and Guattari's social theory: which specific machines do they choose to write about? How might such a choice liberate desire? If their books are filled with the widest variety of theoretical and cultural products, this is not because they have a conception of philosophy as a dustbin, nor because of some anarchic social imperative to value all terms equally, nor because the model of the rhizome functions as some kind of transcendental category. Their thought makes uncoordinated leaps like a dog; it seizes a handful of dice from chaos, but, if chaos is affirmed when the dice are thrown so that it is allowed to determine thought, chance can deliver a winning combination (1994: 75; Deleuze, 1994: 198). Why is the example of Concorde, apparently chosen at random, useful for illustrating the concept of a machine? Because of the network of associations and significations that may be attached to it: it is a machinic assemblage that stands on a concrete runway, a plane that is capable of following a line of flight, circulating between the distant cities of Paris and New York, transferring populations and changing their consistency without mixing them up; its name signifies the international cooperation that made it possible based on the relations of accord that are the aim of desire; but, as a machinic process, it lacks consistency and is haunted by its own abolition. In many respects, Concorde illustrates as a content the concepts of machinic heterogenesis. Expression and content affirm and reinforce each other; they gain a consistency. Concorde becomes a refrain that repeats itself in thought over and over again; it becomes a becoming-other of philosophy, Concorde as a supersonic philosopher thinking at excessive speeds. Instead of content being selected and governed by theory, content escapes itself so as to interfere with the mode of expression and give it an ontological affirmation.

The politics of desire makes use of mythic, phantasmatic, psychotic, and religious elements in the narratives it constructs (Deleuze, 1989: 222; Guattari, 1992: 89). It renounces the claims of consciousness, truth, and knowledge, so as to make thought a place where self-positing others can come into being. It adopts forms of reflexivity or self-referentiality, finding others as foyers of virtual autopoiesis so as to actualize and transversalize them, working towards complexification and processual enrichment (Guattari, 1992: 88). When one considers distributions of desire, a little refrain that finds consistency in a particular environment may be sufficient to transform an entire social field, as did the sign of the cross in the Christianization of Europe (Guattari, 1992: 90). A refrain generates an other as one who inhabits an existential territory: it is through a Bergsonian repetition of memory that mythic, phantasmatic, and religious elements come into play. Of course, if refrains become too dominant, they lead to psychotic dissociation, constructing a universe of reference that has little connection with dominant sociality. Guattari's therapeutic aim, when dealing with psychotics or with sterile models of society and psyche, is to throw bridges that might give consistency to others who lack consistency and existence (Guattari, 1992: 102).

A Winter's Tale (Eric Rohmer): a woman is confused about her choice of lovers. She enters a cathedral and sits in silence. A decision comes to her: she will abandon her current lover and admirer and await the father of her daughter, a man from whom she was separated by accident some five years previously, whom she has no possible means of contacting, and who does not even know that they have a child. Although not explicitly religious, she is like Kierkegaard's knight of faith, or, more accurately, the religious person who chooses to await a religious repetition in the form of a return of the lover, in virtue of the absurd (Deleuze, 1989: 177; Kierkegaard, 1983). Soon she meets her former lover on a bus in Paris – a repetition of the relation is now possible only because she has left her other lover and admirer. What did she see in the cathedral? Who made the decision? Did she have a revelation of providence or destiny? Was the thought that came from outside a revelation of spirit (Deleuze, 1989: 178)? It was her own desire that was able to crystallize in the environment of the cathedral; she does not decide, the cathedral itself decides for her. Desire becomes holy when it witnesses to a possible future that it is able to bring about. The cathedral expresses a possible world that does not exist outside of her own decision and desire. The politics of desire can make use of religious and mythical themes in order narrate its others, so long as these themes are restored to the immanence of a mode of existence (1994: 73–4).

Conceptual personae are the others who populate a minor philosophy: they are the theorists, the people, who are yet to come. They have existential features, as modes of existence or possibilities of life that they invent and bring into existence through repetition of their refrains (1994: 72). They have pathic features, indicating modes of enunciation beyond majoritarian roles (1994: 70). If the philosopher only thinks by becoming something else that does not think, an animal or a rock, a cathedral or a Concorde, discovering something unthinkable that conditions thought, it is because the persona must be taken to a threshold of absolute deterritorialization where it has only intensive features – territories and affects as movements of deterritorialization and reterritorialization. The other belongs neither to expression nor to content; it joins the two as language and possible world on a plane of immanence. Conceptual personae have relational features (1994: 71): a territory is essentially expressive; it never exists alone but only in relations with other territories, and their movements of deterritorialization and reterritorialization. They also have dynamic features (1994: 71), expressing their capacity to affect and be affected. Finally, conceptual personae have juridical features: this is because they constantly lay claim to that which belongs to thought by right (1994: 72). They are not merely facts of thought, but transcendental determinants of the essence of thought. In this respect, all territories are inseparable from a movement of absolute deterritorialization that places them in contact with the Earth. In the same way that lobsters march in a single file on the bottom of the sea, following a religious pilgrimage or line of flight in search of an unknown homeland (1988: 326), conceptual personae lay claim to the absolute as that which belongs to thought by right, even if the absolute is not necessarily the a priori but THE plane of immanence (1994: 85, 72).

Note

1. André Colombat makes style or mode of expression the central feature of his reading of Deleuze. See Colombat (1990).

3

Geophilosophy

Deleuze's empiricism, following Hume, remains sceptical about the possibility of knowledge. For although one may construct models of the world, the scientific tests that one may devise to assess these models are themselves constructions of thought that cannot ultimately be tested in the same way. Instead of concerning itself with procedures of verification, Deleuze's brand of empiricism explores the genesis of thought itself in terms of the intensities, codes, territories, becomings, and machines at work in the thinker. Thought is no longer assessed as a cultural product that can be communicated, exchanged, or marketed independently of its conditions of production – each thought bears its own psychosocial and ethicopolitical implications by virtue of how it is produced and what it subsequently produces. Furthermore, Deleuze and Guattari constructed their own brand of theory that is purified of a negative will to power that dominates others, attaining an affirmative will to power that affects others: a minor philosophy that knows only signs, affects, events, and others. Where Hume replaced the model of knowledge with that of belief, Deleuze and Guattari replaced belief with desire, so as to bring all the pre-human dimensions of subjectivity back into thought: no longer subordinated to a pseudo-scientific paradigm, the simulacra, phantasms, and mythical refrains that fill the mind allow subjectivity, both individual and collective, to be described in terms of an ethico-aesthetic paradigm (Guattari, 1989b: 25).

Each conceptual persona marks out a territory by singing a refrain (1988: 312): it is less a question of putting up placards than of using motifs and counterpoints that express the relation of the territory to interior impulses or exterior circumstances which might be remembered rather than given (1988: 318). Each persona of thought has an ethos which is both abode and manner, homeland and style (1988: 320). The ethos or territoriality expresses a set of affects as relations of deterritorialization and reterritorialization with other personae. If thought is to relate to its social and cultural milieu, then it will not be through internal models, but through a style that expresses a conjunction of its own absolute movements of deterritorialization and reterritorialization with the relative movements of deterritorialization and reterritorialization of a psychosocial, historical, or geographical milieu (1994: 88, 93). Each persona has ecological relations with the surrounding environment: instead of thought mastering nature, it is immanent within nature and society, and its knowledge of such relations is an ecosophy

(Guattari, 1989b: 70). Thought only relates to being through something that lies outside both: a plane of desire.

Given the embodied nature of knowledge for Deleuze and Guattari, one could be forgiven for imagining that their thought is entirely particular to their own social and cultural positions, having little significance for those in very different situations. Yet Deleuze and Guattari's thought does attempt to transcend its cultural specificity, not by attaining some majoritarian universal of Enlightenment subjectivity, but by approaching the immanence of desire as an absolute limit. Their plane of immanence forms an ontology of desire (Guattari, 1992: 160). In recent thought, many have questioned the value of ontology and philosophy as a whole, insofar as these aim to produce a timeless truth, independent and ignorant of its historical conditioning, social and cultural specificity, linguistic expression, and economic and political interests. The possibility of some encompassing, metaphysical metanarrative is brought into question; these critiques, however, are usually conducted in the name of local metaphysics of either history, language, culture, society, economic production, or power, where such concepts are sufficiently ill-defined so as to be able to encompass almost anything. Deleuze and Guattari deny involvement in such questioning: 'In any case, the death of metaphysics or the overcoming of philosophy has never been a problem for us: it is just tiresome, idle chatter' (1994: 9). Their ontology of desire must be understood and evaluated on its own terms, without confusing it with the philosophical moves of their contemporaries.

Deleuze and Guattari claim to escape cultural specificity by distinguishing the relative deterritorialization of a milieu from the absolute deterritorialization of philosophy. If philosophical thought claims access to the absolute by right, this is because thinking takes place in a relationship of territory and the earth – the earth constantly carries out a movement of deterritorialization on the spot, being both deterritorializing and deterritorialized (1994: 85). If personae provide an epistemology (*ratio cognoscendi*) through their relations with their milieu, the earth itself provides an ontology (*ratio essendi*) (1988: 339). The absolute presupposed by philosophy is its image of thought and being: it results from thinking about thinking (noology), or, in Alliez's fortuitous phrase, ' "the Deterritorialized par excellence": the Earth is the concept of the concept of a concept, the Homeland of the philosopher' (Alliez, 1993: 100). This phrase is accurate insofar as it is recognized that the number of repetitions of 'concept' is arbitrary; in fact, the earth is not a concept but thought raised to the absolute through infinite repetition – the eternal return of the concept within the concept. There is a fifth characteristic of Deleuze and Guattari's image of thought: movements of thought are fractalized, raised to an infinite power of repetition (1994: 38).

It is not immediately clear how such a fractalization of thought, attaining infinite reflexivity, could finally establish a relation between thought and being. Why do Deleuze and Guattari conceive of the relation between thought and the social in terms of desire through movements of deterritorialization and reterritorialization? Why are such relations inscribed on the earth as the full body without organs, the 'primitive savage unity of desire and production' (1984: 140)? Indeed, it would appear that in Deleuze and Guattari's thought the earth is fractured into two absolutes:[1] chaos and complexity (consistency, immanence) (1994: 42). Alterity is the primary problem: far from shining the light of consciousness into the abyss of Being, a schizoanalytic ontology is merely content to throw across bridges – 'the schizo fracture is the royal road of access to the emergent fractality of the Unconscious' (Guattari, 1992: 93).

It is possible to trace the heterogeneous emergence of these two absolutes through philosophy's critical engagement with the pretensions of metaphysics. Deleuze learned his critical thought from Kant and Nietzsche. A naive understanding of metaphysics poses the problem of knowledge in terms of analysis: 'What are the essential components of society?' A society could then be understood from the way in which these components are combined within it. Kant's transcendental critique reverses the problem by posing it in terms of synthesis: knowledge of essential components is impossible, since they are not encountered in experience. The question is then a matter of how the human subject imposes its synthetic judgements upon society without encountering them in experience. Nietzsche shifted the problem yet again: he explored the kinds of will, value, or political interest expressed in the synthetic judgements of the subject. All knowledge should be evaluated in terms of the forces which it expresses, rather than its truth or falsehood. Metaphysics is now a symptom of a society's political action upon itself. Deleuze completed critical philosophy by suggesting that society is not simply composed of relations of force; instead, the nature of relations is exterior to both the components of society and the synthetic judgements of the subject, as well as relations of force and interest. In Deleuze's metaphysics, society is not composed of separate beings, nor separate fluxes, nor subjective judgements, nor even relations of force. Relations are exterior, chaotic, unknowable, and absolute. The first limit of critical philosophy is a total scepticism which takes the form of a metaphysics of chaos – the presence of relations of desire is given purely by chance. Chaos is not merely an absolute, indeterminate, undifferentiated morass, however, for it is defined in relation to another limit of critical philosophy. Any metaphysics of chaos must explain the appearance of order in the world.

We can also narrate a different story of critical philosophy. The completion of the Kantian critique occurs through the reflexive self-questioning of knowledge. Philosophy must begin to ask, 'What is philosophy?' Kant criticized analytic metaphysics because its criteria for assessing truth were not given alongside particular truths. Nietzsche criticized Kant's categories because they relied on concepts of being, unity, identity, and universality which are not given alongside particular synthetic judgements; these transcendental concepts express a certain *ressentiment*. Deleuze transformed Nietzsche's thought because the ultimate criterion of the 'will to power' is not encountered within particular modes of existence, except as a synthetic principle. A truly critical philosophy can only be judged by the immanence of its criteria: it must do what it says, and say what it does. It becomes a being-thought: a thought of being and a being of thought (Alliez, 1993: 102). The second limit of critical philosophy is therefore a pure plane of immanence; this is the only possible meaning of the 'end of philosophy'. Immanence does not mean the absence of determination; rather, it implies that all that one is should be put into how one thinks, so that one's entire mode of existence may be changed by encounters and ideas within thought.

Immanence and chaos stand over Deleuze and Guattari's thought as two instances of the absolute. The obvious question which arises, then, is that of their relation – since absolutes are, by definition, not relative or related.[2] Deleuze and Guattari defined chaos in terms of immanence as a lack of consistency, a failure of relation (1994: 42). Chaos is not indeterminate; instead, it can be considered as a vast 'memory' of the future, a repository of seeds of desires which are unable to crystallize by entering into relation with each other. Ideas appear, sketch themselves out, and vanish before they can take on a consistency by being related to other ideas. Immanence functions as a screen placed against chaos which can select a few seeds on the basis of their consistency with other seeds (1994: 42). It provides the environment within which seeds can grow through a repetition of their movements. Immanence allows order to grow out of chaos through a consistent repetition of its differentiations. As with Spinoza's 'common notions', the same becomings are repeated in both a mode of existence and the relations which it forms with others, in both content and expression. The act of knowing, then, corresponds to the act of generating: nature and art, being and thought are united in the emergence of complexity (Alliez, 1993: 44, 95; Deleuze, 1991b: 212). The philosopher-artist becomes a creator of truth: 'there is no other truth than the creation of the New: creativity, emergence' (Deleuze, 1989: 146–7).

The question then arises as to how immanence and chaos relate to desire and the social, for they seem to be purely abstract and formal determinations – they are singular events that change the direction of thought, rather than being 'objects' of thought. This bond is conceivable because Deleuze and Guattari have a philosophy of science (1994: 117–43), which we can only describe in the briefest of terms here.[3] Guattari suggested that there is a double articulation of ontological folds within chaos (Guattari, 1992: 153), the first generating matter and the second generating thought: these foldings are a process of 'chaosmosis'. The infinite speeds of chaos are enabled by their reversibility – as a phantasm, chaos does not exist in linear time. Such speeds, however, are filled with finite speeds that can be selected from chaos through a bifurcation that is inherent in irreversible time: the first ontological fold is a geological process of stratification, somewhat like the baker's transformation, where a lump of dough is folded and rolled out over and over again (Deleuze, 1991b: 169–70) – in spite of having a mathematical description, such a process is irreversible in time because information concerning its initial conditions is destroyed at each fold (Prigogine and

Stengers, 1985: 269–77). Stratification allows a plane of reference to be formed from relative and reversible chaos (Guattari, 1992: 157): each layer has a double articulation, where coordinate axes are defined by being paired off against each other, such as space and time, temperature and pressure, force and distance, mass and charge. Reference becomes fixed and meaningful when pairings of these coordinate axes are defined in relation to an absolute limit where variation is no longer possible: the Big Bang, the speed of light, absolute zero, and Planck's constant (1994: 119). The earth does not pre-exist astrophysical coagulation and geological stratification; as an absolute reference point it has been displaced in science by other absolutes. Since the crystallization of the primitive chaotic soup into spatial coordinates, temporal causalities, energetic levels, and possibilities of cross-fertilization proceeds through stratification, reciprocal determination, and the emergence of complexity, it constitutes an ontological sexuality: desire (Guattari, 1992: 160). It is such crystals of finitude and strange attractors that science semiotizes as functions, constants, and laws (Guattari, 1992: 161). It matters little whether such processes occur in nature or society; they gain a consistency that allows them to become thinkable.

The second ontological fold is the self-positing of thought: an active force of creation that takes desire and the social as its object (Guattari, 1992: 160). For the first fold of matter always appears as the content of thought – but if thought itself is not to be stratified, then that content is taken as a refrain, rather than an object, being repeated in content and expression. For this reason, Deleuze and Guattari constantly appeal to the material world as a source for their concepts, so long as the material world is grasped according to the existentializing function in terms of its affects as movements of deterritorialization and reterritorialization. If thought encounters the unthinkable at its heart, if it calls to a world-people or chaos-people that are yet to come (1994: 218), then these others that populate thought will be foldings of the material world, being, into thought itself. The ontological fracture between thought and being, chaos and complexity, can only be 'bridged' by being refolded and fractalized into a plane of immanence.

Immanence only concerns relations that are exterior to the connected modes. These virtual relations are worked out in practice in the real socio-historical field – chaosmosis works by acting on a pre-existing order in order to produce incorporeal changes. Immanent relations take on a consistency through mutual enfoldment, exchanging aspects of each other's modes of existence. This crystallization is actualized most perfectly in sexual alliance where desire is crystallized into society – each desire is the creation of an incorporeal bond, a new status for bodies rather like a 'marriage', even if such bonds quickly give way to betrayal. The plane of immanence is the social unconscious that connects the purely abstract determinations of desire to the purely machinic determinations of sexual bodies, affecting what they do. Immanence, then, finds its fullest expression in desire and the social.

Immanence gives a pluralist absolute, a singular universal, or an existential ontology. Immanence means that the 'what', 'when', 'how', and 'why' become indistinguishable. While being is always characterized by 'uni-vocity' (an equivalence between thinking and being) and the 'identity' of the abstract machine (an equivalence between composition and function), this universal limit of all thought, matter, and being can only be occupied by certain 'modes of existence', each with its own name and date. Deleuze and Guattari's philosophy of immanence, therefore, gives a voice to this univer-sal limit of thought and being, but the voice it gives is singular. In fact, the immanence of being is the least significant characteristic – it is an empty body without organs that has to be populated by differing intensities. Immanence is merely the zero degree of intensity that all modes of being share. If Deleuze and Guattari speak of being in a voice that is 'universal', therefore, that which they say of being is the least interesting thing that can properly be said. Hence Deleuze and Guattari describe the site of absolute immanence where truth is possible as a pure creation of thought, but they do not speak on behalf of any of the other acts of creation that can take place there.

Deleuze and Guattari's 'philosophy of desire' is not the renunciation but the completion of critical and rational philosophy, where desire oscillates between being a sexual and a deterritorialized term. It gives a desub-stantialized metaphysics of difference, repetition, and consistency. Yet chaos remains alongside immanence as an over-vital element, escaping the attempts of immanence to give it a consistency. Insofar as chaos escapes the plane, one may question the extent to which Deleuze and Guattari's plane is able to comprehend life and society as a whole. Deleuze and Guattari only write from their own shared mode of existence, the arrangement of desire specific to their portion of the plane; they do not speak in the name of universal truths. Their plane is like a cross-section of society taken through their own brains. Yet there is a sense in which their thought claims to 'know' society as it exists outside themselves. This is because they take immanence as a limit: insofar as society produces effects of deterritorialization, it will eventually tend towards this limit of an immanent mode of existence. According to Deleuze and Guattari, society is already tending towards the limit of absolute deterritorialization. Deleuze and Guattari are therefore able to claim implicitly that their own mode of existence, insofar as it attains the plane of liberated desire, is shared with the absolute or ultimate limit towards which society tends. For this reason alone does their theoretical approach claim a legitimacy exceeding its cultural specificity. Deleuze and Guattari's ontology claims a self-legitimation or auto-positing through desire, rather than knowledge or power. It is not a question of whether society really is as they describe, nor is it a question of whether society functions pragmatically through the techniques and strategies they discern in it; it is a question of whether society ultimately desires immanence, whether society is ultimately desire, or, in a manner of speaking, whether society desires desire. Then insofar as Deleuze and Guattari write from the mode of existence on this limit, their thought embodies the assemblage of desire of society itself. In practice, however, they did not claim to attain such a limit; but if someone did, then their thought would attain absolute truth.[4]

We therefore find that Deleuze and Guattari's thought, considered internally, has an ambivalent status: on the one hand, it is derived from a percept of the absolute, which it understands to be the immanent plane of desire, but, on the other, it does not claim to fully embody such a plane within its own mode of existence. It does not arise from the plane of immanence, even though it indicates the existence of such a plane (1994: 59). The desire which is active in it is not the ultimate desire of society as a whole, for society never exists as a whole.[5] Hence Deleuze and Guattari ultimately claim that their work is culturally specific, and only functions in a certain territorial assemblage of society: it belongs to the age of democratic capitalism, even though it maintains a militant assault against this social formation (1994: 99). They therefore use the machinic processes of capitalism as categories for constructing a 'universal history' of social regimes. This universal history shares in the ambivalent status: it is absolute insofar as society tends towards immanence as a limit, but relative insofar as it embodies the tendencies of capitalism.

The earth, the absolutely deterritorialized plane of philosophy, is populated with personae who are yet to come: it is a utopia. In fact, Deleuze and Guattari say that it is utopia that relates philosophy to its own epoch – it is with utopia that philosophy becomes political (1994: 99). The ethos of conceptual personae merges with a politics. Deleuze and Guattari's philosophy should be read as a utopian social theory as opposed to a critical model of our society. If the revolution is a utopia of immanence, it is not a dream that can never be realized, but something that is nowhere as well as now here (1994: 100). Utopia is the only conjunction of philosophy with the present milieu. As a concept and event, revolution is self-positing and self-referential – it can only be apprehended in the immanent enthusiasm of becoming-revolutionary (1994: 101). Yet utopia, for Deleuze and Guattari, is no longer subject to history as an ideal or a motivation: it is a becoming, a society of friends or a society of resistance (1994: 110). The victory of a revolution is a work of art: it is immanent and consists in the new vibrations, clinches, and openings it gives to men and women in the moment of its making, the new bonds it installs between people (1994: 177).

Once we have given a historical account of the production of an ontology of desire through a radicalization of the thought of Hume, Kant, Bergson, Nietzsche, and Spinoza, it may be supposed that we have given a critique of its metaphysical pretensions. This would be erroneous, for history by itself does not produce immanence; only Deleuze's reading of these different thinkers connects them in such a way, and this reading operates by considering their concepts upon a plane of immanence. Once desire is revealed, it shows itself at work in society and history all along, even functioning as the cause of its own repression. Immanence and desire stand at the beginning as well as the end of Deleuze's thought. Having attained a percept of immanence, Deleuze and Guattari may then construct their entire social theory according to the precise political project of the liberation of desire, allowing spontaneous and unmediated relations between people on the plane of the social unconscious. This revolution would transform the nature of social, economic, and ecological relations, spreading by contagion. The success of Deleuze and Guattari's thought can be measured not by its theoretical adequacy, but by the desire present in their relation and the desire it may produce in us.

Notes

1. In spite of Alliez's excellent attempt to reunite philosophy, science, and art into a single, Spinozist etho-ontology (Alliez, 1993). Such a reunion after the manner of Whitehead's panpsychism may indeed be possible, but only through the intuition that the Chaosmosis of Nature can become populated with sophisticated conceptual and ethical personae that unite thinking and acting in both chaos and complexity, constituted by a further passive temporal synthesis that operates beyond the brain – spirits (Goodchild, 1996).

2. This is the ultimate question of desire; while not explored in depth in *What is Philosophy?*, Guattari addressed this problem through the concept of 'chaosmosis' in his final work (Guattari, 1992).

3. Sadly, the philosophy of nature that Deleuze and Guattari had hoped to write (Deleuze, 1991b: 212) was prevented by Guattari's death; it would surely have provided an outstandingly original ontology for contemporary science. One may observe preparations for it in Deleuze's book on Leibniz and Guattari's final work.

4. See the homage rendered to Spinoza (1994: 59).

5. Hence a return to ontology, as advocated by Alliez, must be treated with caution. A pluralist ontology in which modes of being are created never produce an ultimate or final truth. While one can only admire the thoroughness and insight brought to readings of Deleuze by Colombat, Hardt, and Alliez, the concepts governing their thought – 'style', 'efficient causality', and 'ontology', respectively – are too familiar and general, lacking in degree of singularization. Consequently, their readings produce something of a reterritorialization of Deleuze's thought, instead of advancing it by means of further deterritorialization.

PART II

POWER

4

Capitalism and Schizophrenia

What is power? On the plane of immanence of desire, 'power' has no independent ontological status: it is neither an agent, nor an underlying ground of society. Power is not a quality which one can possess, nor a force by which one can be dominated; formations of power in society are merely effects of the workings of desire. Instead, power is a quality of social relation, and it is produced by a complex abstract machine. Power derives from desire, and turns to 'repress' desire. Although the procedure itself is complex, as we shall outline below, we can give an overview by means of a simple and useful model. We may distinguish between two conceptions of power deriving from Deleuze's studies of Nietzsche and Spinoza: a power of autoproduction, in which a relation causes itself, and a power of antiproduction, in which productive relations are prevented from forming.[1] In production, desire is entirely immanent in the process; there is no unrealized capacity left over, and a machine functions as well as it can, consuming and transforming itself in the process – it affects itself. This is the creative power of desire, a spontaneous relation which emerges by connecting up heterogeneous elements, producing some kind of flow. In antiproduction, however, there is not sufficient energy or desire to create a full, consistent, mutually affective relation between assemblages that encounter one another. Instead, the mode of production of one of the assemblages will remain unchanged; for example, codes, habits, or conventions may be applied to a new content, but their mode of encoding remains unchanged; similarly, becomings may be reterritorialized on an unchanging territorial assemblage. The result is an asymmetrical relation: one of the assemblages in the encounter does not change its overall mode of existence, whereas the other draws upon the set of codes and territories given by the former in order to condition itself. Since such codes and territories can no longer be affected and changed, antiproduction effectively stops the conditioned assemblage from functioning as an autonomous machine. For example, an employed person has to accept the fixed relations of production provided by the employer; there is no change or production immanent to the employment relation itself – the codes and conventions in the relation remain unchanged. An alternative example is rape: the body of the victim is forced to submit to the drives of the rapist, while being unable to shape or affect them; the drive belongs to the rapist alone, and is not an immanent desire produced in the relation between them.

Antiproduction, therefore, results from acting out a need, want, or drive that is encoded and territorialized in past experience, and does not pertain to the immanent and present relation between terms. Such motivations may appear to be similar to 'desire', but they are not themselves immanent relations. Something is withheld that remains fixed and unaffected. All fixed orders of society, including conventions, institutions, and impulses, that provide a framework for possible social relations, but which themselves remain unaffected by what happens, are instances of antiproduction. When desire is present, however, it exists as a process that changes the connections and social relations of society, transgressing all fixed boundaries. Desire is revolutionary in its essence, not because it wants revolution, nor because it may be provocative to express liberated sexuality, but because it affects and changes every established order of society. This arises from the immanence of desire: desire fills all dimensions of society – no principle or order can be extracted from society that could be made to stand outside it. All laws, rights, values, and orders can be created and destroyed by society; none can stand outside as an origin or goal. There can be no absolute distinctions or boundaries imposed upon society because these would need to be justified by some transcendent order or 'God'; desire, forming relations between heterogeneous terms, can cross all boundaries. Similarly, there are no pre-social instincts or drives, whether towards aggression or sexual activity, that transcend society. Indeed, the fixing of such drives is a corollary of the formation of a fixed order of society; the drive can only be formed as a desire for repetition of territorial representation. A fixed drive is formed as that which is prohibited and excluded from society. The drive only exists as a 'return of the repressed'; it is shaped by its repression in the image of the repressing structure. The revolution of desire eliminates pathological drives in the same way that it removes fixed social structures.

The result of these considerations is that no established order of society can be formed without the repression of desire. This 'repression' operates through a different strategy from the earlier Freudian model. According to Freudian thought, desire must be repressed through its encounter with 'reality'. The paradigmatic form of this repression is the Oedipus complex: the child desires to be reunited sexually with its mother, but is prevented from realizing this unconscious phantasy (as opposed to conscious fantasy) by the real and forbidding presence of its father. For Deleuze and Guattari, by contrast, desire itself is the source of all reality and truth: 'If desire produces, its product is real. If desire is productive, it can be productive only in the real world and can produce only reality' (1984: 26). Desire is not repressed by reality; instead, desire must be repressed by the power–formations of society mediated through an encounter with another body. The father embodies social authority. Restrictions always derive from without: psychic repression depends on social repression. The interior and private struggles which individuals have with anxiety, guilt, and depression in our society result from the social repression operating within society as a whole. Society imposes its own relations of production and its own needs and drives upon us. Deleuze and Guattari agree with the psychoanalysts who find the Oedipus complex everywhere, that this complex is the chief mechanism for psychic repression at work in capitalist society; they differ, however, by arguing that the complex is not universal in humanity, but merely a product of the mode of repression operating within capitalist society. There is no primal instinct towards incest; instead, the drive towards incest is produced by capitalist society. For Deleuze and Guattari, almost all personal and private problems, particularly those related to mental health and well-being, have social, political, and economic sources. (This would apply particularly to victims of starvation and epidemic diseases who live in poverty.) Much of *Anti-Oedipus*, therefore, is devoted to giving a socio-political 'geology' of the Oedipus complex in terms of a 'universal history' of different social formations and their modes of repression.

Deleuze and Guattari's main problem in analysing the working of power in society is therefore to observe how desire can give rise to power (1984: 29). It would appear that desire is able to turn against itself and desire its own repression. But desire is neither a drive nor a force capable of turning on itself to repress itself; it is not some mysterious substance that can transmute into its opposite. The repression of desire is a quality of social relation that only occurs in complex social assemblages. There is a double genesis to the repression of desire. On the one hand, society is actually structured with a repressive potential. If Oedipus is the mode of repression in our society, then society must contain a virtual oedipal structure in its relations of production. On the other hand, the psyche must have a capacity to invest itself in the repressive social formation; it must have the capacity to actualize Oedipus within itself. Oedipus has an independent, double genesis: it crystallizes when social and psychic repression become articulated together, each taking the other as its content. Moreover, both psychic and social production are manifested in the delirium of schizophrenics, and it is from Guattari's clinical experience of such psychotic delirium with its regular structures, themes, and patterns, as much as from academic studies of psychoanalysis and ethnology, that the theories of psyche and society used by Deleuze and Guattari devolve. Deleuze and Guattari begin *Anti-Oedipus* with a psychic 'geology' of the formation of Oedipus.

Problem 6: On psychogenesis and perversion

The philosophy of desire does not content itself with thinking about sexuality, considering neither the designation of cases, the manifestation of personal histories, nor the signification of complexes (Deleuze, 1990b: 92). If sexuality invests thought, it will be as the surface that is folded and refolded in the act of thinking, the element of thought itself as opposed to an exterior element subjected to the operations of thought (Deleuze, 1990b: 242). Sexuality can invest thought in a manner similar to the investment of fantasy in speech – one is moved to speak by that which is unsayable because of its dream-like character, if only to seek out some indirect expression. Instead of telling the truth about desire, whether one's own or that of others, as is the goal of psychoanalysis, one invests thought with a sexual dimension through the 'powers of the false' – all the resources of language that participate in indirect communication.

How does an infant acquire a capacity to think? How, in general, can physical bodies, their actions and passions, enter directly into thought? The problem of psychogenesis is that of the dynamic genesis of thought within desire, the question of its origin and the problem of its end (Deleuze, 1990b: 217). This problem presents two possibilities: either thought will consider its own psychogenetic origin, after the manner of psychoanalysis, as Deleuze attempted in *The Logic of Sense* (Deleuze, 1990b: 181–249), or else desire will directly invest thought so that thought acts on its desires, as Deleuze and Guattari do in *Anti-Oedipus*. Published just three years apart, the difference between these books is striking, although there is much continuity in use of concepts: from being deeply involved in Kleinian and Lacanian psychoanalysis, Deleuze turned to delimit and reject these forms of psychoanalysis as well as the others; from regarding psychosis and schizophrenia as a perpetual threat of regression (Deleuze, 1990b: 82–93), Deleuze turned to adopt an explicitly schizophrenic image of thought; from granting Oedipus and castration a pivotal role in the development of speech and thought (Deleuze, 1990b: 200–9), Deleuze turned to regard these as the principal obstacles to thinking. In *The Logic of Sense*, Deleuze had sketched out a philosophy of surfaces inspired by the Stoic theory of incorporeals, in contrast to a Platonic philosophy of the heights inspired by absent yet recollected ideals, and a pre-Socratic philosophy of the depths exploring the grounds and mixtures of bodies (Deleuze, 1990b: 127–33). These have some correspondence to Melanie Klein's three psychosexual stages in infancy: the oedipal phase, the manic-depressive phase, and the paranoid-schizoid phase, respectively (Deleuze, 1990b: 186–201; Klein, 1969). According to this scheme, it would appear that Deleuze and Guattari made a schizophrenic regression from the oedipal surface to bodies and their mixtures in *Anti-Oedipus*. The difference between these two books marks the largest discontinuity in Deleuze's thought; it is made more acute by Deleuze's typical reticence in regard to commenting on his previous publications.

The problem of psychogenesis may function as a bridge between these two books. Since it concerns the investment of desire into thought, it may also serve as a bridge between an abstract theory of knowledge and a strategic assault on power. This discussion of the problem will explore the mechanisms by which the concepts of Deleuze's early philosophical work are revitalized in the collaborative publications.

The key question concerning this discontinuity is that of the nature of the distinction between the psychosexual stages of depths, heights, and surfaces: are these images of thought simulacra, presenting an appearance of being distinct on the surface, but in fact being mixed up in depth so that one transforms into another? If so, the regression to a bodily world of desiring-production composed of flows of milk, urine, and faeces in *Anti-Oedipus* (1984: 1) is a satirical subversion of Deleuze's former position. Alternatively, these images could be regarded as ideal models of thought, clearly bounded and exclusively separated, in which case the move should be seen as an ironic conversion to a new model in contradiction to the previous one. The consistent solution, however, is to regard these images as phantasms, erogenous zones, or territories, so that the relation between them is less a question of mixture or separation than of coordination. *Anti-Oedipus* can therefore be regarded as a humorous perversion of *The Logic of Sense*, a continuation and fulfilment of the philosophy of surfaces that falls back upon the depths and the heights, regarding these stages as zones or objects of sexual fascination. Desire is translated onto a plane of immanence (1988: 284).

None of this may seem immediately clear. The conceptual frameworks of the two books, however, can be coordinated by exploring the problem of psychogenesis in terms of concepts consistent with Deleuze's early studies of philosophers. A body is composed of organs that extract and process material flows of food, light, sound, etc. Each organ is defined by a function, a certain capacity for action or passion, for ejecting or swallowing a material flow. According to the Humean synthesis, each of these material processes is contracted into an anticipation – a baby's mouth anticipates milk from the breast. In addition to material objects, therefore, the mental world of infancy is filled with partial objects or simulacra corresponding to the processes of the organs. At this level, there is no distinction between cause and effect, or active and passive roles (Deleuze, 1990b: 3), for the anticipated processes exist only in combination with each other and cannot be attached to particular persons or objects: eating and being eaten, destroying or being destroyed, loving and being loved are indistinguishable – the infant cannot distinguish between its own and others' actions. In this world of simulacra, an infant's drives are frequently frustrated: a breast may be absent or withdrawn, and its good appearance may conceal a bad piece, or too much milk may cause vomiting or indigestion – an infant lives in a world of anxiety because the drives of eating, loving, and destroying are always mixed up. Klein's account of the infant's schizoid solution to this problem is that the child splits partial objects into ideal separate objects, good and bad, so that the child imagines an ideal good breast that it hopes its mother's breast will embody; but Deleuze, drawing on the writings of the schizophrenic Antonin Artaud, discovered a more primitive solution. The ambiguity of partial objects results from their very partiality – they are simulacra of organs dedicated to particular functions, but can always contain surprising additional functions. It is possible, however, to imagine a condition where the mixture is complete: an organism without parts, a complete body lacking in orifices – this body without organs would operate entirely by insufflation, respiration, evaporation, and fluid transmission, as a surface or skin without hidden depths (Deleuze, 1990b: 88). Its functioning would be entirely quantitative, without codes or qualities. Furthermore, it would escape the paradoxes of projection and introjection, eating and being eaten, for it would only measure intensities of eating.

An infant therefore experiences a drive to make a body without organs. This glorious body functions as the support for the later psychosexual stages. The good breast will only be good in virtue of its completeness, so that it no longer conceals a bad or poisonous piece; if the breast that is encountered in reality, as an action or passion, always contains the possibility of its own ambivalence, then the good breast will be an absent and withdrawn ideal that is itself unproductive. Hence the model of completeness upon which the distinction between good and bad is made is the body without organs. Similarly, the constitution of the surface of the skin as an erogenous zone in the vicinity of an orifice requires the flow of pleasure to take on a relative autonomy in relation to the actions and passions that produce it. Pleasure is of course an effect of the actions and passions of bodies; if it is to become a principle of action, as the sexual drive Eros, this effect must be constituted as a quasi-cause – the drive is directed not towards any particular action, but to the pleasure that derives from action. It is a question of constituting a Bergsonian memory as an expressive, sexual territory or phantasm. The surface is fragile and always risks being absorbed back into the depths which caused it (Deleuze, 1990b: 95); for it to take on a relative autonomy, it must be coordinated with other surfaces through imagination, converging on a para-doxical element that is always lacking from its place, being itself neither an action nor a passion – this coordinating element must keep in perpetual motion, for if it were to be fixed on a surface or organ for one moment, then the whole system would fall back into the depths. The liberation of libido from bodily depths in which it is mixed up with alimentary and destructive drives occurs through auto-eroticism (Deleuze, 1990b: 199): perhaps directly, by contact between surfaces, or indirectly, as in Lacan's mirror-stage (Deleuze, 1990b: 200); at any rate, being both active and passive, it posits itself, so that the pleasure appears as the quasi-cause of the desire for pleasure.

Auto-eroticism, in its most primitive form, concerns the constitution of a pure body of pleasure, a body without organs, in which the coordination of zones of pleasure, being both actions and passions, liberates a phantasm as a surface effect that appears to produce itself as its own quasi-cause – one acts for the sake of pleasure, the action being the cause, the reason being the quasi-cause. This is an example of crossing a threshold of absolute deterritorialization: on the one hand, phantasms and traumas are caused by bodily events – children do touch themselves, or observe their parents' bodies, or become the objects of seduction, or are subjected to threats (Deleuze, 1990b: 210); on the other hand, the phantasms produced do not simply remain unpleasant memories, but become compulsions that have a leading role in determining subsequent lives including the actions and passions of bodies. It is possible that the general coordination of surfaces may be vested in the genital zone, the phantasm of the phallus (as distinct from the organ or partial object of the penis) being projected onto the genital zone as the quasi-cause of genital pleasure (Deleuze, 1990b: 200). The phallus becomes a paradoxical element, always in excess or lacking, circulating among the series of erogenous zones. In its pure state, however, the phantasm is the body without organs itself.

Organs function because they express drives – for preservation, for sexual pleasure, or for destruction, for example. These drives are 'principles' as opposed to actions or passions: instead of being forces themselves, they determine how forces operate. Since principles belong to the surface as effects of actions and passions, the surface is already present in the operation of the depths. The drive for preservation, an organ's attempt to continue functioning, is itself dependent on its own auto-eroticism, the pleasure it extracts from its own operation. In material terms, an organ simply aims to produce a product from a flow; as a partial object or desiring-machine, however, the organ expresses a drive insofar as it aims to reproduce itself.[2] The unconscious is an industrial factory (1984: 113), full of machines that grind and stop in various rhythms, beating out and recording their drives like printing presses. The aim itself is the producing, rather than the product; a drive is always self-positing. Such drives for preservation, however, are always threatened at their foundation, living in a state of continual anxiety, for they substitute an internal partial object for the external real object that is necessary for the production of pleasure (Deleuze, 1990b: 198–9). Not only is there a difference in nature between the real object of the organ and the partial object of the drive, so that the drive pursues an object of phantasy that can never be found in the real, but there is also a difference in nature between the intended action or partial object of the drive and its actual result or the event produced (Deleuze, 1990b: 207). Actions determined by traumatic fantasies inevitably produce the wrong effect, not only because they produce an effect of transference insofar as the situation has changed, but primarily because the phantasm differs from material organs. Good intentions are inevitably punished; but it is only because the drive fails that its difference from the real is made apparent – indeed, it is only because the drive fails that it is lacking from its place and can be constituted as a drive, without falling back into the depths of bodies.

'Desiring-machines work only when they break down and in the process of breaking down' (1984: 8). A narcissistic wound or trace of castration – insofar as the phallus is the general phantasm that coordinates all the erogenous zones – is the precondition for desire. The body without organs contains a death-drive, Thanatos (Deleuze, 1990b: 199); it is an experience of death in the unconscious (1984: 330).

How is it, therefore, that Deleuze and Guattari's thought separates itself from Lacanian psychoanalysis, where desire is only possible under conditions of lack, impotence, and castration? There are different ways in which castration can be understood in phantasy. The body without organs, or castrated body, has three different phases. Firstly, in depth, it functions as a total mixture, a complete simulacrum. A product of anticipation and anxiety, it engages in a paranoid repression of the functioning of organs as partial objects (1984: 9); it is a model of death (1984: 329). The phantasm of the phallus can fall back onto the partial object of the penis, which is itself devoured or absorbed along with all other organs by another body, the body without organs that totalizes absorption. Secondly, from on high, the body without organs functions as the quasi-cause of production (1984: 11–12). It is an absent ideal that only gives itself insofar as it withdraws into the heights – castration becomes withdrawal, absence, or lack. Insofar as it constitutes a good object, it will necessarily be attached to a privileged zone such as the phallus, which then functions as a paradoxical and withdrawn element, always lacking from its place. Here castration operates through privation and frustration: the withdrawn one who possesses the phallus is the father, and it is the law of the father in the oedipal phase that both constitutes yet prevents access to desire. Lacanian psychoanalysis remains attached to the philosophy of the heights insofar as it identifies the good object, through which consciousness is able to survey the psychic field, with the model of the Signifier. Desire is turned against itself in psychoanalysis, under the despotic signifier of castration, because it is comprehended from an ascetic point of view that is not itself desire – the impassible perspective of the analyst or the structure of language.

Thirdly, there is a form of castration that belongs to the surface: adsorption, the condensation of a gas on a surface, translation onto a plane of immanence. In *The Logic of Sense*, Deleuze turned Lacanian psychoanalysis against itself: the phallus, the phantasm that is only constituted in and through its own castration, is dissipated in a trace of castration written·on the surface of the body without organs (Deleuze, 1990b: 206). Only consciousness of desire meets its limit in the castration of adsorption; desire itself is redoubled.

On the surface, the body without organs meets the test of the eternal return: the death that it announces is not that of the organs or drives but its own death – oscillating between the model and experience of death, it constitutes desire itself (1984: 331). Here death, instead of having an extreme and definite relation to me and my body as a limit, becomes a pure event, impersonal, incorporeal, and infinitive – in the event of death, it is not I who die, for I am no more (Deleuze, 1990b: 151). Death is impersonal: it has either already arrived or is yet to come, for I can never designate the event of my own death. If the body without organs is now regarded as a surface from the perspective of the surface, it is redoubled in itself and becomes a pure impersonal event:

> this is the point at which death turns against death; where dying is the negation of death, and the impersonality of dying no longer indicates only the moment when I disappear outside of myself, but rather the moment when death loses itself in itself, and also the figure which the most singular life takes on in order to substitute itself for me. (Deleuze, 1990b: 153)

In this phase, the body without organs no longer opposes or appears to cause the partial objects but forms a new alliance with them (1984: 17). Here one should distinguish between intention and result, between the partial objects of the drives and that which is effectively produced. The result is neither an action nor a passion, since it is projected on a surface; but neither is it desired, for it is not the partial object of a drive. Instead, it is a pure event, resting no longer on the sexual surface but on a metaphysical or transcendental surface. There is a sublimation from the partial object to the pure event (Deleuze, 1990b: 208). Insofar as the event differs from the partial object, it constitutes a problem for thought: 'What happened? How did this come about?' The energy of thought is constituted within desire through such a process – the event comes to symbolize the energy of thought (Deleuze, 1990b: 208).

In psychogenesis, the energy of sexuality, as expressed in the drive and partial object, becomes sublimated as the energy of thought. Even though this process is constituted by castration, there is no reduction of energy, for castration by adsorption merely turns sexual energy into the energy of thought. Thought begins by a speculative investment inquiring into the erotic object (Deleuze, 1990b: 238), insofar as the events it produces differ in nature from the object's status as a material object or an object of phantasy. The psychosexual investment in thinking should be clear: a genuine problem is not something one works through to attain a result or fulfil an ulterior motive, nor is it something one considers in order to remove inconsistencies in a total view of the world, nor is it a process undertaken for the intrinsic pleasure it affords. A genuine problem is always an imperative or compulsion to think when a little piece of chaotic reality intrudes into one's mind, interrupting codes, habits, and expectations, sublimating and symbolizing desire. Far from losing contact with reality, problematic thought, having renounced a privileged relation to truth, engages more directly with a chaotic and surprising reality than any theory that tries to subject the real to its own fantasies of control. Thought reinvests an object of sexual interest and therefore resexualizes it in a new way (Deleuze, 1990b: 243). Consequently, the proper object for thought, the sufficient reason for an event, is an unconscious phantasm, being no more a simple state of affairs that could be stated in the form of a proposition than sexual desire is caused by a certain kind of material body.

According to this account of the death-instinct in desire, *jouissance*, the fulfilment of desire, appears to be impossible. This appearance depends, however, on the way in which desire is conceived – whether it is regarded as lacking an object, as transgressing or following a law, or as modelled on a signifying structure or complex (1984: 111). The various kinds of sexual investment are best considered according to the way they organize phantasy life rather than according to the kind of person or object to which they are attracted – self, same sex, opposite sex, child, animal, fetish, etc. Arising from the depths, there is a sexuality of bodies and their interpenetrations, usually focused on genital contact, the sole aim being physical enjoyment. This sexuality is unstable insofar as the partial object of desire is always lacking in the body of the other; it often leads to a serial investment of various bodies, either searching for one that conforms to an ideal borrowed from the heights, or successively exploring differing kinds of bodies, or searching for more extreme forms of bodily contact and interpenetration, or else combining alimentary, sexual, and destructive drives in various mixtures and combinations. In addition, descending from above, there is a sexuality of the heights that aims to re-create the moral ideals of the oedipal family or the subjectified couple, founded on promises, principles, and mutual expectations. This Platonic love is not necessarily unerotic nor unconsummated; its essence merely lies elsewhere. The aim is to isolate and protect the sexual drives from all forces of corruption and destruction. Here, loyalty to a single object of desire, including an obligation to abide by often unspoken contracts and implicit expectations, is of greater significance than the kind of person or object desired: there are oedipal homosexualities, oedipal groups, and oedipal affairs that attempt to re-create the model of the triangular nuclear family (Deleuze, 1991b: 21). Some forms of religious celibacy might belong in this category. Moreover, these separate kinds of sexuality can themselves be mixed, or else the height falls back upon the depth. Deleuze noted that subversive criminal conduct is often inseparable from a voice from above (Deleuze, 1990b: 245), a super-ego command to enjoy oneself.[3] The sexuality that is constituted around transgression of laws, taboos, and standards of purity is no less a sexuality of the heights than those which follow a moral ideal.

These kinds of sexualities fail to attain complete *jouissance*. Finally, there is a sexuality of the surfaces which does not seek consummation in the penetration of bodies nor in imitation of an eternal idea of marriage: this immanent sexuality aims at the constitution of plateaus of intensity – a continuous, self-vibrating region avoiding any orientation toward a culmination point or external end (1988: 22, 158). Such a sexuality continually enfolds its intensities into every movement, word, and touch: its aim is to isolate the event of sexuality as a phantasm that subsists in every moment, 'saturating every atom', without this phantasm being actualized in an exchange of bodies or promises. Indeed, every desire is initially of this nature, before being caught up in the depths of bodies or withdrawing into the ideal heights. The sexuality of surfaces operates through perversion (Deleuze, 1990b: 133, 206): one surface is always substituted for another – the search for the phantasm yields something else of a different nature as its result, but this result can be made into a new object of desire, producing new phantasms, maintaining the plateau of intensity.

Thought, invested with desire, also has perverse devices for adding to the explicit meaning of a proposition and saying more than it means. Satire is speech from the depths, where bodily drives and functions rise up to engulf and subvert intended meanings with sexual and anal references, showing them as a regressive investment of drives (Deleuze, 1990b: 246). Irony is speech that invokes the heights, alluding to an ideal through relations of eminence, equivocity, or analogy (Deleuze, 1990b: 247). The problem here is that one is perpetually caught in the ignorant position of dramatic irony, unaware of the events that pass by around one. Humour, however, like perversion, is an art of surfaces (Deleuze, 1990b: 248): there is a perpetual substitution of one phantasm or surface for another. In a certain sense, all desire is perverse, for something else is always substituted for the phallus or desired object. In this sense, all desire is bisexual, by right, insofar as it involves the coordination of at least two kinds of phantasms or objects of desire, even if the second sex must also be substituted for in a process of double deterritorialization, so that sexuality is ultimately the production of a thousand sexes (1988: 278). Similarly, humour is a perversion of thought that explores a problem by answering each question with an element from a foreign category (Deleuze, 1990b: 136). The aim here is to disengage the pure event that always escapes actualization in states of affairs by blocking both the depths and heights. When Deleuze and Guattari write about creatures and characters from the domains of nature and history, there is an essential perversion to their thought – in order to disengage the pure event, it is necessary to discover the psychosexual and speculative problems to which these characters respond in intensity, without regarding them as existent bodies or ideal categories. Humour is the art of expressing intensity on a surface; one will never find a contradiction here because the meaning is always a paradoxical phantasm, escaping the domain of thought – the unthinkable that nevertheless causes us to think.

Psychic Repression

The most significant set of dichotomies which Deleuze and Guattari bring
into question by means of their immanent approach is that between words
and things, theory and practice, meaning and matter, mind and body, the
artificial and the natural, the social and the physical; there can no longer be
any transcendent principle maintaining a distinction (1984: 2). Following the
Freudian revolution, the psyche can no longer be regarded as relating to
social experience by means of the imposition of a fixed set of rational,
Kantian categories on its representations (1984: 25). For Deleuze and
Guattari, however, the psyche cannot even be regarded as a realm of
interpretive consciousness generating its representation of experience
through the presuppositions of a phenomenological subject. Consequently,
the psyche is composed of the same kind of material as society: bodies,
relations, productions, events – Deleuze and Guattari call these 'desiring-
machines'. The psyche must be produced in the same way that society is
produced; it has no primacy or originality in relation to experience. It is
filled with encounters and relations where anything can meet anything
else.

   Having removed the barrier between interior and exterior, ideas are
liberated from the model of logic and can come to behave like bodies.
Deleuze and Guattari's thought calls itself 'schizophrenic' because their
ideas follow this paradoxical behaviour (Deleuze, 1990b: 129). It is a
question of attaining the primary process of 'orality', where there is no
longer any distinction between eating and speaking, or thinking and being
(Deleuze, 1990b: 186–95; Guattari, 1992: 123–4). A word becomes an
asignifying material substance. They then appear to construct a phenomenology of schizophrenic experience in terms of 'desiring-machines', the 'body
without organs', and the animating energy of 'desiring-production'. This is
not intended to turn the schizo into a postmodern hero; instead, schizoanalysis aims to tackle all modes of being in the light of psychosis (Guattari,
1992: 118, 92). The emphasis on psychosis derives from combining Deleuze's Nietzschean and Spinozist ontology with Guattari's clinical experience.

   Within this model of the psyche, one is able to conceive of the primary
repression that will make possible the repression of desire. The explanation
runs something like this: a desiring-machine functions by connecting
together other machines that will form its parts; it is like a spirit that
'contemplates' them, producing a flow of its own which is the extracted
synthesis. A productive machine follows this first passive synthesis of time;
it is an organ, like an eye, that views the world from its own perspective and
produces an output. Now, in processes of production, when desire connects
machines together in order to produce flows of output, the process itself,
production, is a product which exists alongside the machines as one of the
outputs of the process (1984: 6). Deleuze and Guattari reject the category of
expression for this phenomenon; production is not merely an idea added to

the process. By contrast, what is implied is that the machine, the schizophrenic object, has no ontological status in itself; it can only be considered according to the processes that produce it (1984: 6). Rather than hypostatising things and words as objects with their corresponding ideas, a working machine or organ may be regarded from two perspectives: its process of composition, and its process of functioning; it cannot be regarded as an existent object in itself. Next, effacing any distinction between existence and essence, Deleuze and Guattari refuse to distinguish between these two perspectives: 'There is no need to distinguish here between producing and its product' (1984: 7). The process of composition is also the functioning of the machine, for there is only one synthesis at work.

Deleuze and Guattari also extract a third term or perspective on machines: in addition to composition and functioning, there is the perspective that identifies the two. The event of production is a paradoxical identity of producing and one of its products; it is also a body, although a smooth and inert one, lying alongside the other machines. Deleuze calls this a 'body without organs'; it is a moment of antiproduction, or a model of death in the unconscious, for it produces nothing itself – its lack of output is its lack of organs (1984: 7). This is a totally schizophrenic logic: it deliberately confuses words and things, turning transcendental categories into empirical events: 'production', apparently an idea of a process, becomes a body. This allows a first distinction: we can contrast a field of differences, composed of partial desiring-machines, each of which comes into existence and functions by connecting others together, with a field that grasps the machinic process all at once as an identity. This latter perspective is that of the Bergsonian disjunctive synthesis, producing a quality and a drive: the field is surveyed as a whole, and regarded from the perspective of composition as a territory with an expressive quality, while from the perspective of function it is regarded as a drive. There are therefore two poles to this whole without working parts or 'body without organs': an empty body or quality, which does not affect production at all, and a full body or drive that falls back upon the desiring-machines.

Deleuze and Guattari make two assertions about this process of production: the body without organs is not merely an unproductive body extracted from production – it encompasses the whole of production sufficiently to be able to make the whole process stop 'for a moment' (1984: 7); furthermore, this stoppage makes the whole process function (1984: 8). The full body is a principle of repetition (Deleuze, 1994: 108–9) – it aims to produce the body without organs once more, and therefore conditions the productive machines to function in such a way that they will eventually produce the unproductive body. Desiring-machines are haunted by a desire for their own abolition. The drive to continually produce production is merely an indirect means to produce antiproduction. In this way, the drive 'represses' production: through repetition, one passes from the model of death, as an ideal to be repeated, to the experience of death, as a state to be attained (1984: 330). Desiring-machines only function by breaking down, and in the process of breaking down (1984: 8); desire only comes into the world through 'repression'.

We therefore find two functions of the body without organs: on the one hand, the dead body repels or represses the machines by causing them to stop working for a moment; on the other hand, it appears to attract the machines to itself, record them, and cause their functioning, synthesizing them as a territory. There is also a third function: since attraction and repulsion spring from the same source, they can be reconciled at a further stage:

> The experience of death is the most common of occurrences in the unconscious, precisely because it occurs in life and for life, in every passage or becoming, in every intensity as a passage or becoming. . . . Every intensity controls within its own life the experience of death and envelops it. And it is doubtless the case that every intensity is extinguished at the end, that every becoming itself becomes a becoming-death! Death, then, does actually happen. (1984: 330)

The two drives are reconciled in the experience of death as an intensity.[4] Here we come to a third synthesis: a conjunction experienced as an identification of the two kinds of bodies without organs: 'So that's what it was!' The conjunctive synthesis has the effect of producing a residual subject of identification, 'So it's me!' This subject consumes the relation produced by the conjunction, deriving an immediate sensual pleasure from it. What it consumes, however, is neither a process, nor a quality, but a conjunction of these – an experience of intensive quantity. Intensities are states of passage between qualities, or pure affects:

> There is a schizophrenic experience of intensive quantities in their pure state, to a point that is almost unbearable – a celibate misery and glory experienced to the fullest, like a cry suspended between life and death, an intense feeling of transition, states of pure, naked intensity stripped of all shape and form. (1984: 18)

Deleuze and Guattari take these schizophrenic experiences of unbearable intensities as the primary level of existence (1984: 19). For only at this level is the subject identified with and immanent in the disjunctions it presupposes.

This experience of intensity gives meaning to the humorous, abstract, and dead model of desiring-production and its machines, and not the inverse – Deleuze and Guattari's thought is produced as an effect of an experience of intensities, and only simulates a concept of 'intensity'. Indeed, the collapse of the distinction between mind and matter, so that ideas behave like bodies, merely reflects the behaviour of intensities as exterior relations. Consequently, their theory is not a phenomenology of schizophrenic experience; it is a delirium that expresses schizophrenic experience.

Instead of being cut off from society, the schizo is able to experience underlying social relations and forces at the transcendental level. For an intensity is not some kind of internal, consumed product extracted from the real; instead, it is the tension of attraction and repulsion between divisions such as the psychic and the social, or the virtual and the actual. Although the delirium accompanying such intensities may seem 'irrational', making unexpected jumps and transitions across the entire fields of nature and history, these are real relations of production that affect the psyche: intensities combine processes and qualities, enfolding the whole process of production with its transitions and opposing forces, within themselves. The schizophrenic is the one who is best able to name the abstract social processes of desire and repression which impinge upon his or her body; indeed, the schizo no longer speaks in the name of some individuated ego constructed within the social field, but speaks in the name of the collective assemblage of enunciation, the specific assemblage of social relations localized and focused upon his or her life. For example, many schizo-phrenics believe that there are agents of a foreign power controlling their thoughts by sending subtle messages through the television set – such delusions express profound symbolic truths, both about the schizophrenics' own states of mind, insofar as they lack control over their own thoughts, and about real social processes, insofar as thoughts are largely subject to external influence.

Any explanation of repression should therefore be considered at the level of intensities: here it is no longer an 'explanation', but a production and an experience of repression. Desire turns to repress itself because of the unbearable affects and intensities it produces; repression is ultimately a way of sheltering from unbearable affects. Primary repression is a functioning part of desire; but, when it becomes unbearable, primary repression may turn back upon itself to repress itself. Instead of converting the model of death into an experience of death, the drive now works the opposite way: it aims to convert the experience back into the model so as to shelter from suffering in abstraction. It makes the dead and abstract body into its goal, as opposed to the live, unconscious body, so that the latter begins to proliferate as a cancerous body (1988: 163). In practice, this means that an intensity will 'turn on itself' to 'repress' its social conditions of production: the intensity takes itself as an autonomous product, detachable from its socio-historical conditions of production. One loses sight of the real forces that control thought, taking shelter in delusion. A disjunction is introduced between the process of production, with its component machines or organs, and the produced quality of the body without organs – the organs are now treated as enemies.

The initial result is a schizophrenic free play of consumed intensities as qualities, producing nothing; they appear to be ultimately symmetrical and reversible, external to the passage of time, since they no longer have any conditions of production (as in Lyotard, 1993). This way of thinking leads to chaotic delirium. It is all too easy to leap into the philosophy of desire, to dispose of history, and not to maintain the tension between producing and product which is desire itself. By contrast, the repression of desire should be considered from the point of view of its production. All intensities are positive, and must be considered according to their positive processes of production, but some processes produce diminishing intensities. Such pro-cesses are the 'death-instinct' in desire, and their ultimate product is the body without organs, the zero degree of intensity (1984: 19). Hence 'repression' is really a positive production of diminution; it is a product of desire.

This is the theoretical model of the psychic repression of desire that underlies Deleuze and Guattari's thought. Its consequences may then be explored in terms of different kinds of uses of the syntheses of the unconscious that generate psychic repression, on the basis of a diminution in intensity (1984: 68–112). In each case, something is extracted from the immanent plane of production, becoming 'transcendent' or unproductive. Firstly, repression begins with the conjunctive synthesis, for it is through this synthesis that desire relates to the social field. The intensity of the conjunctive synthesis always has a political, cultural, world-historical, or racial content: it is composed of proper names designating events, changes, and transitions, and the way in which these events affect the schizophrenic (1984: 85–6). The social unconscious is mapped out on the body without organs in terms of proper names that designate intensities. When antiproduction comes to dominate, the passage between intensities stops, and simulation is replaced by an identification with one particular quality, having a particular political, cultural, world-historical, or racial content. Conjunction is no longer a polyvocal process of continual transition between a multiplicity of meanings; it becomes a biunivocal conjugation or pairing of flows in the manner of a signifier and signified. The signified is an incarnation of the race, culture, or society in person; the fixed intensity becomes a transcendent signifier corresponding to it. There is no longer a relation of desire or becoming between social and psychic fields; the drive is now 'invested' in some fixed or transcendent manifestation of the social field. This reactionary investment becomes segregative, for the immanently produced desire will be unchanged by the investment, there being no relation of production here: 'I am of a superior race, class, sexuality, or political persuasion.' This involves a fundamental dissimulation: the antiproductive social formation is not the source of the desire invested in it, but it does appear to be. This reactionary investment of desire then bases its phantasy upon a social formation that both transcends it, in the sense that it cannot be produced or changed by it, and appears to cause desire, leading to an identification. This segregative or fascist investment of desire forms the basis for other reactionary investments.

Secondly, once segregation is introduced, we have a different use of the disjunctive synthesis. Formerly, the distribution of inscription on the body without organs did not affect production: one distribution would amount to the same as another in terms of result. The disjunctive synthesis separates terms such as alive or dead, male or female, parent or child, but these stand as poles or limits of a transition. The schizophrenic does not identify with both at once, but is always in a state of passage: 'He is not simply bisexual, or between the two, or intersexual. He is transsexual. He is trans-alivedead, trans-parentchild' (1984: 77). These states are differential positions in a field inhabited by the schizo as a whole. Once antiproduction makes the machinic process stop, however, the residual subject is no longer in a state of passage between poles. The segregative force means that absolute boundaries can be erected between differential positions. Disjunctions become exclusive: one is 'either/or' (1984: 76). The boundaries between terms become fixed; an order or grid is imposed upon the world. Such boundaries have the effect of imposing a law upon desire: 'You shall not cross the boundary.' Indeed, the boundary is traced by the signifier: law is a product of signification. Consequently, the social formation that imposes such boundaries adopts the position of a transcendent God, a creator of principles, boundaries, and order in the world, and who then issues a law to prevent any crossing of the boundaries of nature or society. Indeed, the law appears to create the boundary, for one does not find out what was prohibited until one is punished for transgression. Such a law, however, is merely a product of desire.

This exclusive disjunction imposes a double bind upon desire: either you will accept the imposed differentiations, or you will fall back into the abyss of an undifferentiated or non-signified (1984: 78). To be outside the imposed realm of order is to collapse into madness and chaos. Here, however, the threat of madness is invented at the same time as the order. The exclusive disjunction creates its own representation of an outside of reason and culture, but this representation bears no resemblance to the schizophrenic processes of desiring-production that exist prior to signification. Desire can be fooled or captured as follows: the suffering of primal repression is represented as a consequence for transgressing the law; if, then, the law is obeyed, production ceases along with the primal repression that goes with it. Suffering is a punishment for sin. Boundaries appear to be justified by experience because they give meaning to suffering – instead of being inexplicable and chaotic, it is the result of transgression, attached to signification. Desire then has a choice: either neurotic identification with one of the terms separated by the law, in relation to which any production or movement will be represented as transgression; or else 'internalization' of the law through identifying with its significations, so that one reimposes the law upon the social field, repressing the desires of others. Cultural reproduction results from the passing on of internalized laws and prohibitions; the threat of violence against transgressors may now take the place of primal repression. One should note that the law or principle, in this double bind, enters into one of the alternatives: either one internalizes the law, or else one suffers its punishments. The exclusive disjunction only generates an illusion of its transcendent status; in fact the entire disjunction or double bind is immanent within one of its terms.

Thirdly, such prohibitions and exclusions are the source of the formation of complete objects or persons. Prior to such prohibitions, names designate singularities or events in the social field, or sites between which the residual subject of desire can pass; all desiring-machines were partial objects which could only function when connected up to others. Yet prohibitions constitute individuated objects or persons; they separate an 'I' from others (1984:

70–1). This 'I' is only able to think in terms of representations; its thought produces nothing. It represents objects and persons as separate, individuated, and complete. They are regarded as transcendent to the representation in which they are connected, and this transcendence produces the illusion of their 'reality' which is lacking in the representations. This is our normal mode of conscious thought: when we connect representations of global objects or persons together, they do not function together to produce anything, but lie together as inert ideas. Indeed, in our representation, they seem to lack something: the full presence of reality – the object is never present in its representation. When desire is represented in this way, it appears to lack what it desires. Desire is then regarded as a quest for something which it appears to lack: a lost totality or unity, which can never be made actual within representation. The formation of the ego takes place at the same time as a lack is introduced into desire: the ego is defined by a castration-complex, by something which it is lacking, even if this lack is merely the signifier of a missing reality.

The Psychic Production of Oedipus

The present human condition is founded upon a repression of desire through the 'transcendent' or fixed uses of the syntheses. The way in which we think is based upon these uses: the conjugation and fixing of flows so as to produce representations of a biunivocal nature between signifier and signified, identifying a certain phantasy content with a fixed representation; the introduction of principles, laws, and boundaries to divide up the field of representation; and the construction of imaginary or represented relations between complete and detached objects or persons, which themselves are lacking or can never be represented. In addition, the institution of the family is regulated by the same syntheses: a fixed conjugation between individuated persons, in which desire is subordinated to reproduction, leads to the filiation of new individuals by exclusive disjunction. Gestation, birth, and growth become more than just the production and emission of a set of desiring-machines: the child is separated from the mother's body by means of the socially imposed prohibitions which found their separate identities. The same set of prohibitions then determine the possible alliances which can be made between complete, detached persons. These transcendent uses of the syntheses, or law, lack, and signifier, are the three instances by which desire can be subjected to psychic repression (1984: 111). Yet one is dependent upon another: desire cannot lack anything until its object has been prohibited; and desire cannot be subjected to a law unless this law is founded upon a signifying structure enabling representation. The structure of the signifier lies at the heart of the repression of desire. It is therefore through structures of meaning that power operates in our society. The revolution of desire will not take place until desire has challenged dominant structures of meaning.

The psychic and social dimensions of the repression of desire are inseparable. If the psyche is formed as a signifying structure, it is potentially repressible; but desire will not actually be repressed until a social product plays the role of the signified that will activate and produce the structure. The actual repressive social formation lends its shape to the psychic structure of the signifier, but, because the relation between signifier and signified is arbitrary, a substitution is possible that will lead the psyche to relate repression to imaginary causes, making it impossible to unravel. Psychic repression, operating through representation, can then gain a four-fold structure: desire; the representative of desire; the repressing representation; and the displaced represented (1984: 164). For repression, the formalism is all important, even though it has no content or meaning in itself. All a dominant social formation has to do to introduce repression is make an arbitrary substitution of meaning or 'signified', perhaps through issuing its own sanctions that turn suffering into punishment, in order to conceal the operation of power through a displaced representation. Power needs a minimal level of 'force'; it operates through structures of significa-tion. Insofar as desire embraces the signifying structures offered to it by a dominant social formation, it invests itself in that formation and desires its own repression.

The best example of a purely signifying structure is the figure of Oedipus produced in Lacanian psychoanalysis. Lacan saved Freud's model of the Oedipus complex from its dependence on an imaginary history, as well as the worst excesses of its chauvinism, by extracting the signifying or symbolic structure from the imaginary story. For Lacan, the unconscious is structured like a language; the triangular relationship of the family is translated into a symbolic structure devoid of imaginary content. The resolution of Oedipus means an internalization of its structure into desire, and an acceptance that desire will always lack something, the transcendental signified which restores it to reality. By investing itself in the search for the transcendental signified, desire lives out the Oedipus complex. The solution to this neurotic search is a regression from the signified to the structure: when desire embraces the oedipal structure as the law of society, it resolves and internalizes Oedipus. The resolved and internalized Oedipus can then function as the basis of both our participation in society and the way in which we think.

This structural version of Oedipus is taken by Deleuze and Guattari to be the prime agent of repression in our society. For instead of referring to imaginary histories or identifications, it is explicated at the more primordial level of structures of meaning. Nevertheless, it can only be passed on when it is actualized in specific social institutions; a signifying structure is nothing without the social formation that gives rise to it. Deleuze and Guattari take the family to be the delegated agent of psychic repression in our society: 'Inscribing itself into the recording process of desire, clutching at every-thing, the family performs a vast appropriation of productive forces; it displaces and reorganizes in its own fashion the entirety of the connections and the hiatuses that characterize the machines of desire' (1984: 124). The family reorganizes desire so that it becomes intra-familial. The desire for incest did not occur until it was prohibited and parents were separated as detached and complete persons. One resolves Oedipus by internalizing the structure of desire which it presents; one can then participate in the rest of society through the family as a model, so that authoritarian figures are extensions of the father, and sexual attraction is a repetition of desire for one's mother. The structure will be repeated in the rest of one's experience, so that the child eventually constructs its own oedipal family.

Where families do not function successfully enough to internalize Oedipus, children will grow into adults who are not quite adjusted to society. They may suffer from neurosis or some form of obsessive fear of castration. Psychoanalysis may then complete the work of the family by helping the neurotic to resolve unfinished oedipal conflicts. If psychoanalysis is not successful, then isolation from society may be necessary – either in a psychiatric hospital or prison, or through alternatives such as major tranquillizers, poverty or unemployment. Where Oedipus does not take root at all, then schizophrenia will arise. The liberation of desire allows the development of a phantasy not normalized or inscribed by the dominant structures of society. Schizophrenia, for Deleuze and Guattari, is above all a process – the process of desiring-production. It is not a medical diagnosis. If Deleuze and Guattari are asked whether or not they have seen a schizophrenic, they lie (in spite of Guattari's decades of clinical work): 'No, of course not' (1984: 380). The catatonic or autistic people one meets in psychiatric hospitals have had their process interrupted, their desire stopped or even re-oedipalized. They produce nothing. The real schizo, for Deleuze and Guattari, is someone who temporarily enters a process, a transition, or a voyage in intensity. Schizophrenia is a move to a different quality of consciousness: the fantasy of desiring-production.

Social Repression

Power is acted out in a physical form through violence; indeed, it is easy to assume that the essence of power is violence. Yet social repression operates more commonly through the threat rather than the commission of violence. It is therefore mediated by the psychic domain of meaning; social repression is inseparable from psychic repression. A psyche, however, is formed in a specific way through its social experience; indeed, all impulses towards violence arise from some kind of socially produced meaning. Society and psyche are interdependent; if one must posit some form of primal, neutral, pre-social exercise of force, then this would be accidental suffering. The operation of power, therefore, is to be discovered as an element of meaning extracted from an association of processes, signs, events, and relations (1988: 445); it is relatively independent of the specific contents of particular societies. Deleuze and Guattari's account of social formations turns away from their varied contents towards their regimes of expression, where psyche and society meet and become indiscernible. The claim is not that differing societies share universal structures of signification, but rather that they share universal machinic processes for the production of expression. The same kinds of syntheses are at work in differing societies to produce and repress desire.

In *Anti-Oedipus*, Deleuze and Guattari examine three such social machines of expression. These share a rare characteristic: in each social formation, the mode of economic production, the mode of representation, and the mode of reproduction all derive from a single machinic formation that gives to each society its consistency. A society is therefore defined by the mode of representation given by its machine of expression or 'regime of signs', rather than its material relations of economic production and exchange. So, according to Deleuze and Guattari, society is not primarily a milieu of exchange or circulation, but 'a socius of inscription where the essential thing is to mark and be marked' (1984: 142). People ultimately relate to each other by means of a primitive communication or expressivity.

The first form of social machine is a territorial machine of primitive inscription (1984: 139–65). The primitive exercise of power, violence, gains meaning if it makes an inscription. The various operations of tattooing, excising, incising, carving, scarifying, mutilating, encircling, and initiating ensure the entry of the body, or its particular organs, into the collective investment of desire of the whole tribe. The marks function as codes to designate the social status and roles of the bodies. The purpose of such practices is to create an alliance between the tribe and its marked member that will endure independently of any fluctuations of desire. There is, however, no repression at this stage. Deleuze and Guattari borrow from Nietzsche the notion that the infliction of pain causes pleasure: the tribe gains a certain pleasure from observing the marking (1984: 191). In Nietzschean thought, the exercise of power over another is a primordial form of pleasure.[5] There is no mutually affective relation of desire here, for the expressions of pain of the victim simply reassure the perpetrator of his power. This has a strange result: the victim is normalized to think in the same way as the perpetrator. For although the experience has a different affective content for each party, the visible scar that remains encodes the power of the perpetrator; the traumatic memory held by the victim reinforces a belief in the power of the perpetrator. The scar warns both parties of a possible repetition of the event. Now, at the purely expressive level of codes, it becomes impossible to distinguish between the agent and the victim in events (Deleuze, 1990b: 33). An alliance of meaning is therefore created in the non-affective form of a code or convention, along with a tendency to repeat such a marking process on others. Deleuze and Guattari interpret this as a supremely economic instance: in the event of marking, those watching gain a 'surplus value' of code. Marking is not enacted against actual or potential debtors, but instead is the primordial creation of debt: debt is a shared expectation of repetition. Paradoxically, against the laws of exchange, the victim becomes indebted to the tribe; pleasure cannot be exchanged for the mark because its only external and exchangeable representation is the mark itself. Marking creates a memory that makes the victim capable of consistent, conventional behaviour along the lines given by the tribe. In this way, marking is a kind of primitive appropriation, like planting a flag on a newly discovered territory or signing one's name on a piece of private property. Once such marking behaviour becomes habitual, so that each member repeats the marks that they receive, then there is no unmarked perpetrator, and all are victims of the 'socius' or collective memory of the tribe. The collective memory of the tribe functions as a divine quasi-cause of marks, alliances, and production within the tribe.

Marking is a kind of appropriation: the victim is appropriated into the tribe. Indeed, one can also mark objects as well as persons: the marks indicate that the marker has power over the victim. Encoding can therefore form the basis for the economy of primitive society. The political economy of tribes operates through exchanges of differing kinds: women, consumer goods, ritual objects, rights, prestige, and status. Indeed, such exchanges may themselves be regarded as commutative encodings: a man is coded by his property, and his scars are his property, in just the same way that he marks his property. The giving of gifts is therefore another way of exercising power over a recipient: at the material level, giving endows property; at the psychic level, giving endows obligations. The property, like a scar, records a gift, and a 'debt' or obligation owed to a giver: such gifts and codings create alliances between people (1984: 150). Social bonds and obligations are created by gifts that themselves play the role of marks. This differs from an economy of value in that there is no aim to equalize and cancel out the exchange; although gifts are frequently given in the direction of debts in an attempt to gain more power, the debts are also passed on to others rather than being repaid, and the system functions to maintain its state of asymmetry, along with the consequent production and circulation generated. For example, a chief emerges: his own wealth indicates that he is the one to whom gifts should be given. Inequality in exchange, and the surplus value of wealth and prestige gained by some, is necessary for such an economic machine to function at all; like any economy of desiring-production, it only functions through breaking down (1984: 151).

The reproduction of members of the tribe, through alliance and filiation, operates through similar exchanges of debt. The social order as a whole can be determined by the status of individual members in relation to marital alliance and reproductive filiation (1984: 146). Filiative lineages are both hierarchical and administrative: there is a hierarchical order of lineages, and each lineage is assigned a certain role or function within the tribe. Matrimonial relations of alliance are independent of these, and constitute the most important exchanges between lineages: they often follow a circulatory pattern of exchanges in terms of relations of debts and alliances. Indeed, not only is reproduction part of the primitive economy, but it is also part of the machine of territorial representation. For alliance and filiation constitute the process of marking: a body is detached from a filiative stock of a tribal lineage, and a mark is detached from a signifying chain of marks used in the tribe, and the two become conjugated together. The mark designates the body in the socius according to a segregative use of the conjunctive synthesis: 'So she's this!' The mark, also, designates the place of a body within the marital exchanges of the tribe; it encodes the lineages and alliances. Inscription, here, makes the primitive socius itself the divine quasi-cause of social reproduction, the source of all alliance and filiation, and hence it can be mythically expressed as the mother of the tribe as a whole.

There are limits to this primitive territorial machine that it must resist. The greatest threat would be the presence of decoded flows escaping social control, as in capitalism. A second threat emerges from an excessive accumulation of surplus value of code in the person of the chief, leading to the rise of an imperial system; for this reason, the division of lineages through multiple filiation, and the relative impotence of the chief in relation to the group, are necessary to maintain the social order. To a large extent, however, such tendencies for the system to break down can be reincorporated easily by the encoded systems of exchange: the chief can be killed, or decoded flows can be marked. A final threat is a stoppage in the system of circulation: if alliances are made within a filiative lineage, as in the case of incest, then no circulation or encoding can take place. The alliance takes place outside the socius because it is not regulated by the markings and debts within the socius. A flow becomes completely detached from the socius. Once alliance and filiation are reunited, they are no longer independent; the flow is no longer subjected to exclusive disjunctions. Primitive society must therefore prevent the escape of such flows by means of a prohibition against incest.

If incest does occur, however, then the representation on which it is founded breaks down. The concept of incest is founded upon an exclusive disjunction; once this is broken in practice, it is also broken in representation (1984: 161). 'Incest' as such is only possible between detached and complete persons who are encoded or named as having specific roles in relation to each other. By means of incest, people escape these roles. Since incest does not distinguish between alliance and filiation, it can be employed to represent the primal autoproduction of desire, by which desire produces itself. Indeed, while primitive myths may often portray an intensive filiation or autoproduction as the origin of the tribe, this liberated desire can no longer function within the codings of the socius. Society determines where and when the autoproduction of desire can occur by using incest as the displaced representative of desire (1984: 166). The law prohibiting incest appears as the apparent foundation of primitive society, displacing the marking that incorporated all productive bodies into the relations of production, filiation, and alliance coded within the tribe. Yet there is no real law, repression, or desire for incest at this stage, but only the machinic relations that constitute and produce the tribe.

It is through incest that the next kind of social formation can come about: the 'imperial, despotic machine' (1984: 192–216). The despot leaps outside the tribal socius, installing himself at the limit or the horizon. The despot begins by marrying his sister; this endogamous marriage places him outside the tribe because it is not an alliance between separate filiative chains. In this way he escapes the codings of debt, and is able to enter into new alliances anywhere within the tribe. Then he marries the mother; this is as though he had married the mother of the tribe, for it results in a direct, intensive filiation (1984: 200–1). He simulates the mythical alliance between the goddess earth and her progeny. According to his coding, he becomes the father of the tribe. He is now able to extract a surplus value of code from anywhere within the tribe; effectively, the debt owed to him can become infinite. The despot is therefore constituted by two poles: as a magician-emperor, he bonds people to himself through a representation of direct filiation; and as a jurist-priest he creates new alliances as pacts or contracts (1988: 351).

The despot gains the freedom to carry out his own productions. It is important to note that this double incest is carried out within territorial representation at the level of codes: it does not necessitate another regime of representation, although it will eventually produce this; nor does it necessitate a literal incest, although this would be helpful – the incestuous alliances must be carried out at the psychic level of codes. The result is that the despot does not replace the old alliances and filiations, but subjects them to an additional coding, an overcoding, with a new alliance and filiation. Since the despot is capable of an autoproduction of his own codes, he stands in a relation of direct filiation with the god of the tribe; since the despot is capable of forming a relation of alliance anywhere within the tribe, the entire surplus value of code becomes an object for his appropriation. The former alliances furnish the material of surplus value, but now this is owed to the despot in the form of tribute.

The despotic machine of overcoding repeats the double incest at the level of representation. This overcoding no longer inscribes the debts on the earth, together with the organs and bodies it produces, but on a detached and decoded flow: the despot introduces a decoded flow of abstract signs which are marked with signs of his own body. This abstract sign is money – flows of metal which have become encoded with the sign of the despot. Metal escapes the codings of the primitive socius because it can be melted down and recoded: by encoding the flow of metal with his own signs, the despot produces a flow from his own property, performing the representational equivalent of marrying his own sister. This new inscription can then be used to overcode previous relations of alliance or debt. The despot repeats the founding moment of society: he begins by abolishing debts, paying them off with money, as though all debts were owed by the despot. In return, however, the despot expects a return of the gift in the form of money, as opposed to other surplus values; it is the representational equivalent of marrying the mother, for all exchanges can now be overcoded and evaluated in terms of money as a quasi-cause of social relations. The apparent gift of the payment of debts, however, initiates the interminable duty of service to the despot or his State, usually in the form of taxes. Through the circulation of money, the State becomes an infinite creditor claiming a debt of existence owed by its subjects (1984: 197). The State gains power by overcoding the desiring economy of its subjects; but where taxes are not sufficient to ensure the investment of desire in the despotic machine, then the despot may ensure order through the primitive method of cruelty – execution, by which he inscribes his law upon the bodies of his subjects (1984: 212). To live in such a socius is to live under an indefinite reprieve, under threat of execution. Nothing can escape the power of the despot, for he stands at both limits of the tribe: at the beginning, in a relation of direct filiation with the god, and at the end, as a decoded flow outside the tribe. Both gift and cruelty, creation and destruction are needed in order to construct a despotic socius. This imperial formation then has the capacity to impose itself upon other tribes by overcoding their peculiar codes with its own abstract flow.

The imperial formation functions according to a different economic regime from primitive societies. Instead of alliance proceeding according to the differential exchanges of marked debts, aimed at passing on and proliferating the surplus value of code, exchange now proceeds through the generation of the surplus value of a single code, money. The imperial formation requires the continued existence of territorial formations which it overcodes in order to generate the surplus value which it will extract. Now, however, bodies no longer belong exclusively to the tribe; they also belong to the State. The despot functions as a quasi-cause of all production, the source of all blessings; this is because all the processes of production are represented in terms of the overcoding given by the State. A different regime of representation is also at work here. Incest itself becomes the repressing representation of desire (1984: 201). Each member of society is in an alliance of infinite debt with the despot, and seems to exist by means of a direct filiation from the despot. The desire of each member of society is now invested in the despot – a desire to share his glory and radiance, to obey his will, to give back his generously endowed gifts; this desire is essentially incestuous. This migration of incest within the structure of representation is only possible with the introduction of a new regime of inscription. Whereas in the primitive regime marking was written directly onto bodies so that signified and signifier were always conjugated, in the imperial formation writing is deterritorialized, taking place on decoded flows of matter: metal, papyrus, parchment, paper. Legislation, bureaucracy, accounting, the collection of taxes, the State monopoly, imperial justice, and historiography are included in the modes of writing performed by the State. Such a writing functions by overcoding: its signs refer to the marks or signs already implanted on bodies. Such signs are regulated by the imperial socius: they are aligned no longer on bodies, but on a detached and fictitious voice from on high which issues its decrees (1984: 205). Writing is composed of the signs emitted by a fictitious voice which no longer needs to express itself except through writing – a revelation.

This form of imperial writing is able to become completely deterritorialized, detaching itself from the marks of the primitive socius. The occasion for this complete deterritorialization is the encounter between imperial formations by which a dominant system overcodes another. Now the signifiers of the dominant language refer to the signifiers of the other language; there is no longer any contact between the signifier and the earth. For the first time, one can begin to ask of representation, 'What does it mean?' (1984: 206). Instead of meaning being produced by specific marks and events, such codes can be forgotten and appear to emanate from the transcendental voice itself. One moves from one chain of signifiers to that of a more dominant language, eventually looking beyond the chain of signifiers to the voice producing them all. Since desire is invested in the despotic signifier, it is from this transcendental signifier, standing at the limit of all the chains, that one expects to find meaning. This transcendental signifier is nothing other than incest itself; it is the simulated marriage of the signifier with its signifieds. Full meaning is only possessed by the incestuous despot; such relations are forbidden to others since the despot, the object of their incestuous desire, always remains above and beyond them.

The meanings which the despot generously grants to his subjects are all simulated: they do not replace any real meanings, but they are produced as apparent meanings. These meanings issued by the despot take the form of law, this being the juridical form assumed by infinite debt: one has an infinite obligation to act in accordance with the law. Law is also the language of the signifier: the law signifies without designating anything; it decrees abstract boundaries, but it does not designate when such boundaries are crossed. Where cruelty had been the creation of debt, punishment takes its place as a vengeance exercised in advance. The imperial formation gains its strength from issuing such punishments; it initially writes its law, which is not knowable in advance, by means of the punishments it imposes – this happens in the conquest and subjugation of other peoples. Such punishments are no longer interpreted as accidents or events happening to specific bodies; nor are they interpreted as habits, codes, or conventions. On the contrary, they are now signified: each punishment leads to the erection of a universal rule. Where cruelty is still a production of desire, the law, once accepted, crushes any desire and production flowing outside of the imperial formation by means of its threats. Everything passes into the latent state of vengeance and counter-vengeance, or *ressentiment*. Only at this stage does repression begin.

Such imperial states rarely exist in actual history (1984: 217–21). Instead, they function as ideal formations. The despot is threatened by any organ which breaks away from the socius and escapes overcoding. In the same way that the despot first became detached from the primitive socius, the private citizen can become detached from the State, and rise up against the despot. The law is no longer merely decreed by the imperialism of the signifier in the punishments issued; it is recorded as a memory according to which society will function. The question of what the law signifies, its interpretation and its true meanings, becomes important to jurists who demand that the despot also obeys the law. The democratic signified can assert itself against the despotic signifier. Although we may have a completely different distribution of power in society arising from such a privatization, the same regime of signs is at work. The infinite debt is merely internalized and spiritualized – one owes a debt to the transcendental signifier which is always carried around with one; the despot has merely become incorporeal and invisible. The State fragments into a multiplicity of differing private individuals, each with an infinite claim over their private property as their own domain where each has the freedom of a despot. Such relations of ownership are quite different from primitive property, which implied a certain responsibility and obligation towards one's own property. The State is not so much a real social formation, therefore, as an ideal origin of society which attempts to realize itself by overcoding the existing social formations. It is an abstraction which can only be realized as an internalized abstraction; it only attains concrete existence when it serves other interests such as those of the dominant classes. It is no longer a transcendent law depending on a pure signifier; the law is immanent, following behind its signifieds. This abstract State may be internalized in a field of decoded social forces such as private property, commodity production, and class relations; it may also be spiritualized in a metaphysical or religious system which overcodes everything. The despot becomes democratized, oligarchized, segmentalized, monarchized, internalized, or spiritualized, becoming 'natural right', 'private property', 'reason', or 'God'. Everywhere desire is repressed, but it still functions through the desire for the State, and the desire for the actualization of the State. Desire turns towards its own repression.

Fragmentation and decoding resulting from an internalization of the law lead to the next regime (1984: 222–61). Decoded flows of sold property, circulating money, social and technical machines, and deterritorialized workers may meet together in a contingent conjunction that allows a new system to be born: capitalism. This generalized decoding of flows is necessary to constitute a new desiring-machine and a new form of social production. Deleuze and Guattari refer to the encounter between two 'principal' elements in Marx's *Capital*: the deterritorialized worker, able to sell his labour capacity, generating a flow of abstract labour; and a flow of decoded money that has become capital and is capable of buying it (1984: 223–4). Society no longer works by connections of production, as in the primitive territorial machine, nor by disjunctions of inscription, as in the despotic machine, but by conjugations of consumption. Instead of production being consumed by a ruling class, it is apparently consumed by the deterritorialized body of capital itself. Previously, the value of money only derived from the overcoding inscriptions to which it was subordinated. It was essentially a capital of alliance or exchange, overcoding according to a general equivalence of value. Capital begins when money generates its own surplus value: money begets money, becoming autoproductive. Only when capital becomes filiative, reproducing itself, does it become an independent substance operating at a new threshold of deterritorialization, separate from the overcoding socius. Here it becomes the new socius, the quasi-cause that appropriates all productive forces. The filiative quality of capital makes it a simulation of the autoproduction of desire itself.

Of course, the notion that capital is able to reproduce itself is an illusion; it can only do so when it is conjugated with relations of production. To begin with, labour cannot work as a decoded flow; it must first be coded by a primitive territoriality, becoming a specific kind of labour performing a specific task, before being overcoded by a capital of alliance. At this stage, labour is exchanged for money. Abstract labour can then be considered as capital. The production of a surplus value of code is now seen as an increase in capital; the surplus value of code is transformed into a surplus value of money, a decoded flux. Capital is invested by making an alliance with labour through exchange; the surplus value of code produced by labour results in an increase in the return on invested capital. Capital must therefore utilize and depend on previous social systems of territoriality and overcoding.

For Deleuze and Guattari, there is a dissimulation here which functions as the motor of the capitalist machine (1984: 229). There are, in fact, two different kinds of capital at work, functioning in two different regimes of exchange. Alliance capital, circulating in terms of exchange and payment, is not the same as filiative capital, circulating in terms of investments and profits. The money which is paid to the worker is not capable of reproducing itself; it can only be exchanged for consumer goods. The money written on a balance sheet of a commercial enterprise, however, is financial capital, able to increase itself over a period of time through investment. Financial capital has a different mode of inscription; it can be lent on credit, created by banks, provided that it may be returned with interest on a later date. It is dematerialized, without needing to be inscribed on any countable flow of marked metal or paper. Capitalism functions, then, according to a principle of convertibility of these flows of entirely separate inscriptions. The inscriptions belong to different games; they play on different boards or territorialities. The conjugation takes place between exchange and financial capital; it is an alliance between flows of alliance and filiation – the autoproduction of capital is the 'incest' committed by abstract, decoded flows. The desire for incest lies at the heart of the capitalist socius; incest, at last, becomes the true representative of desire because desire now takes the structure of incest.

All this has a number of consequences. Firstly, it solves the Marxist problem of the tendency to a falling rate of profit whereby wages increase in relation to total capital (1984: 230). Since a different kind of money is at issue, wages can increase to an unlimited extent without surpassing the total amount of financial capital, for this is written on a different board, and plays a different game. The value of financial capital is never fixed, but is given by its rate of increase; so long as there is a return on investment, this investment can be increased indefinitely. There is no common measure between the two kinds of capital. Thus the limit is internal, and can easily be displaced every time that it is approached. Secondly, the surplus value of money ultimately depends on a surplus value of code from which it extracts its profit. Filiative capital therefore needs to export itself, so as to open up more traditional sectors or archaic territorialities from which it can extract a surplus value of code. Primitive accumulation is continually reproducing itself in the form of 'globalization' or an integration of more and more sectors into the capitalist economy. Thirdly, production has to be consumed or realized in order to maintain the demand for production, for while capitalists aim at the accumulation of financial capital, such accumulation is dependent on rates of credit and profit as opposed to totals of exchangeable products. Mechanisms of absorption or antiproduction are required to remove the surplus value, ensuring its convertibility back into capital (1984: 235). Advertising, civil government, militarism, and imperialism are obvious forms by which production can be consumed. Capitalism does not function alone, therefore; it requires a State as a source of antiproduction to prevent an accumulation of surplus value of code which could not be converted.[6] Capitalism needs to maintain anachronistic sectors of reterritorialization in order to absorb production. According to Deleuze and Guattari, taxes and wars are good for the capitalist economy; the contradictions within capitalism are its strength. The consumer society is a similar formation of antiproduction; it creates new needs and wants in order to increase the differential relation of flows which is filiative capital. Similarly, recessions are good for the capitalist economy because instability of employment can keep wages low and increase the rates of profit. Capitalism can draw strength from almost anything that happens; the idealized State is merely an antiproductive pole of the capitalist economy. Finally, capital conditions the production of learning in the form of the invention of new technologies, both to facilitate the means of production and to create new needs for consumption; this intelligence, however, is consumed by a stupidity or antiproduction of knowledge that directs technological means towards useless ends such as military expansion (1984: 235–6).

Capitalist representation does not operate according to codes or signifiers; it operates through the conjugation of decoded flows. One of these takes the role of expression, while the other takes the role of content; there are no longer any signifieds or signifiers, defined in relation to a memory of meaning. Instead, there are only points–signs, 'schizzes' (divisions of flux into separate flows), and points–breaks (1984: 242). Electricity can be considered as the realization of such indeterminate flows, and the computer as the technical machine which operates such a decoding of flows. Abstract labour and capital can be considered as reservoirs of potential, like electric potential. The signs produced in capitalist society are asignifying; their production and recording are determined by the need for capital to repro-duce. An advertisement merely means that a company is trying to increase its profits. Such signs flow, break, split, and conjugate under the mode of capitalist production, determined by desire. Only secondarily are they

reterritorialized onto signifiers and images by which advertising and information communicate. Capitalist representation operates by simulation alone:
its simulations have no intrinsic meaning because their distribution is
completely determined by the capitalist relations of production that produce
them. The material of capitalist representation is the differential relation
itself, the conjunction between a flow of alliance and a flow of filiation.
Unlike other social formations, however, capital figures itself as a directly
economic instance (1984: 249). Nothing is concealed in capitalist representation. Its simulations are antiproductive because they cannot enter into
relations of production by themselves; they can only be made to function as
parts of an economic machine. Antiproduction ceases to be a transcendent
factor added to production; instead, it pervades all production and becomes
coextensive with it. Production only takes place where there are flows of
capital, and the extraction of surplus value.

Capitalism is the limit of 'universal history', the outside of all societies,
because it is the socius of decoded and deterritorialized flows. It is unique in
being able to enclose and reincorporate its own limits: it can always surpass
its limits and survive, because it can displace them through other reterritorializations. Capital does have one exterior limit, however: schizophrenia
(1984: 246). While capital produces unlimited quantities of decoded flows,
it binds these to itself when necessary by inventing a new axiom to quantify
such flows. No flow can be purely productive or filiative; it is bound to a
regime of equivalence or antiproduction which forms part of the capitalist
regime itself. Capital is powerless, however, to prevent the conjunction of
deterritorialized flows and the creation of new desiring-machines. Indeed,
capital produces schizophrenics, machines of immanent desiring-production,
in the same way that it produces anything else (1984: 245). To prevent
capital from being overturned by schizophrenia, and the free exercise of
desiring-production, it must find a way of capturing desire. Capital's power
depends neither on violence, nor belief in its ideology, nor demonstrations of
its productivity. The 'American dream' and fantasies of a better life arise
where production is blocked. Capital needs a way of injecting antiproduction
everywhere, into every private sphere such as the family, personal life, free
time, and perhaps even fantasy and dreams, so that desire will be invested in
its process as the only available mode of production (Guattari and Negri,
1990: 25). This means is Oedipus (1984: 262–71).

The Social Production of Oedipus

Capital takes upon itself directly relations of alliance and filiation – it
governs connections and reproduction. Representation no longer relates to
distinct objects or persons, but is inscribed directly upon forces and means
of production. Production is purely economic; it no longer requires the social
form provided by the family (1984: 263). The family becomes privatized,
placed outside the field of economic production, providing only a human
matter or labour pool for the processes of production. On the one hand, the

family remains as an archaic territoriality to be overcoded by a flow of abstract labour; on the other, its internal relations do not figure directly in the capitalist socius. This process of 'privatization' is a product of capitalism: families are produced as deterritorialized and decoded flows of human matter, outside of any territorial or signifying socius, irrelevant for the organization of society. The family is no longer able to participate in social production; its privatization is a 'castration' splitting it off from the productive conjugations of economic relations, with their alliances and filiations. Yet human reproductive relations of desire could now constitute a danger to capital insofar as they can create their own desiring-machines and alternative socius, independent of the control of capital. Decoded flows of labour must be reterritorialized on a private, nuclear family to prevent other social formations from growing. Hence capital is not content to leave the family to its own devices; it must extract its own profit from familial reproduction. Even if the family as a concrete institution breaks down, it becomes all the stronger as an ideal or a signifier in a process of 're-familialization' (Guattari, 1989b: 63). The abstract machine of the family does not produce itself; it can only be produced by the real relations of production in the social unconscious.

In capitalist representation, persons are individuated in terms of abstract roles first of all: the capitalist, the worker, the banker, the trade unionist, the lawyer, for example. Each of these images is a 'signified', but such signifieds are distributed not by overcoding, but by the flows of production in which the person participates. The family, placed outside of the economic field, may then model itself on capitalist representation, composing itself through images of images, or simulacra: the roles in the family may be distributed according to the autonomous requirements of the reproduction of the capitalist socius. The separate roles of father, mother, and child within the privatized family do not have any essence in themselves – they become simulacra of the images of the capitalist machine, with the father as simulacrum of capital, the mother as simulacrum of the earth, and the child as simulacrum of the worker (1984: 264). In the same way that capital governs a worker's access to the earth's resources; the father coordinates the possible relations of production a child may have with its mother. Although the family is merely a simulation, it enables capitalism to colonize each individual psyche.

This production of roles extends to the colonization of desire itself: the social field as a whole is applied to the family, so that through an operation of flattening and folding, the family becomes a representation or simulacrum of desire invested in capital (1984: 265). Previous formations included a representation of incest, but did not depend on any such desire. Now, however, it is essential that one desires something that is unobtainable except in fantasy, or one desires a fantasy whose realization gives no pleasure. Each desire that motivates capitalist production, based on the postponement of pleasure, repeats the oedipal structure. The child desires the mother in imagination, and is threatened with castration by the father in imagination; the child resolves the Oedipus complex by accepting the castration of its imagination, so as to internalize Oedipus as a symbolic structure. Once the symbolic structure is attained, the capitalist machine of representation has been reproduced – as a regime of signs. Consequently, every phantasm is now merely a simulacrum, with no means of reacting back on its conditions of production. Every image, thought, and person becomes compartmentalized – the repression of desire suffuses the entire social field, in which agents and images are now 'castrated', cut off from their conditions of production so as to be incapable of changing themselves.

One may well wonder who the victims of capitalism are, since nothing is concealed: workers are remunerated, consumption is distributed, and desire is invested in the socius. Capital has, however, incorporated the previous social regimes into itself, so that in some ways it still operates like an imperial formation, repressing any decoded flows at its global boundaries. Now, however, the socius is purely economic: it does not extend over the field of human persons. Indeed, it expels deterritorialized flows of human matter whom it is not able to overcode as abstract labour, and it deprives these of the means of production. It can afford to maximize the rate of profit by keeping wages as low as possible, for reluctant workers can always be threatened with expulsion from the economic socius altogether. While capital is able to tolerate and profit from the coexistence of archaic economic sectors, operating according to primitive or despotic regimes, it is also able to enforce an effective antiproduction on the deterritorialized flows which it expels. Consequently, economic growth is also accompanied at a global level by an increase in absolute and irreversible poverty in the form of famine, unemployment, marginalization, child-labour, and regression in the condition of women (Guattari, 1989b: 14–19). Perhaps conjunctions of flows of labour with flows of garbage enable a certain level of production at the fringes of the capitalist economy, but there are not sufficient means of production here for the construction of a new society (Guattari, 1989b: 62).

A similar effect is produced at the level of desire. Capital invites the investment of desire, since desire naturally longs for the production and conjunction of flows. Yet desire is only able to invest itself in capital so long as it engages in a repression of all desiring-production that cannot be overcoded or bought. The capitalist machine produces a desire that functions in terms of the representations of images; there is no effective distinction here between the public images of style and advertising, and the private images of dreams and fantasy. Production is conditioned by the consumption of images; private fantasies are one of the principal commodities of late capitalism. There is now a radical separation, however, between this level of desire, which is the social field where everyone acts and is acted upon as a collective agent of enunciation, and Oedipus, where everyone is now divided into two kinds of individual subjectivity. The 'subject of the statement' is the 'I' who is represented in discourse, a public and social person sharing in the collective play of images; the 'subject of enunciation', by contrast, is the private person, the 'I' who speaks, and who lives in a private world of fantasy images. The only difference between these subjects is their access to the means of production. One passes from the collective to the individual regime of desire by castration, the internalizing of Oedipus. Oedipus functions as a selective screen admitting only the desiring-production of images that can be conjugated with capitalist relations of production; these become components of the public world. All the remaining images that cannot be overcoded or subject to capital investment make up the private world of the imagination; by means of its flattening, interpretive power, psychoanalysis can map all these images onto the oedipal triangle, so as to construct their signification of the private family romance. There is a double displacement at work here: the imaginary representations of desire are first called 'private', and separated from the social realm; they are then mapped onto Oedipus, and subjected to repression. Here, at last, we have uncovered the complex mechanism for the repression of desire. Far from being a primal instinct that turns against itself, desire invests itself in Oedipus as its only mode of access to social production and the entire social field.

The oedipalized mode of consciousness experienced within capitalist society is composed entirely of images, and images of images. Whereas in previous forms of representation, thought was linked into the entire social field and the relations of power and desire at work, now the images of images merely relate to the private realm of the individual. When, in mass-media society, the individual is bombarded with a stream of public images, these acquire a kind of pseudo-eternity that only endures for a moment, for the individual is unable to respond to and change such images, being involved in separate processes of production (Guattari, 1989b: 45). Consequently, the individual is merely a product of capitalist repression; he or she is not an autonomous source of creativity and imagination. The way in which the individual produces images and participates in the social world of representation and meaning is determined by the selective screen of the capitalist economic socius, and its agent of colonization and repression, Oedipus. The ways in which we are able to think, and the entire cultural production of images, will be determined in the last instance by the possibility of integrating such thoughts into the capitalist economic machine: one may only work with fantasies that can be bought and sold. Even critical theories of society and revolutionary discourse will be incorporated into capitalist society as commodities to be bought and sold. In terms of desire, the question of their truth or falsehood in representing, legislating, and interpreting society is irrelevant. Oedipalized consciousness is separated from the real world of economic production, sign production, power relations, and desiring-production by castration; it is not a case of the inadequacy of language, the ubiquity of power, or the fictional status of the real world preventing any link between thought and the real. On the contrary, consciousness produces the real, but it can only do so under determinate conditions of production. So long as theory is oedipalized, spoken by the private individual and reterritorialized on some signifier of utopia as an absolute value, then it will merely be a play of images under the governance of capitalist production.

For this reason, Deleuze and Guattari see 'schizoanalysis', a theory that produces images through the unlimited conjunction of deterritorialized flows, as the escape route from the oedipal repression. Schizoanalysis, with its 'universal history' of society in terms of abstract flows of production and desire, is self-consciously produced by the socius of capital – but as an exterior limit escaping any reterritorializations or overcodings. One finds that the logic of Deleuze and Guattari's social theory is that of a vicious circle, conforming to the eternal recurrence: capitalism and the stratification of desire produce schizoanalysis, but only schizoanalysis can describe this production. The criteria of schizoanalysis are entirely immanent: it cannot be critically assessed to see whether it conforms to some model of 'truth'; by contrast, it can only be assessed according to whether it is able to effect a production of desire. The remarkable magnum opus, *A Thousand Plateaus*, provides the evidence: it escapes comprehension and recoding according to any existing mode of discourse.

The theory contained within *Capitalism and Schizophrenia* is therefore merely a simulation, the delirium of a pair of 'schizos', but this simulation is entirely immanent. Instead of appealing to the transcendental signified of a 'real world' to justify its claims, or a transcendental signifier such as 'truth', 'Being', 'I', or the 'Signifier' to legitimate its practice, it attains the conditions of the immanent experience of intensities and the production of desire. Any 'truth' of the simulated theory is given by its own immanence in its psychic material of being (1984: 87; 1988: 3–5, 11). Any transformation of society that it may bring begins with a transformation of the subjectivity of a thinker. The intellectual no longer claims the right to be a critical conscience for society; he or she merely becomes a worker in the collective production of subjectivity (Guattari, 1989b: 25; 1992: 179–80).

Notes

1. These are *puissance* and *pouvoir* in French respectively, derived from Spinoza's *potentia* and *potestas*.

2. cf. Žižek's account of the drive in Lacan (Žižek, 1991: 5).

3. Here Deleuze anticipates the 'obscene father of enjoyment' that Žižek finds as an alternative anti-Oedipus in the later Lacan (Žižek, 1991: 24). Žižek himself is clearly a thinker of the heights who hopes for liberation when the truth of everyone's desires is brought into the clear light of consciousness. His own work therefore provides the reader with much obscene enjoyment through participation in his analytic omniscience with regard to others' desires, but, lacking in an appreciation of surfaces and their substitutions, leaves unliberated desire in the dilemma of either the impossibility of enjoyment or an obscene enjoyment.

4. In Guattari's later work, 'death' is replaced by chaos, so that production only occurs by virtue of a 'plunge' into chaos (Guattari, 1992: 109–22).

5. Such a pleasure would appear not to be socially conditioned. One might invoke de Sade, but only insofar as the actions of a Sadist constitute a demonstration of his reasoning (Deleuze, 1971: 18). Such reasoning is not yet explained. Instead, it is better to invoke a conjugation of

Nietzschean types – the noble who takes pleasure in expressing his power through action, and the priest who constructs an interiority: the feeling of enjoyment is already a reactive sentiment, where the suffering of the victim is a displaced representative of primordial suffering, now neutralized and harmless to oneself. In a sense, therefore, the despotic form of sovereignty must pre-exist primitive territorial representation, although not as a social machine.

6. Capital is not the sole global power. There are also military–industrial complexes, motivated by archaic representations, producing power through terror (see Guattari and Negri, 1990: 53–66).

5

Escaping Dominant Discourses

Deleuze and Guattari aimed to counter the effects of power by constructing a revolutionary discourse which is liberated from the effects of repressing antiproduction. Since power is mediated through representation, the only way in which repressive structures of society can be removed is by changing the way in which we think, and hence the way in which power operates in society.[1] This strategy will eventually distance the style of thought adopted by Deleuze and Guattari from all their contemporaries – as evidenced in *A Thousand Plateaus*. Their thought is remarkable for freeing itself from representation, legislation, critique, and interpretation. Instead, Deleuze and Guattari aim to extract a positive force from a wide variety of differing fields and styles of discourse. In this chapter we shall examine how their thought can be differentiated from other contemporary theoretical options with which it interacts. Most of these have a productive force which is extracted and utilized by Deleuze and Guattari; there is, however, a dominant mode of discourse which makes antiproduction coextensive with the field of thought. Oedipalized representation is the one mode of thought which prevents production, and is therefore subjected to a direct critique.

Oedipalized Representation

Anti-Oedipus is not primarily directed against psychoanalysis; it is directed against the dominant capitalist economy of production, representation, and desire that introduces repression on all levels. As a theoretical text, it assaults the dominant way in which people think. The analysis of oedipalized representation is continued in *A Thousand Plateaus* according to a different conceptual vocabulary, no longer in terms of capital, Oedipus, desire, and repression, but in terms of immanent regimes of signs and pure, abstract lines. For the discourse of *Anti-Oedipus* situated itself in relation to abstract quantities: labour, production, capital, and desire. Instead of desiring-production providing an ultimate ground, however, it explains nothing, and only emerges at the end of capitalist representation as a liberated and expelled flow (1984: 101). *A Thousand Plateaus* uses a different technique: instead of assembling on a monistic plane of desiring-production, it begins by subtracting monistic concepts, tracing lines of flight that dismantle the assemblages. For one will produce nothing by asserting that Oedipus is everywhere – it merely becomes a dead machine. The vital force of Oedipus as a machine for repression can be recovered when it is analysed in relation to its function of composing signs. *A Thousand Plateaus* still concerns capitalism and schizophrenia, however, for the sedimentations of power it explores are specific to capitalism, and the smooth space of multiplicity where desire is produced is the schizoanalytic unconscious.

In *A Thousand Plateaus*, the production of a dominant mode of subjectivity is described in terms of 'faciality': the imposition of a certain appearance upon bodies, and the subsequent internalization producing the subject (1988: 167–91). We have noted previously how the electric current, with its passage of decoded flows, is exemplary of the capitalist mode of representation. The computer constructs meaning not through flows of current, however, but by means of stoppages; it constructs representation by means of antiproduction. Oedipalized representation can be considered in terms of the binary logic of information theory applicable to computers. The claim here is not that a reterritorialization of social representation on the technical machine of the computer conditions us to think in the same way as computers; on the contrary, the development and extreme utility of the computer in capitalist society is due to its conforming to a pre-existing oedipalized representation. This is the 'informationalized subjectivity' that operates in mass-media society (Guattari and Negri, 1990: 58).

Oedipalized representation operates by giving people faces; a person is recorded on the socius and participates in society according to the appearance which he or she is given, and by which he or she is recognized. Capitalist culture is largely concerned with the investment of desire in the production, recording, and consumption of faces. The capitalist subject wishes to produce a face of his or her own, to be recognized and acclaimed; films, television, newspapers, and magazines operate less as 'media' than as machines for the production and recording of faces; the consumer gains an immediate pleasure from the recognition and consumption of a famous face by virtue of the numinous quality of 'fame' attaching to it. Deleuze and Guattari analyse the production of faces in terms of two elements drawn from information theory. In the first place, a grid is constructed composed of exclusive alternatives: a face is a man or a woman, rich or poor, adult or child, a leader or a subject, heterosexual or homosexual (1988: 177). The distinction is 'biunivocal', in the sense that the alternatives refer to a single distinction. The subject which judges and recognizes will always be placed on one side of the distinction. Secondly, there is a selective response in the form of a binary choice: a face either passes, or is rejected, in a simple 'yes' or 'no'. These two operations can combine to give a tolerance at a more removed level: a face is neither white nor black, is it Asian? Or Arab? A face is neither male nor female, is it a transvestite? Faces which do not pass the first distinction may become acceptable and recognizable at a later level of choice. This mode of thought is majoritarian: it assigns every face a place in relation to a constant norm which always receives a positive evaluation, such as a white, adult, rational, male, heterosexual, married speaker of a major European language, dweller in a town. The use of 'majority' does not imply that most people are of this kind, but rather that it is the dominant norm from which faciality is defined, and according to which everyone can be located. This way of thinking is unproductive: such simulacra cannot be connected together to assemble a productive machine. Instead, processes of biunivocalization and binarization must be adopted by a transcendent machinic apparatus exploiting them for its own interests.

Faciality lends itself to two directions of thought. On the one hand, society can be recorded in terms of information, which then has to be handled statistically. The real relations of production that compose society, with their multidimensional machinic processes, remain invisible; society is described in terms of statistics and trends, the movements of vast molar aggregates. One constructs a 'knowledge' of society in terms of fluxes of large numbers of subjects from one face to another. Secondly, the face can be internalized to form a subject defined in terms of facial representation: the face becomes a perspective, so that everyone is required to have their own opinions and choices. In capitalist democracies, everyone is required to have a point of view, an opinion on everything; everyone expresses their identity in terms of the choices which they make. A second social theory is the statistical analysis of subjects, internalized faces, according to opinions polled on multiple-choice questionnaires. Even the 'don't knows' are given faces.

In a later interview, Deleuze suggested that since the Second World War we might be passing from Foucault's 'disciplinary' society to a society of 'control' (Deleuze, 1991b: 240–7). Enclosing institutions such as the family, school, psychiatric hospital, prison, and factory are in crisis, and are replaced by a dispersal of their roles. Modes of domination are internalized firmly within the subject, so that a fragmented Oedipus becomes all the more effective in investing desire within privatized relationships, in continuing education, in normalized rationality, in cooperation with the law, and in private enterprise. The mode of control is no longer enclosure but faciality, or an informational form of it, a number such as those printed on a credit card. The dominant mode of representation is the pass-word: a face or a figure allows access to the means of production, information, and consumption according to a simple binary scheme. The pass-word itself represents an abstract quantification of the degree of financial or cultural accumulation, one's credit or credibility, which itself can be regulated by salary and degree of access to the production of information. Once the social can be rendered in the form of data, it can be exploited and controlled scientifically by external machinic apparatuses (Guattari and Negri, 1990: 49).

For Deleuze and Guattari, these simple processes of thought and styles of subjectivity are formed from the conjunction of complex regimes of signs. Since such machinic processes cannot be represented in terms of information, they appear within oedipalized representation as redundant information, or repetition. One component of the face is the despotic regime of the signifier.[2] Applying this notion, faces gain cultural accumulation or 'fame' according to frequency of repetition (1988: 115); a face frequently repeated in the homes of many people gains a certain surplus value of cultural code.[3] Yet faces, like signifiers, can refer to each other: a face can accumulate surplus value through repetition of appearance alongside more famous faces. Hence chat-show hosts have some of the highest surplus values of codes; they can confer such value, like barbarian despots, by inviting faces onto their shows. All such faces are overcoded by being inscribed on the transcendental signifier, the white wall of the blank projection screen, the inverted Big Brother which never ceases to be watched.

The second component is the post-signifying regime of subjectification which we shall describe in detail because of its importance in the formation of a redundant subjectivity. It begins with the breakdown of the signifying regime of overcoding: the transcendental signifier fails to overcode, the despot's face is averted, and a packet of signs is expelled in the manner of a scapegoat (1988: 123). This group of signs still carries a signifying structure, but no new overcodings are possible, punishments issued by the despot are indefinitely postponed, and the signified or meaning of the law can be turned against the despot. The subject begins as a passionate grievance or resentment maintained against the absent despot. Desire is entirely invested in the aim of revenge, the attempt to bring the despotic power to justice. A kind of mirror-image or internalized despotic regime is carried away from the previous social formation; yet it is determined by the previous regime. The despot, with his overcoding and punishments, acts as a point of subjectification; this transcendental signifier becomes fixed without the freedom of the despot. The State operates an effective repression upon its scapegoats because it emits them as solitary flows, without leaving them any possibility of encountering other flows and forming productive relations. It can no longer issue new laws: the State has become an abstraction, a lost origin, which one can only attempt to reconstitute. This is an internalization of the transcendental signifier, a fixed source of meanings, which becomes the subject of enunciation, the 'I' who speaks. This subject uses the same signifying language of the law, but it only speaks in order to make its grievance heard against the despot; the subject is emitted, while still being repressed by antiproduction. The subject may be liberated from the power of the State, only to become subjected to the abstract power of an internal State as a lost origin. Yet because this 'I' is a fixed point, formed out of the transcendental signifier, it is incapable of any production of its own laws or meanings. It is post-signifying. Corresponding to this fixed subject of enunciation, there is also a transcendental signified, the 'I' which is represented in language. This is the subject of the statement. The post-signifying regime is therefore only composed of three points: a point of subjectification, a subject of enunciation, and a subject of the statement. This subject lives in a world of representation or dominant reality given by the regime attaching to the point of subjectification.

Such processes can structure both consciousness and passion (1988: 131). Each subject carries with it its own world-view, perspective, or regime of signification. One becomes enslaved to oneself, and the power of one's own reasoning (1988: 130). Yet subjectification is not a process which can only happen once: dominant subjects can function as new points of subjectification for others. Encounters between decoded flows of subjects are possible, but they relate to each other through their antiproductive regimes. This process happens in education: a teacher will issue statements whose subjects are interchangeable, so that 'we think that' can always be substituted for 'it is thought that'. These statements can function as new points of subjectification, so that the subject of enunciation recoils into the subject of the statement, and the student becomes incorporated into the dominant reality shared with the teacher. Subjectification begins when one is addressed as 'you' (1988: 130); the statement is repeated by the learning subject, substituting 'I'; finally, this statement may give the new subject of enunciation, making its own perspective from the signifying regime of such statements. Faces are always given from without, before they are interiorized as perspectives. Education is a process of incorporation into the dominant reality, so that whatever face one may have, one is forced to think like a majoritarian, even if one has a grievance against the majority. Redundancy here is a matter of resonance: one subject resonates with another, and one perspective resonates with another. Majority is therefore defined by resonance rather than frequency.

The point of subjectification always operates through some kind of impulse or marking: a shock, force, or punishment by which it establishes its dominant role. A gift may also have a disorientating effect as a result of the new alliance it produces. Later, it will be sufficient to recall a previous pain by making a threat, or a previous gift by making a promise. Such points do not always receive a negative response: if the overcoding takes, as in the despotic regime, the point of subjectification may be invested with passion, or positive desire. Since the despot has withdrawn, however, desire is merely invested in the black hole of a transcendental signifier; it cannot produce anything. The process of oedipalization does not need to take place within the closed, despotic regime of the nuclear family; any point of subjectification can awaken a passion for a transcendental signifier or another human face. Passionate subjectification can take a wide variety of forms: one can form a conjugal love-couple, in which each subject provides statements for the other to identify themselves with; one can follow a segmented chain of passions, passing from one subject to another, searching for a transcendental signifier which cannot be found in any of them; one can follow a similar segmented chain where each point provides a new point of subjectification, a new dominant reality, with its passion eventually leading to betrayal; one can construct one's sexuality from a particularly traumatic point of subjectification, leading to unfortunate repetition, either as victim or despot; one can even internalize the traumatizing point of subjectification in such a way as to conduct one's grievance against oneself, so as to make of oneself both despot and victim; finally, one may invest desire directly in the signifier, so that a grievance is conducted by the other against oneself, leading to infinite ethical responsibility for the other. All these sexualities are developed from a fragmented Oedipus; it does not matter whether they are heterosexual, homosexual, bisexual, celibate, temporary, or permanent – they are produced by the same machinic processes as those which produced Oedipus.

Oedipalized representation directs thought and sexuality towards the face. Both thought and desire are trapped between the white wall of the transcendental signifier, and the black hole of the transcendental signified (1988: 167–8). Under such conditions, desire is castrated, and is unproductive: it invests either what it lacks, or the law, or the signifier, or a combination of these three. This antiproduction is a dissociation: thoughts are unable to encounter other thoughts, and desires are unable to encounter other desires, because their flows are blocked by white walls and black holes. They are stratified by external machinic processes which only allow thought and desire to produce in order to extract a surplus value. Capital uses oedipalized representation to control thought and desire for the sake of its own reproduction. The forces of production which operate through such a mode of consciousness and passion are entirely external; they will not be evident within the content of desire. It is not that the machinic unconscious is hidden, censored, or concealed beneath something else, but rather that it has no need to present any kind of image of itself within consciousness. Thoughts and passions can be turned in all kinds of directions, concerned with all kinds of issues, fantasies, needs, or subjects, but no productive relation is established.

Deleuze and Guattari are pessimistic about any mode of thought concerning itself with some objective, real world, outside of thought but designated by it, as well as any mode of thought concerning itself with some subjective, imaginary, interior realm, internal to thought but manifest within it. The reason is political, rather than epistemological: the claim is not that we cannot construct approximate models of the behaviour of external reality or internal imagination, nor that we cannot test the truth-value of our information and opinions, but that the mode of reasoning which does so has no productive force of its own. It therefore allows itself to be produced only under the conditions tolerated by the dominant capitalist social machine for the purpose of extracting surplus value. The most revolutionary opinions remain 'castrated', deprived of any revolutionary investment or productivity.

In oedipalized representation, thought is staged as a melodrama or even a farce. Strange debates can take place between metaphysical realists and anti-realists, and between upholders of traditional values and nihilists, over the existence of entities that withdraw from representation. Many debates over political and moral opinions are little better than those concerning various kinds of cheese. In such debates, nothing can ultimately be decided because speaking precludes eating, and representation masks production. Even pragmatists appeal to what is done to legitimate truths and values, without facing the practical problems of doing.

Theoretical Discourses

Few academic discourses in France, contemporaneous with Deleuze and
Guattari, were quite so antiproductive as oedipalized representation. Deleuze
and Guattari engaged with and utilized the theoretical products of many of
their contemporaries. It may appear to many readers that Deleuze and
Guattari were entirely immersed in their theoretical culture, making a
contribution to an unfolding history of ideas. This appearance is as one
would expect from a philosophy of immanence; one should not expect to
find entirely new theories or opinions. Nevertheless, cultural, historical, or
sociological approaches to understanding Deleuze and Guattari would miss
two vital distinctions which separate them from their contemporaries. In the
first place, Deleuze and Guattari rarely write about the same matters as their
contemporaries, even if many of the same words are used. They have their
own way of constructing and selecting knowledge, so that they are only
concerned with such things as intensities, codes, territories, machinic
assemblages, and abstract machines (see above, Chapter 1, 'The Emergence
of Desire'). Every name, concept, or problem which appears in their thought
has been translated into their own idiom or language. Secondly, their
thought is governed by an imperceptible abstract machine functioning in a
different way from other theoretical discourses (see above, Chapter 2, 'The
Abstract Machine'). A consideration of the strategies and desires at work
gives the impression that their thought emerges from outside its historical
context – and its origins may be sought in Hume, Bergson, Nietzsche, and
Spinoza. One therefore finds comparatively little explicit debate, discussion,
commentary, interpretation, and critique of contemporary theoretical perspectives in Deleuze and Guattari's work – their attention is turned away
from the interior battles of theory to politics, art, and life.

In the following sections, we shall examine the relation between Deleuze
and Guattari and some other significant theoretical discourses. The aim is
not to set up a debate between differing positions, but to note the productive
elements selected by Deleuze and Guattari and incorporated into their
theoretical machine, as well as the ways in which they escape such
discourses by following their own lines of experimentation. Structuralism,
Marxism, psychoanalysis, and Nietzscheanism are regarded as collective
assemblages of enunciation – their function and practice can be altered by
each taking the other as its content, in a process of machinic heterogenesis.

Structuralism

The intellectual movement dubbed 'structuralism' which emerged in France
in the 1950s and 1960s was a major reference point for all subsequent social
and philosophical theory. Structuralism developed in reaction to the previously dominant humanistic modes of thought such as existentialism,
phenomenology, and Hegelian historicism which had based thought on

exploring the freedom, experience, and progress of subjectivity.[4] Instead of examining human culture as experienced subjectively, structuralism returned to culture as an 'object' to examine its intrinsic properties. Analogous sets of problems and methods were explored in diverse fields, so that, rightly or wrongly, the work of Roman Jakobson in linguistics, Claude Lévi-Strauss in anthropology, Jacques Lacan in psychoanalysis, Michel Foucault in history, Louis Althusser in Marxist political theory, and Roland Barthes in literary theory were grouped together as 'structuralists'. In 1967, Deleuze wrote an article entitled, 'A quoi reconnaît-on le structuralisme?' (Deleuze, 1972) in which he describes the common characteristics of structuralism in terms of a differential ontology and epistemology which he subsequently used in his own *Difference and Repetition* and *The Logic of Sense*. The main characteristic of structuralism is a triadic structure afforded to cultural experience so that in addition to human data designating an extrinsic, objective reality, and manifesting an intrinsic, subjective imagination, there was a third, symbolic dimension composed solely of differential relations between given terms. For Deleuze, the symbolic dimension was a virtual, topological space of relations and singular points which could produce actual experience through its own development; Deleuze relies on a Bergsonian ontology to describe this differential realm. This symbolic dimension, composed only of relations between the data, could be taken independently of the field of inquiry. The structural relations of fields as diverse as ethnology, psychoanalysis, and economics were expressed in terms of the symbolic domain, constituting structuralism as a universal human science.

Since human data could only be communicated through language, although occasionally a hidden or non-verbal one, then linguistics came to be dominant in structuralism as a whole. Symbolic relations were considered in terms of the signifying structure of language first outlined by Ferdinand de Saussure, in which a signifier gained its associative meanings through its differential relations with words which could be substituted for it. The result of this way of thinking was that actions could no longer be attributed to individual agents, since combinations, roles, and attitudes were already mapped out by a subject's place in the symbolic field pertaining to language, culture, political economy, etc. The human subject was now regarded as a product, a site produced within language and designated by the linguistic signifier 'I'.

The positive ways in which structuralism coincided with Deleuze's own selective ontology, developed through Hume, Bergson, Nietzsche, and Spinoza, are clear: it only considers relations, differences, and displacements; it rejects the self-presence and agency of the human subject; it bypasses history and the Hegelian dialectic; it draws upon interdisciplinary sources, constructing regimes of signs utilizable in diverse contexts; and its structures can be self-regulating, generative, and transformational. Nevertheless, the grouping 'structuralism' proves to be too broad and general when it emerges that the element considered as the 'symbolic' is something rather different for each theorist. As received in the English-speaking world, structuralism was often considered to be a science of constant, uniform, universal, and synchronic structures of human experience. As such, structure merely gave a form to the matter of human cultural products. The structures themselves were regarded as transcendent instances, belonging either to the nature of things themselves, or to the nature of ideas by which the world is understood. The symbolic was not considered as an independent domain, but lapsed back into a formal designation of the real or the imaginary. 'Structuralism' became inadequate to account for change; it had no relation to Deleuze's empiricism, vitalism, or Nietzschean philosophy of force and becoming. Those thinkers who developed a generative and transformational understanding of the role of the third, symbolic or structural dimension in such terms as 'writing', 'power', 'desire', or 'culture' were dubbed 'post-structuralists' by English-speakers, while still often being regarded as 'structuralists' in France. Hence Deleuze and Guattari's thought can be distinguished from other thinkers of their generation by the different way in which they understand the operation of the virtual, unconscious, or structural element. Deleuze and Guattari retained from structuralism the translation of culture into expressive signs, which will later come to form the machinic unconscious. They also learned to understand the operation of power in the form of the State according to the logic of signification elaborated by structural linguists. They did not, however, take the linguistic turn themselves, for this only enshrines the values and associations already found within current uses of language. For if structuralism is to be understood in its own terms, then paradigmatic and syntagmatic chains of signifiers cannot have any privilege; there merely remain singularities and topological relations as instances of difference and repetition.

Deconstruction

Structuralism allowed a productive, associative movement horizontally from one signifier to another, escaping fixed conjugations of signs with manifested intentions or designated objects, as found in oedipalized representation. The meaning of any cultural product is given not solely by what it explicitly says or what it secretly intends, but also by all the associations which are carried along with it through the substitutability of signifiers. Saussure had already termed such signifieds linguistic 'values', and Barthes and Althusser explored how ideologies operate through signification (Althusser, 1971; Barthes, 1972; Saussure, 1974): a bunch of red roses signifies a passion; a salute signifies the greatness of the nation. The structural field of differential relations is not neutral, therefore, but invested with all kinds of operations and effects of power. This means that a certain direction is introduced into the associative substitution of one signifier for another; the texture of a text composed of chains of signification tends to run in a particular direction which we have called that of the 'majority'. The presupposition of a real world, about which true propositions can be formulated, and the presupposition of a conscious subject, present to itself and responsible for itself, are ultimate effects of such ideological prejudices produced by the fixing of significations. These presuppositions are taken as targets of Jacques Derrida's deconstructive thought.

If language is entirely composed of chains of signification, then it instigates an unlimited movement of meaning – Derrida's method is to expose the occluded significations of each signifier. A subject which is present to itself can never be manifested or made present within a differential structure; neither can an object be designated which is really present. Both subjects and objects, therefore, remain transcendent to the signifying effects of language. They may be intended as transcendental signifieds, but they can never be made present. For this to happen, one would have to fix once and for all the meaning of the verb 'to be'; only as such could we understand designation of an object, 'It is here', and manifestation of a subject, 'I am present'. Derrida deconstructed the 'metaphysics of presence' by noting the effect of the flow of signification: meaning is never present, because it is always given by a possible substitution of another signifier, different from the previous one, or because its meaning is deferred until more substitutions can be made. In this respect, Derrida commented upon Martin Heidegger's heroic attempt to capture the meaning of Being, and how in Heidegger's later work the quest is found to be impossible, so that Being can only be written crossed out (Derrida, 1976: 18–26). Being is the transcendental signified, the meaning which can never become present within language. This part of Derrida's work accords with structuralism.

Derrida did not merely leave the signifying structures in place, however; he actively dismantled or deconstructed them. For structures are built on certain distinctions and evaluations; these evaluations will be subjected to revaluation (Derrida, 1981). An example is the privileging of speech over writing (Derrida, 1978); in speech, it is assumed that the speaker is present who can explain the true meaning of what is spoken. In writing, by contrast, the speaker is absent, and is unable to prevent meanings and interpretations from wandering off in all directions. Derrida, when deconstructing the metaphysics of presence, took 'writing' as a metaphor for a field of signification which can operate its own free play of substitutions, without being determined in advance by some transcendent author. In order to deconstruct the structured distinction between speech and writing, Derrida showed how speech depends on a prior field of signification or 'archi-writing' in order to present its meaning at all (Derrida, 1978). Deconstruction, therefore, is a political activity which involves the dissolution of the fixed boundaries that shape hierarchical structures. In addition to declaring that the search for truth or presence is impossible, deconstruction subverts the desire to pursue such a search.

One can then imagine that deconstruction would privilege the free play of signification or the element of 'writing' by which meaning is produced. This would involve attributing a transcendental signified to a signifier such as 'différance', meaning the signifying process of differing and deferral. The logic would be that of a kind of negative theology, by which the absent process of *différance* creates all meanings (Derrida, 1982: 6). One occasionally finds this privilege accorded in Derrida's readers, but not in Derrida's writing, which does not keep referring to *différance* by this, or by other names. By contrast, Derrida always discovers polysemic signifiers within the text under his consideration at any particular time. Even deconstruction must be deconstructed. As a result, the signifying field is not accorded any conditioning or transcendental status. This dimension of exploration would be as barren as those of reality and imagination. In practice, however, the signifying field does gain a certain privilege in deconstruction insofar as it is able to incorporate any thought, object, or product of culture within its chains of associations. Deconstruction is only able to operate insofar as it effectively privileges the field of signification because it knows of no other possible field of meaning. It is therefore caught in a self-conscious and deliberate performative contradiction, always deconstructing itself.

Deleuze and Guattari's thought developed in parallel with Derrida's. In some respects, it seems like a naive deconstruction which does not deconstruct the origins of its own discourse. Deleuze and Guattari do not merely deconstruct hierarchical dualisms, they overturn them so as to value the lowest term or the minority. They reverse the chains of signification so as to take them off along lines of escape towards the transcendental field giving rise to them. Instead of privileging the transcendental signified, they privilege the transcendental signifier, an empty space circulating between chains of signifiers and chains of signifieds, distributing singularities and roles. In practice, however, the field of meaning used has an entirely different nature. For Deleuze and Guattari, the meaning of language is not produced by the structural field of relations between signifiers and signifieds. In *The Logic of Sense*, Deleuze isolated a fourth dimension to add to the structuralist triad of the powers of language (Deleuze, 1990b: 17). In addition to the designation of objects, the manifestation of subjects, and the signification of concepts, Deleuze found another dimension which he calls 'sense'. This derives from an immanent methodology: language is required to function a priori from within. Deleuze combined two arguments to indicate this fourth dimension. The transcendental field cannot be encompassed by language because it also involves the material domains of economics and culture. In practice, the realm of words or statements does have some kind of interaction with the realm of bodies or visibilities. Language works. Deleuze then argued that this relation cannot be given by designation or manifestation, since both of these presuppose signification, but neither can it depend on signification alone, for this requires designation in order for a signified to relate to an object. The immanent and transcendental field, for Deleuze, is not signification, with its active powers of substitution, but 'sense' (Deleuze, 1990b: 105). Sense appears to be a sterile and unproductive surface effect of signification which could only be given by an infinite regression (Deleuze, 1990b: 28). In practice, however, it is the empty place which circulates along signifying structures. It appears to be nonsense, a breakdown in signification, but it is the term which makes the practical relation between language and bodies possible. Sense also appears to be a surface effect of bodies: it is a pure event, a membrane without thickness through which a change passes. For example, 'the tree greens' (comes into leaf) is an event which possesses its own sense (Deleuze, 1990b: 6). The 'greening' of a tree cannot be located in a specific place and time; instead, it is a meaning which is extracted from its actualization in a body. Deleuze and Guattari's machinic unconscious is only concerned with sense-events: these include micropolitical instances such as promising, ordering, advising, giving an assurance, praising, taking seriously or lightly, sneering, and so on – they organize bodies through an asignifying semiotic that cannot be reduced to signification (Guattari, 1984: 104). Deleuze and Guattari escape structuralism by supplementing the chains of signification with pragmatic gestures, by which language affects bodies and social presuppositions (Guattari, 1992: 23).

At the heart of the transcendental field is a transcendental signifier or empty place which circulates along series of signifiers and signifieds in order to produce meaning. The circulating element constructs the differential relations between signifiers and signifieds. Here it exhibits the logic of *différance*, except for a crucial difference: where '*différance*' signifies the emptiness of the place, where meaning is different and deferred, Deleuze was concerned with the empty place insofar as it actually produces meanings or relations between series of terms – such meanings are only evident when language is actually used in statements. More important than its circulation between series of signifiers and signifieds is the circulation of the empty place between signification and bodies. When such heterogeneous series begin to function together, structure merely expresses machinic effects. Meaning never comes from language as such; it is determined by an outside of language – the real social power formations that can easily be identified in terms of territories (Guattari, 1984: 169). The empty place itself has no meaning at all; it merely functions by the substitution of a body when a signification is required. Deleuze cites the example of the ancient philosopher Diogenes the Cynic who, when asked 'What is philosophy?', went about carrying a cod on a piece of string (Deleuze, 1990b: 135). When asked deconstructive questions, this is the proper Deleuzean response. It is also the procedure followed throughout *Anti-Oedipus*: the product 'production', the empty space within meaning, becomes a 'body without organs'. Of course, it is possible to deconstruct Deleuze and Guattari's texts insofar as they make use of propositions that designate an 'outside'. Such attention to signification, however, misses the meaning of the speech-acts and order-words enunciated in their texts.

Deleuze and Guattari agree with Derrida that every language presupposes a 'writing' system from which it originates. But there is a decisive break between inscription as a synthesis of recording on the body without organs, and the signifying structure of a major language. There are kinds of 'writing' which do not exhibit the logic of signification: the mark inscribed on a body is not a sign of a sign, but a self-validating event. The signifying structure of a major language belongs to a different regime of signs; it has a different machinic arrangement, and a different system of repression (1984: 202–6). The transcendental signifier to which all signs point is the body of the despot, the empty space which now functions as a quasi-cause. In fact, Deleuze and Guattari do not privilege the transcendental signifier – they see it as the quasi-cause of repression in the signifying structure of the State. They aim to overthrow this despotic power by inverting the hierarchy, so that productive relations between signs can be formed by immanent processes of encounter. The major difference between structuralism and Deleuze and Guattari, therefore, is a difference in understanding of the nature of the structural or transcendental field. For structuralists, it is a question of meaning, or a theatre of representation. For Deleuze and Guattari, the machinic unconscious is merely a business of production, posing only problems of use.[5] While one may suppose that machines have a 'structure', a particular arrangement of parts or assemblage, a machine, for Deleuze and Guattari, is identified with its process of autoproduction rather than its parts. 'A machine is like a set of cutting edges which insert themselves into an assemblage' and 'draw variations or mutations of it' (1988: 333). Deleuze and Guattari therefore mutate the structural field so that it becomes autoproductive and self-transformative, overcoming all dichotomies between 'doing' and 'thinking' (Guattari, 1984: 100). It attains to a level of Nietzschean becoming. Stable structures are called 'stratifications'; Deleuze and Guattari use structuralism to explore repressive social formations in the form of a 'geology of morals'. Structuralism, however, does not tell us about desire and its liberation. Beyond structuralism, they return to Marx and processes of production.

Marxism

Deleuze and Guattari explore a Marxist understanding of the transcendental field of culture.[6] Production is considered in terms of an abstract process of labour; it is divided into the three primary processes of production, recording, and consumption. In order for the field of political economy to be related to the field of meaning, on a single plane of immanence, it must be considered in a form abstracted from the real and the imaginary. Deleuze and Guattari are not concerned with designating the material production and consumption of goods in particular factories and cultures, except insofar as these produce events with meaning. Neither are Deleuze and Guattari concerned with understanding the essence of humanity in terms of its 'species-being' of productive labour. For them, production is considered not in relation to objects or subjects, but as an abstract, machinic field composed of relations of production. One is not concerned with who operates such machines, nor with what is produced, except insofar as these can form parts of other machines. Structuralism and Marxism encounter one another and transform each other: structuralism is deterritorialized from the field of signification, under the dominance of language, only to be reterritorialized on the field of economic production. Meaning is now only a part of the total process, deriving from the synthesis of recording; it does not encompass production and consumption. Political economy significantly expands the possibilities of the transcendental field.

In *Anti-Oedipus*, Marx is frequently cited as an authoritative source, and treated with a rare reverence. Deleuze and Guattari's dependence on the Marxist analysis of the workings of capital is too pronounced to remark upon in all its detail. A few points may be made. Firstly, like Marx, Deleuze and Guattari construct a 'universal history' of different social formations in terms of the categories given by capital. This is only possible because capitalism is the limit towards which all societies tend; it therefore gives a privileged understanding of the way in which previous societies function. Nevertheless, it is clear the argument here is circular: capitalism is only a limit according to its own globalizing terms; its concepts are as effective at representing all social formations as capital is at decoding all societies. This Marxist theme is merely a mask operating in Deleuze and Guattari's thought; behind Marx and capitalism one finds the figure of Spinoza and immanence. Capital is a distorted double of a Spinozist plane of immanence, translating all determinations into the single, monistic, quantitative equivalent of money. The immanence of schizophrenic desire is the true limit of society. Secondly, Deleuze and Guattari rely upon the Marxist understanding of machines in terms of abstract labour. Machines are not understood purely according to a scientific or technical code, but also in terms of the 'work' which they can do. This allows Deleuze and Guattari to break down the dualism between humanity and machines, the natural and the artificial, humanism and materialism. It also allows them to take up the notion of a 'machine' as an immanent agent of production, a process which does not stand above its product but which can be affected by it. Consequently, exploitation may take place through the 'alienation' of labour, but labour is never alienated from a pre-existing essence, human or otherwise. The 'alienation' of labour is merely antiproduction, a failure of machinic production. Thirdly, Deleuze and Guattari make much of the false equivalence of monetary exchange. For Marx, the false equivalence between money and goods in the exchange relation allows the extraction of a surplus value because prices are set in relation to money, according to the law of supply and demand. Deleuze and Guattari use this false equivalence as an opportunity to explore a different false equivalence in banking practice between credit money and exchange money; this they regard as a return to the Marxist theory of money (1984: 230). They find the essence of the capitalist system, the extraction of a surplus value of a deterritorialized flux no longer inscribed on quantifiable objects, in terms of this false equivalence by which material or real money is exchanged for a differential or structural relation. Fourthly, they draw upon the Marxist notion of primitive accumulation as a precondition for the development and investment of capital. Instead of regarding this primitive accumulation as a stage now complete within European history, they observe how this primitive accumulation continues in the economies of developing countries at the fringes of capitalism. While capital functions by producing the deterritorialized and decoded flux of credit, it can only do so through the deterritorialization of other, overcoded fluxes in the form of the production and distribution of commodities. Developing countries therefore continue to supply developed countries with wealth, as in the days of colonialism. Finally, Deleuze and Guattari are concerned with the economic limits of capitalism as described by Marx, in the form of the tendency to a falling rate of profit. Yet they write from a vantage point in history at which it becomes evident that capital is in some sense able to confront and overcome its limits. This tendency to displace its internal limits, as theorized through the false equivalence of investment capital and exchange capital, becomes one of the essential features of capitalist society for Deleuze and Guattari. Capital now becomes a limit towards which all societies tend because its own limits are merely relative. Each time it approaches one, it can displace it by various means, such as a recession together with a drop in wages of the lowest paid. Capital is much more invincible than in the classical Marxist account because its internal contradictions now only make it stronger.

The above points are merely modifications of classical Marxism. When it comes to a programme of revolutionary action, however, Deleuze and Guattari effect a much more significant subversion of Marxism. The critique is perhaps all the more far-reaching for not being made explicit: Marxism is deterritorialized by being analysed in terms of itself – the categories of Marxism, such as classes, the party, ideology and alienation, will be explained in terms of machinic processes of production, recording, and consumption. To begin with, revolutionary action is no longer considered in terms of the 'real' components of society: relations of power are no longer interpreted in terms of the class struggle (Deleuze 1988d: 25). The classes of 'capitalist' and 'worker' are merely roles assigned by the functioning of capital; class revolution, allowing workers access to the means of production, does not change the machinic mode of production. Power does not operate through dominant classes, but merely produces such classes as its effects. Class struggle will therefore be ineffective in challenging the dominant regimes of power. In the place of class struggle, revolutionary transformation occurs in the creation of a new subjective consciousness born of reconfiguration of the collective work experience (Guattari and Negri, 1990: 19).

Secondly, the State apparatus is a repressive power formation which functions as an agent of the antiproduction effected by capital, even though it pre-dates the capitalist system. Any party formed in the image of the State apparatus, with the express purpose of seizing control of the State apparatus, has a similar repressive and antiproductive character. Revolutionary action will not be effective if it collects together the masses in the form of a political party, for this mass behaviour is part of the system of power which it is necessary to resist. Instead of power being localized in a state, it is diffuse and microphysical, spreading throughout the social field, where each subject reproduces the ideal form of the State (Deleuze, 1988d: 25). Deleuze and Guattari implicitly pose a Nietzschean challenge to the motives underlying revolutionary action: much Marxism springs from resentment (Lyotard, 1977: 17). The exploitation carried out by the bourgeois State functions as a point of subjectification, and the revolutionary exercises his or her grievance against the State by attempting to overthrow it and seize control. The Communist Party indoctrinates revolutionary workers into its own dominant reality, forming subjects out of their resentment against the capitalist system. Resentment and opposition, however, are antiproductive: they cannot change the machinic operation of power in society.

While the revolution is not to be fought out in the real realm of class struggle and power relations between subjects, neither can it be fought out in the imaginary realm of ideology. Deleuze and Guattari uphold in part the Marxist principle of ideology, that the way in which people think is determined by their position in the processes of production. They also accept that a certain dominant 'majority' are able to determine how one should think in order to participate properly in society, and that this bourgeois world-view has little effective truth-value. What they deny, however, is that power operates through the illusions it produces. For where a certain mode of producing recording holds sway, then no alternative strategies of thought will become available. Power operates through the way in which it produces consciousness, rather than by maintaining a false consciousness (Deleuze, 1988d: 28). Capital no longer needs to be believed in order to be the dominant social reality; even if one is educated as to one's true class interests, and allows one's thought to be formed from one's own economic and material site of production, one can still continue to desire one's own repression. This seemed to be the case after May 1968 in France: the people were no longer fooled by ideology, but they still voted for a reactionary government. Capitalism is the age of cynicism: one does not have to believe in the system in order to see that cooperating with it is the easiest way to fulfil one's immediate economic interests. All recording, ideology, and imagination is produced by the dominant mode of production in society – power may operate through simulation rather than ideology. There is no Marxist 'science' containing a liberating truth, for such economic 'truths' will be expressed in pragmatic terms that reproduce the dominant machinic mode of production (Guattari, 1984: 106, 163). Instead of power operating through ideology, it operates through desire. This can be seen in the success of capitalist regimes, having little censorship, as compared with Stalinist regimes, with their diffusion and molecularization of propaganda and secret police via party officials and informers. The desire for repression is not a conscious want or need – people do not want their repression – but it is a state of the social unconscious to which people are subjected by their very formation as subjects with needs and wants. Revolutionary theory cannot liberate anyone by telling the 'truth' about political economy; the only true liberation occurs at the level of desire.

Deleuze and Guattari effect a powerful deterritorialization of the Marxist theory of political economy. They remove power-relations from the objective realm of class struggles and the subjective realm of ideology to place them in the structural realm of the machinic unconscious. At first sight, this might seem like an encounter between Marxism and structuralism. Yet Louis Althusser had previously been able to give a structural account of the workings of the class struggle and ideology (Althusser, 1969). Not only is the structural order displaced in favour of a Marxist economic infrastructure in Deleuze and Guattari's thought, but this economic infrastructure is also displaced in favour of the machinic unconscious of desire (Deleuze, 1988d: 26–7). Behind the masks of structuralism and Marxism there is another logic at work, a materialism which extends beyond the real, the imaginary, the structural, and the productive. Power cannot be comprehended in terms of these levels because it operates through the logic of desire. Deleuze and Guattari's thought deterritorializes Marxism by means of an encounter with psychoanalysis. Yet they retain some very significant Marxist themes: capital is a repressive social order; capital gives the categories for a universal history of society, even if this history is arbitrary, contingent, and singular, without proceeding through necessary stages; thought is derived from a specific site of enunciation within the order of production; and revolution is possible through some form of collective action, leading to a free 'society of artists'. The kind of revolution aimed at by Deleuze and Guattari will be explored in later sections.

Psychoanalysis

Deleuze and Guattari's critique of psychoanalysis is outspoken and sustained. This has the double effect of concealing the dependence of their thought upon psychoanalysis, especially that of Jacques Lacan, and of appearing to exaggerate the importance of their opponent within French culture. As we have noted, Guattari trained as a psychoanalyst under Lacan, and worked for almost four decades in an enclosed psychiatric establishment, La Borde Clinique, in which experiments were undertaken with 'institutional analysis' during which the staff would participate alongside patients. In some ways, therefore, Guattari's attack on psychoanalysis can be regarded as an attempt to reform it or redirect it from within. Following Freud, Deleuze and Guattari make desire, the activity of a specifically sexual energy, universal to all social, political, and psychological processes. Marxist production is reterritorialized on desire. Desire is neither a biological impulse, nor a metaphysical energy, nor a symbolic structure. Desire is a plane of immanence: production does not rely on external agents or materials, but is an autoproduction – it produces itself when certain machinic parts are brought into a relation with each other. Deleuze and Guattari also rely on a late text by Freud in which he divides the instincts into two fundamental principles, the sex-instinct and the death-instinct, Eros and Thanatos (Freud, 1955). For them, however, these two instincts have the

same immanent origin: antiproduction is always produced alongside production, and belongs to desire itself. A second element which Deleuze and
Guattari take from Freud is that psychopathologies, dreams, phantasies, and
deliriums are produced by desire and can function as symptoms of the
current state of desire. The 'liberation of desire' is a process of psychic
regeneration which will have just as much effect on psychic structure as it
will on social structure. A third element which Deleuze and Guattari borrow
from Freud is the importance of Oedipus in the everyday life of the
bourgeois, capitalist citizen.

It is easy to believe that the importance of the Oedipus complex has been
exaggerated by psychoanalysis. Deleuze and Guattari's attack on Oedipus as
a reductive formula of interpretation, unable to grasp the multiplicity of
desires presented to the analyst, seems to accord with this belief. Yet their
view is much more nuanced: *Anti-Oedipus* is not merely an internal debate
within psychoanalysis on the importance of the Oedipus complex; instead, it
is an attack on the foundational structure of contemporary consciousness.
Deleuze and Guattari almost agree with the interpretations of the psychoanalysts: Oedipus is to be found everywhere among 'normal' people, but not
necessarily in psychopathologies. This agreement is all the more striking
because Deleuze and Guattari reject the theoretical basis according to which
such interpretations are made: psychoanalysis is shown to rest upon several
'paralogisms' or internal contradictions (1984: 68-129). They can then argue
that the social repression found within capitalist societies operates through
Oedipus as formed within the nuclear family. While Oedipus has a purely
despotic status within psychoanalysis, it has a perfectly vital function within
social theory. Indeed, it becomes the most important enemy which Deleuze
and Guattari are able to attack.

Deleuze and Guattari follow Lacan in noting the importance of a
structural understanding of Oedipus. This obviates the need for a real,
historical genesis of the Oedipus complex in the form of some primordial
murder of a father, as theorized by Freud (Freud, 1950). More significantly,
it moves away from metaphysical and imaginary conceptions of the unconscious as a psychic place housing a certain set of contents, for such an
unconscious, by definition, can never become evident within consciousness.
There is no mysterious, Jungian quest for some spiritual or other-worldly
realm hidden within the depths of human nature. For Lacan, the unconscious
is structured like a language, and only becomes evident in the psychoanalytic session through the actual speech which is used (Lacan, 1980). The
unconscious does not belong to an individual subject, but is made present
through the play and lapses of signification within discourse. The unconscious can now be considered in terms of series of displacements and
repetitions. Lacan therefore separates Oedipus as a symbolic structure from
the imaginations and phantasies of incestuous desires experienced by
neurotics. Desire follows the sterile, symbolic structure, but it can never
fully attain this for the structure itself has no desire. The symbolic structure
is a displaced limit of desire which it can never attain; desire is separated

from the signifying structure by castration. Oedipus does not arise, therefore, because a boy desires his mother, either in reality or as an object of phantasy. Instead, the symbolic structure of Oedipus is enacted in the family. Desire seeks that which is prohibited by the law of the father because desire is identical with the structure of the law itself: it is always the desire of another. It is through Oedipus, therefore, that one can internalize the desire of another, even if this is the desire of the State itself. Desire always comes from outside – not from a relation between bodies or from a subjective realm of phantasy. With the discovery of the structural unconscious, the autonomy of the subject is shattered.

Deleuze and Guattari make a clear distinction between Lacan's theory and the practice of psychoanalysis as followed by Lacan's 'disciples', showing a continuity with the Freudian practice (1984: 52–3). The aim of such psychoanalytic sessions is to make psychic progress by 'resolving' the Oedipus complex. This resolution means internalizing the symbolic structure so as to leave behind the neurotic phantasies. In practice, such psychoanalytic treatments become interminable – one can never fully move to the structural level. Moreover, 'resolution' of Oedipus is an intensification of its effects: it means accepting the castration, and then ordering one's life according to the oedipal structure. Psychoanalysis, therefore, acts as a support for the capitalist socius by normalizing and reconciling its citizens to the necessary psychic repression (1984: 119). Lacan, in contrast to his disciples, is regarded by Deleuze and Guattari as effecting a 'regression' to the symbolic order so as to discover the cause of the oedipal structure in the form of the 'phallus' as a transcendent signifier – the element that is always lacking from its place (1984: 217). This regression to the signifying structure from the signified meaning is almost sufficient to carry Oedipus to the point of its autocritique.

While Deleuze and Guattari's respect for Lacan is clear, their verdict on his thought is unambiguous (1984: 217, 268). Lacan discovered the semiotic regime by which power uses Oedipus to conduct its repressions; he did not overthrow such a regime, nor discover the true nature of desire. Deleuze and Guattari mention the story of the resistance fighters who, wanting to destroy a pylon, balanced the plastic charges so well that the pylon blew up and fell back into its hole (1984: 268). Although Lacan no longer analysed the unconscious in terms of hidden meanings, looking instead for a signifying structure, he did not turn to look at the power-relations at work through such a structure. The unconscious is no longer a theatre of representation, posing questions of meaning, but it has not become a factory or machine, posing questions of use: how is Oedipus used in capitalism (1984: 109)? This is Deleuze and Guattari's strongest objection against psychoanalysis: it does not examine the pragmatic relations of power and production at work in the unconscious that might, for example, produce forms of sexuality (Deleuze, 1988d: 76). It does not properly connect the unconscious to the social field. The Lacanian signifying structure deforms desire in three ways, uprooting it from its field of immanence. Firstly, desire is subjected to lack, so that it always desires what it lacks, and cannot desire anything without lacking something. Secondly, desire is subjected to a law, so that it only desires what is forbidden it, and therefore only desires when it is repressed, assuming that it would be assuaged and fulfilled if the repression were lifted. Thirdly, this law is constructed by the signifier as a transcendent ideal, so that desire always seeks a pleasure which transcends it and can never become present. The transcendent signifier is internal to desire itself (1988: 154). Desire is defined negatively as the limit structuring consciousness, while itself escaping reality and consciousness; it is not encountered in its own positivity, outside of the subject, as the machinic social unconscious.

Deleuze and Guattari adapt the Lacanian account of the oedipal structure of desire in order to analyse the workings of power in despotic and capitalist societies. They deterritorialize the psychoanalytic account of psychic repression so as to connect it up to Marxism and problems of social repression. In this respect, they follow a former breakaway figure from psychoanalysis, Wilhelm Reich, who had explained psychic repression as dependent on social repression, and not the converse. Reich interpreted the operation of power in society in terms of the repression of sexual desire, and preached a sexual revolution as the key to psychic and social revolution (Reich, 1969). In many respects, Deleuze and Guattari follow Reich's thought closely: it leads to their fundamental political problem of fascism, how the masses can be led to the point of desiring their own repression (1984: 29). Deleuze and Guattari differ from Reich, however, in terms of their concept of desiring-production: desire is able to directly invest the social field. Consequently, any revolutionary programme requires a schizoanalysis of the libidinal investments prevalent in the social field. Reich, by contrast, confined his psychoanalysis of desire to the subjective, negative, and inhibited qualities of psychic repression, and relied on Marxist ideology to explain reactionary investments in the social field (1984: 118–19). The role of repression, as an operator of power, will not have the central place in the thought of Deleuze and Guattari that it does in that of Reich. For Reich, desire is the cosmic energy of the universe, functioning as some kind of primordial and universal instinct (Reich, 1961). Deleuze and Guattari have a rather different conception of desire: for them, desire is not a pre-existent instinct, subject to repression, but something which must be produced within social production. The unconscious is not some transcendent source of energy, but an immanent 'factory' which has to be made at the same time as it invests social relations. For Deleuze and Guattari, therefore, the unconscious does not refer to some subjective or interior realm; instead, interiority is an effect of the internalization of antiproduction.

In many ways, therefore, Deleuze and Guattari take on board the psychoanalytic teaching concerning Oedipus. The evaluation of Oedipus, and psychopathologies as a whole, differs because Deleuze and Guattari evaluate Oedipus in relation to a completely different field. In psychoanalysis, psychopathologies can be judged in terms of their relation to 'reality': in neurosis, the requirements of reality are obeyed and the ego has to repress the drives of the id; in psychosis, by contrast, the drives take charge and break with reality (1984: 122). The aim of psychoanalysis, therefore, is to aid the repression of the drives and strengthen the ego's adaptation to reality. For Deleuze and Guattari, however, such a 'reality' has no ontological status: it is merely an effect of oedipalized consciousness. Psychoanalysis therefore works on neurotics to foster the illusion of 'dominant reality'. For Deleuze and Guattari, there will be no absolute distinction between neurosis and psychosis (1984: 125–7). Indeed, the effect of a 'loss of reality' encountered in patients diagnosed as schizophrenic is an effect of their enforced oedipalization, rather than a product of the free play of desire. It is because they do not produce and share in 'dominant reality' that they have to be subjected to it; schizophrenia as an illness arises from an interruption of the processes of desiring-production by the dominant mode of social production, leading to the responses of autism and psychosis (1984: 135–6). Guattari links schizophrenia with political revolution by thinking of the latter as an 'ungluing' of dominant realities, in order to allow people to make their own territory as in the schizo process (Guattari and Negri, 1990: 141). For the signifying structures that shape thought and desires are effectively produced by machinic processes in society. The schizophrenic, who experiences this factory of desire directly in intensity, apart from signification, is therefore in touch with reality itself (1984: 19, 26–7, 87).

It is clear that, for Deleuze and Guattari, the reality which they call 'desiring-production', functioning as a synthesis of abstract flows of psychic desire and social labour, does not have its origins in either Marxist or Freudian thought. 'Reality' is not to be found, in its fullness and positivity, in either the conception of desire advanced within psychoanalysis, since here desire is subordinated to a 'reality principle' formed on the basis of Oedipus, nor the conception of production advanced within Marxism, since this does not account for the investment of desire in the socio-economic field of production. Neither does Deleuze and Guattari's thought derive from a Freudo-Marxist synthesis, for an ontology cannot be derived from a synthesis of elements which do not themselves possess a full reality. The synthetic term 'desiring-production' is therefore merely a mask for an empty space which is circulating through the series of Freudian and Marxist themes. Deleuze and Guattari's turn to ethnology to explain the geology of Oedipus indicates the ontology which underlies their thought: production and sexual desire are merely effects of the power-relations which exist between people in society. More significant than Marx or Freud at this stage is the influence of Nietzsche.

We can now return to an anomaly in Deleuze and Guattari's treatment of psychoanalysis: they emphasize the role of Oedipus as the structure of psychic repression utilized by capitalism, and so exaggerate the significance of psychoanalysis in culture, while rejecting the psychoanalytic theory describing the formation of Oedipus. Beneath the mask of Oedipus we can begin to discern the shapes of other characters. It is not for nothing that the title of *Anti-Oedipus* alludes to the title of a work by Nietzsche, a title given the greatest of emphasis by being taken up again by the last paragraph of Nietzsche's 'autobiography', *Ecce Homo*: 'Have I been understood? Dionysos against the crucified ... ' (Nietzsche, 1979: 134).

Nietzscheanism

It may seem strange to explore Deleuze and Guattari's differentiation from a dominant mode of discourse dubbed 'Nietzscheanism', for the French revival of an interest in Nietzsche, through such leading figures as Georges Bataille, Maurice Blanchot, Pierre Klossowski, Michel Foucault, Jacques Derrida, Sarah Kofman, and others, owes as much to Deleuze's own work on Nietzsche as it does to anyone else. Furthermore, 'Nietzscheanism' never became a coherent school or movement in the way that Marx and Freud became authoritative texts for a number of theorists, partly because Nietzsche's texts discourage a systematic reading (although Deleuze's work comes closest to imposing one), and partly because they discourage trust and belief in any evident 'truth', especially their own. In a sense, therefore, there were few true 'Nietzscheans' in France in the 1960s and 1970s, and many of those with an interest in Nietzsche were of a leftist or feminist political persuasion in direct opposition to Nietzsche's own views. Nevertheless, it will be useful to differentiate Deleuze and Guattari's thought from Nietzschean social theory as a preparation for elucidating Deleuze's complex relation with Foucault, and as a way of examining a transition to a non-Nietzschean form of politics.

Nietzsche, for Deleuze and Guattari, was the foremost theorist of schizophrenia. His philosophy explored the implications of distrusting all pious metaphysical beliefs which constitute the illusion of reality. Once these are stripped away, one sets sail on a sea of flux without fixed identities, where there are only becomings, leaps, transitions, conflicts, chance, and chaos. As an author or subject of enunciation, Nietzsche passes through countless ironic transitions and leaps, frequently expressing paradoxes and contradictions, and leaving his 'true' intentions and meanings indecipherable (Nietzsche, 1973: 203–4). In Nietzsche's exploration of the implications of the eternal return, and in the letters immediately following his 'breakdown', Deleuze and Guattari find a manifestation of schizophrenic thought (1984: 21). Yet such schizophrenic thought does not seem to give us a coherent social theory. Deleuze and Guattari also describe Nietzsche's *The Genealogy of Morals* as the 'great book of modern ethnology' (1984: 190). The influence of Nietzsche can be seen most clearly in their 'universal history' of the development of Oedipus. Behind Oedipus there stands revealed Nietzsche's man of *ressentiment*, the Christian (1984: 215). Although this character is not the same as the psychoanalytic Oedipus, since it does not function as a repressing representation, it is the genealogical origin of Oedipus.

Nietzsche's ethnology is used by Deleuze and Guattari to trace a further regression: we are led from private phantasies, through the law of the signifier, to the cruelty of marking bodies. The transcendental field is now turned back onto the physical power-relations existing between bodies. The signifier becomes merely an effect of pre-existing codes or marks upon bodies. While there is some dependence on the Nietzschean method of 'genealogy' here, it is important to be clear about how it is used. Genealogy refers to descent or filiation: it implies that the past, in the form of 'ancestors', continues to exert an influence in the present. Notions of 'essence' and 'origins' are replaced by 'history': the nature of a phenomenon, such as Christianity, is determined by its marks: the past and contingent events which have shaped it, such as a 'slave revolt in morality' (Nietzsche, 1973: 100). This notion of genealogy, which seems to have some role in Nietzsche's texts, is only valid for describing phenomena which depend on some form of continuous history, memory, or tradition. The genealogist then gains a privileged site of interpretation from which he or she can reveal the hidden 'truth' about a phenomenon through a knowledge of its political history. Deleuze and Guattari do not adopt this form of historicism for their social theory as a whole; for them, the nature of a phenomenon is not completely determined by the historical layers of accretion of events which form its memory or essence. For them, genealogy in terms of descent and alliance applies to only one particular social machine: territorial representation. Their understanding of the primitive socius derives almost entirely from Nietzsche.

The aim of territorial representation is breeding: marks are made upon bodies so as to fashion a memory for humanity, and to breed people who are capable of making promises (1984: 144). This memory is the territory itself, the primitive socius of inscription. Deleuze and Guattari are concerned to argue that society is inscriptive, not exchangist, and its first inscriptions take the form of painful marks inflicted upon the body. A casual reading of Nietzsche's *Genealogy*, by contrast, seems to indicate that such punishments only arise within the context of contractual and exchangist relations (Nietzsche, 1956: 194–8). Deleuze and Guattari therefore have to add ideas concerning the priority of marking over debt which are not explicit in Nietzsche (1984: 191). Nevertheless, the deliberate infliction of pain does occur earlier in Nietzsche's account for the purpose of breeding memory, and contractual relations must be based upon memory (Nietzsche, 1956: 189–94). Deleuze and Guattari are therefore justified in deriving a social theory composed of the arbitrary infliction of cruelty from Nietzsche; this is exemplified in his ontology of the will to power. Yet it is important to notice in their thought that territorial society is constituted by a memory of the marks, rather than the physical acts of violence themselves. We are not in the realm of an ontology of violence, therefore, but in the realm of representation; a 'theatre of cruelty' as opposed to a productive machine (1984: 189). This mode of representation makes the genealogical method possible: it looks for the acts of territorialization or marking which constitute present social formations.

Michel Foucault distinguished a second strand to genealogy in Nietzsche's method: in addition to 'descent' (*Herkunft*), Nietzsche is also concerned with 'arising' (*Enstehung*) (Foucault, 1986a: 80). Through contingent historical encounters between social formations with differing memories, new power-relations can come into play. This second element is taken up by Deleuze and Guattari when they cite Nietzsche's description of the 'founders of states' (1984: 191). These despots always emerge from outside the territory of the tribe, and can overcode many different tribes; Deleuze and Guattari do relate these despots to filiation, however, by tracing their genesis through incest which places them at once outside the tribe and at its origin. Such despots can bring in radical discontinuities and deterritorializations through their conquests. Yet in many ways, overcoding uses a similar operation of power as coding: although the violence is usually latent and threatening, it appeals to a memory of past violence in order to ensure that the overcoding will take. In some sense, the figure of the despot becomes the new memory. Representation is established through successive overcodings, and the meaning of a phenomenon is given by the dominant overcoding, through a process of one code (or signifier) replacing another. Since the despot always comes from outside, and in some sense remains absent from territorial representation as an abstract possibility, there remains room for an internalization of the dominant code, a 'slave revolt in morality' turning the dominant code against itself, and the development of such phenomena as bad conscience, the ascetic ideal, the Christian, and Oedipus.

Genealogy has a different role here. It aims to interpret signs as symptoms of the dominant force which is in operation. To this end, it follows the history of contingent encounters in the form of a chain leading from one overcoding or signifier to another. The aim is not to discover some original territorial representation beneath all the overcodings, for this no longer gives the essence of the social phenomenon. Rather, the aim is to establish where the most recent breaks and overcodings have occurred. It is a matter of separating out mixed regimes, so that the figure of the most recent and dominant despot can emerge clearly into view. Genealogy no longer attempts to construct a memory, but a 'counter-memory' which will effect a further deterritorialization from the despot. It examines the representations produced by the current despot, not in order to decipher some hidden meaning or even to name the transcendental signifier, but in order to discover the power-relations at work within such a regime. Power-relations, of course, concern the territorial markings latent within any regime of overcoding. The distinction between specific acts of cruelty and their territorial memory becomes relevant here, leading to differing politics of genealogy.

In the first approach, the genealogical attempt to interpret dominant forces is an attempt to construct a new theatre of representation opposed to the previous regime; the despot can now be represented in all his nakedness by the genealogist. This is an attempt to overpower and dominate the previous despot; genealogy is motivated by a will to power which wishes to impose its own scale of meanings and values on society. A significant proportion of Nietzsche's texts follow this direction: Nietzsche aimed to subordinate the arbitrary historical succession of powers and rulers to a primitive territorial assemblage. Indeed, this is what the genealogical method of interpreting phenomena in terms of relations of force means: to harness a despotic regime of overcoding in the service of a lineage or primitive regime. Nietzsche's 'overman' is a despot of territorial representation who must be formed by breeding: Nietzsche aims to breed founders of states, and so reimpose a continuity onto the discontinuities of history. Deleuze and Guattari reject this Nietzschean, aristocratic politics of a despotic chain of 'Caesars' (1984: 215). Likewise, they must also reject the genealogical method which is inseparable from it, that of representing society in terms of its relations of power. Deleuze and Guattari are interested neither in breeding overmen, nor in founding new states (1984: 199).

Deleuze and Guattari only utilize Nietzschean genealogy, which is inseparable from a will to power, to describe the negative and repressive operations of power in society. For even the pleasure obtained by cruelty is only the result of a negative will to power. This negative will to power is the source of all our different modes of representation, and so is the only mode according to which the will to power can be known. Power, in the form of production, escapes representation. Deleuze and Guattari will therefore effect a displacement and relativization of Nietzsche's thought so that it is grasped from a different perspective; they escape the Nietzschean theoretical territory in the same way that they had escaped from those of structuralism, Marxism, and psychoanalysis. A different form of 'genealogy', no longer concerned with filiation and therefore only retaining the name somewhat anachronistically, can still deal with society in terms of its power-relations. This requires, however, a further 'regression' beyond primitive territorial representation to the acts of inscription or violence constituting it. Power is no longer to be considered from the perspective of the territorial marks inflicted by cruelty; instead, it is considered according to the strategic distribution of marking representations or 'statements'. In their 'universal history', Deleuze and Guattari look for singular machinic operations of production which work not merely in the realm of language and representation, but simultaneously in the realms of political economy and biological reproduction. There is a link here to the alternative form of 'genealogy' offered by Foucault. In *The Order of Things*, Foucault had examined the relation between regimes of statements in the three areas of philology, economics, and biology (Foucault, 1966). Yet while Foucault sought a single discursivity operating in all three of these 'human sciences', Deleuze and Guattari return to the content and seek a single abstract machine operating within the fields articulated by these discourses, in language, production, and bodies.

Foucault

Deleuze and Foucault became personal friends and the most enthusiastic admirers of each other's work (Deleuze, 1991b: 128; Foucault, 1977: 165, 196). The extent of their mutual influence is immense and difficult to disentangle. Foucault's academic career progressed more rapidly than Deleuze's, following the publication of *Madness and Civilization*, and because Foucault was then in a position to aid Deleuze's advancement, together with the fact that Foucault's work has attained a much wider degree of recognition due in part to its greater accessibility, Deleuze has occasionally been regarded as a 'disciple' of Foucault. This view ignores the fact that Deleuze's philosophical development, together with some very significant publications such as the works on Hume and Nietzsche, occurred prior to his friendship with Foucault. It is not very interesting to explore who was the 'author' of the various ideas with which they worked in common. More remarkable, however, was the decisive break which occurred between them in 1977, so that they were never to see each other again (Erebon, 1992: 258–62). The occasion was an apparently trivial political difference; the break was deeply regretted on both sides as time went by, but a misconstrual of each other's feelings on the matter prevented further contact as if by accident, without interrupting their mutual admiration. This break is perhaps symptomatic of a theoretical difference which did not fully emerge until the publication of Foucault's *History of Sexuality Volume I*. After Foucault's death, although Deleuze would still describe Foucault's thought as 'the greatest philosophy of the present age', Deleuze acknowledged a 'difference of method and perhaps even of goal' (1991b: 128, 117).

We can trace the emergence of this difference from their considerations of power. For Foucault, the Nietzschean play of forces and dominations were constituted by non-relations:

> What Nietzsche calls the *Enstehungsherd* of the concept of goodness is not specifically the energy of the strong or the reaction of the weak, but precisely this scene where they are displayed face-to-face. It is nothing but the space that divides them, the void through which they exchange their threatening gestures and speeches ... a 'non-place', a pure distance, which indicates that the adversaries do not belong to a common space. Consequently, no one is responsible for an emergence; no one can glory in it, since it always occurs in the interstice. ...
> This relationship of domination is no more a 'relationship' than the place where it occurs is a place; and, precisely for this reason, it is fixed, throughout its history, in rituals, in meticulous procedures that impose rights and obligations. It establishes marks of its power and engraves memories on things and even within bodies. (Foucault, 1986a: 84–5)

The argument of this passage is that relations of power arise from 'outside' of the territorial representations and practices of the super-imposed rivals. Foucault was always fascinated by the 'outside' of confining and disciplining regimes of power in the form of a madness outside of reason and society (Foucault, 1989). Here he discovered power-relations operating outside the realm of knowledge and representation. The transcendental field becomes truly transcendent when considered in terms of the physical operations of cruelty. Yet there is no way in which this 'outside' could be represented in terms of reason, for all reason is constructed by such relations of power (Boyne, 1990). The outside is the realm of chaos, of the contingent, arbitrary, and singular; an unthinkable which conditions thought itself. Yet Deleuze had already explored the conditions under which such an unthinkable could be thought: the 'pure distance' or 'non-place' described by Foucault is developed from the concept of 'difference' elaborated by Deleuze in *Difference and Repetition*.[7] There is no question of crossing the boundary or entering the outside; instead, one merely has to map the surface. The plane of power is a plane of exterior relations, or plane of immanence; this is the strength which Deleuze recognizes in Foucault's work. One does not have to attribute any essence, meaning, or representation to the 'forces' which emerge from outside; one merely marks their effects and examines their strategic distribution. 'Force' is merely a name for a certain strategy of emergence surrounding the void.

Genealogy adopts a different political strategy here. One cannot escape from the field of knowledge; Foucault later defined genealogy as 'the union of erudite knowledge and local memories which allows us to establish a historical knowledge of struggles and to make use of this knowledge tactically today' (Foucault, 1980: 83). Where Nietzsche had opened thought to the outside in order to breed the singular despot who would be capable of overcoding all representation, Foucault aimed to open thought to the outside at a multiplicity of diverse sites in order to form local discursivities or strategies of knowledge that resist despotic overcoding. Resistance is a necessary part of power itself: it plays the role of 'adversary, target, support or handle in power relations' (Foucault, 1979: 95). Power has no substantial essence, and cannot be resisted itself; it is the very strategy of force and resistance. Micropolitics is concerned with the formation of local and partial 'truths' which resist the encompassing claims of some overcoding truth. Instead of a single lineage trying to seize control of the State, a multiplicity of local memories and lineages begin to resist the overcoding power of the State. The result is a proliferation of 'tribes' and codes; struggles are fought out in all the different dimensions of everyday experience. The aim is not to escape from power-relations, but to enact tactical oppositions and liberations. This mode of thought is still 'genealogy': the lineages constructed are local and partial, but they are still memories all the same.

The place of desire arises within such a strategy. For Deleuze and Guattari, the primitive territorial regime had apparently effected a repression of desire by using the incest prohibition as the displaced represented of desire. In this way, the primitive socius was able to control alliances, and to determine where sexual relations were permitted. In 1977, Foucault began to attack what he called the 'repressive hypothesis': that the control of power over sexuality is purely negative, in the form of prohibition, with the result that liberation will result from a trangression of sexual laws and taboos (Foucault, 1979). While not mentioning Deleuze and Guattari by name, he does refer to the 'Reichians', as well as those who explore links between psychoanalysis and ethnology. Those who preach the 'revolution of desire' come in for some considerable criticism.[8] It would appear that the movement surrounding Deleuze and Guattari, at the height of fashion in the early 1970s, is one of the main targets. Foucault then went on to argue that sex is not completely repressed, that the workings of power have a positive and productive role in the formation of sex, and that the critical discourse which addresses itself to repression is part of the same power network as the thing which it denounces (Foucault, 1979: 10). The different volumes of Foucault's *History of Sexuality* explore the strategies by which power is able to produce and shape sexuality as a disposition, a set of physical practices, and a set of sexual attractions.

Do these points find their mark in the thought of Deleuze and Guattari? Certainly, concepts such as 'desiring-machines' are dropped, as well as nearly all reference to desire and repression in *A Thousand Plateaus*. Rather than regarding this as a substantial theoretical shift, however, it is possible to maintain a continuity between the two volumes of *Capitalism and Schizophrenia*, and believe that Deleuze and Guattari are simply being more precise about what they mean by 'desire' – the plane of immanence, with its intensities, lines, and abstract machines. Since desire was never an instinctual or metaphysical force, it cannot strictly be 'repressed' in their thought; their use of traditional psychoanalytic language is unfortunate and misleading. In *Anti-Oedipus*, the body without organs only 'represses' the desiring-machines because of its smoothness, absence of organs, and lack of productive relation to other bodies. The body without organs is located at the same non-site as the arising of power: it is a void, or non-relation, between separate formations. It is an immanent plane of exterior relations. In effect, Deleuze and Guattari accept the force of Foucault's critique, and change their subsequent language accordingly, without needing to introduce any major changes to their immanent philosophy of desire. The charges which Foucault brought against representatives of the 'repressive hypothesis' miss their mark with Deleuze and Guattari: repression belongs to the strategy of power which operates through law and discourse, but Deleuze and Guattari translate law and discourse back into writing on bodies; the incest prohibition is the fundamental law in those repressive hypotheses that link psychoanalysis and ethnology, but Deleuze and Guattari regard this prohibition as a product of a regime of alliance and filiation, derived from the debt produced by violent marking. For Deleuze and Guattari, therefore, there are normative strategies for the production of certain kinds of discourse and sexuality; power is not merely negative and antiproductive, but has a positive role in the creation of strata. Deleuze and Guattari are much closer to Foucault than is sometimes believed.

There is, however, a substantial difference that remains concerning the nature of the outside or the non-relation between forces. Foucault only conceived of two kinds of power relationships: the Reichian hypothesis of repression and the Nietzschean hypothesis that 'the basis of the relationship of power lies in the engagement of hostile forces' (Foucault, 1980: 91). Foucault asked a rhetorical question: 'Isn't power simply a form of warlike domination? Shouldn't one therefore conceive all problems of power in terms of relations of war?' (Foucault, 1980: 123).[9] He therefore rejects or forgets the Deleuzean reading of Nietzsche which had sought an affirmative will to power (Deleuze, 1983: 175–94). In Foucault's ontology, the only possible basis for relation is hostility and resistance.[10] Yet one wonders whether local discursivities are able to engage and interact with each other apart from relations of domination: alliances are possible between differing minorities who are not in competition for a limited space of representation. This would imply that the outside, the non-site where force arises, could become a specific site for the arising of a different kind of relation: desire.

Foucault's thought was deeply concerned with an 'outside', a place outside of reason and society constructed by the exclusive and disciplinary operations of power through discourse; the same power can also be at work in bodies, unmediated by discourse, as a formative network for such things as sexuality (Foucault, 1980: 186). Since this 'outside' is constructed by power through exclusion, it becomes impossible to bring the excluded 'others' back into knowledge. Foucault is only able to trace the boundary; there is no possible knowledge of that which is excluded from knowledge by power. Ultimately, therefore, the 'outside' does not really exist, except as a non-site, a non-relation between contesting forces. In Foucault's later work, he explored the possibility of a deliberate construction of forms of subjectivity and self-mastery (Foucault, 1987, 1988). The aim here is to gain self-mastery, to become a dominant force as well as a strategy of resistance to oneself. Foucault explored a discipline of sexuality giving autonomy over the network of power-relations in which one finds oneself, allowing one the space not only to act as a dominant force, but also to control the arising of pleasure within one's body. Interestingly, Deleuze's reading of Foucault's later books and interviews is ecstatic: Foucault has discovered a way of 'folding the line of the outside', a way of producing subjectivity so that a small portion of the outside is contained as a memory within the self (Deleuze, 1988d: 97). It is a question no longer of crossing the line, so as to attain that realm excluded from rationality, but of folding it, so that the arising of relations of force can be controlled and included within power-relations. According to Deleuze, when the line of force is turned back upon itself it is no longer a question of power (Deleuze, 1991b: 150). Instead, it is a question of creativity, of the arising of thought within oneself: the invention of new modes of existence, new possibilities of life (Deleuze, 1991b: 156). 'To think' is to fold the line of the outside, to make it liveable, practicable, and thinkable, in a violence which one exercises against oneself, where reason confronts madness and life confronts death, so as to produce life as a work of art (Deleuze, 1991b: 151, 140, 127). This practice of thought lies outside of knowledge and power.[11]

Deleuze and Guattari do not have the same struggle with the outside as a limit to be displaced or folded. We can draw out that which is implicit in their thought. For them, power is merely the zero degree of desire; it is not an absence, but has its own intensity which can be measured in terms of degrees of stratification and the death-instinct.[12] The boundary or line of the outside is merely an effect produced by stratification; for Deleuze and Guattari, the outside is simply a smooth space of multiplicities. The plane of desire lies outside of power-relations; desire is only encountered insofar as it escapes power along 'lines of flight'. For this reason, only minorities have access to desire. It will therefore be necessary to distinguish between the stratified forms of sexuality constructed by power, and concerning which one can have knowledge, and the 'plateaus of intensity' where multiplicities meet, and creations replace the productions of power (1988: 35). Deleuze and Guattari transgress the boundaries erected within Foucault's thought: they displace and relativize relations of knowledge and power in favour of desire. They describe their only points of disagreement with Foucault as follows: (1) assemblages are of desire, not power; (2) the abstract machines have lines of flight which are primary, not phenomena of resistance (1988: 531). Desire is discovered when multiplicities enter into pacts and becomings.

Feminism

Deleuze and Guattari claim access to the 'outside', the other side of the narcissistic mirror of reason. Here they encounter minorities who have always been excluded from the majoritarian ideal of pure reason, and first among these is the women's movement. Deleuze and Guattari's assessment is largely positive: 'Women's Liberation movements contain, in a more or less ambiguous state, what belongs to all requirements of liberation: the force of the unconscious itself, the investment by desire of the social field, the disinvestment of repressive structures' (1984: 61). The women's movement advanced most successfully the new synthesis of the concept of production with the social field that Deleuze and Guattari seek (Guattari and Negri, 1990: 44). The forms of collective action and consciousness-raising found in women's liberation movements are exemplary for the revolution of desire: women learn to speak in the name of their own desires. In many ways, Deleuze and Guattari's analyses of the ways in which power operates in thought and society concur with those of feminists: the strategies of power at work are particularly violent and masculine. Nevertheless, many strands of the women's movement, like other minority and revolutionary movements, carry repressive structures within them: they merely seek the freedom of the oedipalized woman, participating as an autonomous subject within society. Discourses of liberation based on identity, essentialism, rights, equality, opposition, resentment, or an absolute and primordial gender distinction have little interaction with Deleuze and Guattari's thought. While Deleuze and Guattari acknowledge that women's struggles have to proceed at such levels in order to attain recognition, they are interested in a more clandestine struggle (1988: 471).

It is particularly difficult for male theorists to address the problem of sexual difference because they risk muffling women's voices: either by speaking on behalf of women; or by remaining silent and ignoring the issue, perpetuating the absence of women's voices; or else by listening, followed by 'recuperation', reinscribing women's thoughts within male discourse. Deleuze and Guattari do not avoid this triple dilemma; consequently, their work is not regarded by many feminists as a source for liberation (see, for example, Braidotti, 1991; Irigaray, 1985; Jardine, 1985; Spivak, 1988). In some respects, this is because their work is not intended or able to fulfil all of the expectations laid upon it: it is not primarily a forum of representation, in which women's voices might claim a place among others; it is not an authoritative political programme, which lays down places, roles, strategies, and tactics; it is not a master-discourse, which claims to tell the truth about the whole of reality; and it does not operate by the exclusion of experience and desire, but rather invites the addition of other minority discourses, experiences, and desires to its own theoretical assemblage. Deleuze and Guattari do not write about the nature of 'woman', nor do they tell us what it is like to be a 'woman'; there is no glorification, mystification, or denigration at work here.

They do, however, write about 'becoming-woman'. It is not our purpose to explore the utility or threat of such a notion in relation to women's movements.[13] The hostility aroused by such a notion may reflect its role in a theoretical discourse that relativizes and displaces the claims of much feminist discourse, regarding the liberation of women as part of a broader emancipation – as such, it cannot be harmonized with all feminisms. Yet there are some striking parallels, particularly with theorists such as Luce Irigaray. Irigaray explored the nature of the sexual difference between men and women: the first difference which she noted is that while male sexuality is centred on the single organ of the penis, female sexuality has no single equivalent – instead of being an absence or a hole, as theorized by psychoanalysis, there are two labia which touch each other. No manipulation or mediation is required for the expression of virginal, feminine sexuality. Women's sex is not 'one', but at least two; moreover, the additional erogenous areas through which a woman can take her pleasure mean that female sexuality is multiple (Irigaray, 1985: 29). Sexual difference, therefore, is manifested in the incapacity of masculine reason to think of 'otherness' in ways which are experienced by women: the otherness of women from men, the otherness which a woman contains within herself by virtue of her sexuality, the otherness between generations of women in the form of the mother–daughter relation, the otherness of women's differences from each other in general, and the otherness of women in discourse, so that they 'never say what they mean'.[14] Women's sexual multiplicity and otherness allow them to escape oedipalized subjectivity. This multiplicity is evident in the variety of different forms of feminism that exist; consequently, it will not be possible to differentiate Deleuze and Guattari's thought from any totalized 'feminism'.

These themes of sexual multiplicity and difference are also taken up in Deleuze and Guattari's thought. For them, 'becoming-woman' is the first kind of becoming because it is the entry into a world of multiplicity, of collective assemblages of enunciation which change as they operate. Where Irigaray avoids biological essentialism, regarding the sexual difference as something which has to be constructed by the women's movement, Deleuze and Guattari regard 'becoming-woman' as a task which is necessary for both women and men (1988: 470). While for many forms of feminism that do not merely aim at oedipalized equality between the sexes, the sexual difference is absolute and irreducible, there are no such irreducible differences for Deleuze and Guattari. Instead, there are only affects and becomings that can spread by contagion; 'woman' does not have an essence, but she expresses a territory and processes of deterritorialization. Some recent feminisms try to avoid the poles of the social construction of gender and biological essentialism by looking towards a different field in which the sexual difference can be drawn: perhaps a potential becoming of women, a sexual unconscious for women, a different way of speaking and thinking open to women, or a different historical lived experience.[15] Deleuze and Guattari, however, draw the consistent conclusion from an abandonment of essentialism: the sexual difference is not irreducible, and becoming-woman must be available to men as well as women. There are an unlimited multiplicity of sexes, of which 'woman' is merely the first coherent multiplicity. Feminist commentators regard this abstraction as a move towards a 'neuter' sex, a colonial expansion of a single sex which again effaces the specificity of women (Irigaray, 1985: 140–1).[16] This is certainly a misreading, for Deleuze and Guattari write about a multiplicity of sexes, not a monistic 'neuter' sex; they aim to multiply differences, not efface them.[17] The sexual difference is not removed; it is merely relativized and displaced by the addition of a host of other differences. What is at stake in these objections, however, is perhaps a protest against Deleuze and Guattari's method of abstraction: if men are able to experience a 'becoming-woman', then this latter is no longer connected to the lived histories of oppression experienced by real women. A certain theoretical and sexual discourse replaces the site occupied by real women, perpetuating the assimilation of woman to a masculine stereotype of sensuality and irrationality. The abstract theoretical discourse appears to deprive women of their voices once again (Braidotti, 1991: 119–24).

In effect, therefore, the feminist charge laid against Deleuze and Guattari is analogous to one laid by Foucault: the abstract philosophy of desire relies simply on certain affirmations and schematizations which replace any precise historical analysis (Foucault, 1980: 139). Deleuze and Guattari's most scandalous theoretical move is to produce a 'universal history', even if a singular and contingent one, obviating the need for any precise analysis of given data.[18] Deleuze and Guattari appear to have discovered their own immanent absolute from which they can construct an a priori cartography of all abstract machines. Deleuze and Guattari's thought remains inextricably linked to the extremities of abstraction or absolute deterritorialization. It deliberately pursues the schizophrenic state of desire in which the 'reality principle' breaks down; it has nothing to say about real, historical, lived experience. The position of 'woman' is relativized and displaced by that of the schizophrenic. Their claim, however, is that, far from cutting them off from the 'real' fields of nature and history, the plane of abstract machines is all the more real for being abstract.

Here we must remember the point at which their thought turns (see above, Chapter 2). To reach the abstract machine, machinic assemblages must be dismantled. The image which we form of a plane of abstraction is dead; one must follow a line of flight from such an abstraction, passing through various becomings, in order to construct the true immanent plane. The question, for Deleuze and Guattari, is not whether 'becoming-woman' represents the real, lived, historical experience of women – it has no such intentions – but whether it is effectively produced. They would like feminists to assess this 'becoming-woman' on whether or not it works. For example, Braidotti lists certain 'traces' of the becoming of women which are identified by Irigaray: 'a privileged relation to play and laughter (rather than seriousness of meaning), to what is ''near'', to tactile apprehension (rather than the gaze), to touch, and especially the caress (rather than take) [sic] and to resistance to normative unification' (Braidotti, 1991: 259). Are these traces present in the style with which Deleuze and Guattari think and write? Certainly, Deleuze and Guattari never cease to emphasize an asignifying 'outside' of language (Deleuze, 1993: 16). The only faithful way to read their texts is to seek this realm outside of signification.

The main difference between Deleuze and Guattari and most feminisms, therefore, is not primarily over whether the gender difference is absolute or relative, essential or cultural, but whether singularity is to be found in concrete, lived, historical experience, or whether it must be constructed by a process of 'singularization', through becomings. It is a question of ontology: is existence pre-given by spatial, temporal, bodily, historical, social, and cultural coordinates, or must it be constructed by an 'existentializing' function (Guattari, 1989a)? For Guattari, the above axes of existential location are given by 'universes of incorporeal reference' or ideas, and hence are based on the broadest of generalizations. To simply live, even as a woman with a concrete story of oppression, is not yet to attain a singular existence or any absolute difference, nor any position outside of majoritarian reason by right – such women are still missing; their oppression constitutes their absence. In contrast, a singular existence must be constructed by ahistorical and machinic processes of becoming.

We shall explore such becomings of desire in a later section. But becomings do not happen all by themselves: they require exterior relations, encounters, pacts, deterritorializations, the construction of collective assemblages of enunciation. The question then remains of how many real women are present in Deleuze and Guattari's collective assemblage of enunciation. This is not easy to answer, since they do not all have to be mentioned by name.[19] Yet Alice Jardine's observation is revealing: Deleuze and Guattari hardly ever cite women authors (Jardine, 1984). One may assume that the role of women in their collective assemblage of enunciation is minimal; they are not 'represented' at the machinic level. This is one of the strongest points of the feminist critique of Deleuze and Guattari: they have not been sufficiently deterritorialized by encounters with the thought of women.

Postmodernism

Deleuze and Guattari's thought follows a line of flight that emerges between other significant kinds of discourse. For this reason, one may believe that Deleuze and Guattari's thought cannot be properly understood through historical, sociological, or cultural contextualization of a conventional kind, but only according to the cultural theory which it provides itself. Nevertheless, others have also formed a style of thought out of an assemblage of these various discourses. In many respects, such a way of thinking would simulate the effects found in Deleuze and Guattari's own thought. If one does not write from the imperceptible position of the vital creativity of desire, however, one will no longer have a basis for thought, meaning, power, and desire. Thought will lose its consistency, and circulate around a black hole. Deleuze and Guattari's line of thought and experimentation is in some sense doubled by contemporaneous theoretical projects circling around the unproductive black hole of 'postmodernism'.[20] The implosive and engulfing force of such styles of thought has proven immensely attractive in the English-speaking world, obscuring the more difficult path trodden by Deleuze and Guattari – with the amusing consequence that Deleuze and Guattari are now often read because their thought is believed to anticipate and resemble the postmodernism of Jean-François Lyotard and Jean Baudrillard.

Lyotard's thought was conditioned by many of the same formative influences as Deleuze and Guattari, particularly Marxism, psychoanalysis, and Kant. Lyotard was also a professor of philosophy in the same university as Deleuze. He produced his own 'philosophy of desire' around the same time as Deleuze and Guattari, examining the investment of desire in the social field (Lyotard, 1971, 1993). Deleuze and Guattari were particularly impressed by Lyotard's work as the 'first generalized critique of the signifier' (1984: 243). Beneath the realm of meaning and signification, Lyotard discovered a figurative dimension of thought – both visible and plastic – which is subject to a direct manipulation in dreams, without needing to pass into the realm of meaning. This figurative domain is constructed from the processes of desire, where desire 'works' without needing to think (Lyotard, 1989a: 19–55). The 'work' of desire can then be used to construct a libidinal economy. Although Lyotard's later work abandons the philosophy of desire in order to consider other issues, one can observe traces of this early work still present throughout his thought. For example, his work on narratives and language-games raises questions concerning the reference and legitimation of such narratives; his work on judgement explores the irreducible abysses (*différends*) between kinds of discourses and narratives; his work on modern art and the aesthetics of the sublime concerns the presentation of an unpresentable source of hetero-geneous judgements which can produce differends. As previously, where Lyotard sought the work of desire which lies outside of thought, his later thought is still concerned with negotiating the boundary between thought and an outside which is more present, more real, more of an event, and more differentiated than thought (see the use of 'micrology' in Lyotard, 1989a: 208). This outside only becomes present by making a difference to thought: for this reason, Lyotard favours the creation of new works of art, new discourses, new narratives, and new judgements which aim to show their differences from previous forms. This is the only form of resistance to capital, for capital operates by indifference, reducing all determinations to the same phrasing of money (Lyotard, 1989a: 353).

This concern with the outside of thought shows the common inquiry which Lyotard's thought shares with Foucault and Deleuze. An attentive reader can observe many issues common to Lyotard and Deleuze cropping up in the later works of both, independently, such as a concern for the presentation of the pure form of time in the visual arts, and the existence of difference in the form of incompossible worlds of meanings and judgements (see Deleuze, 1981, and Lyotard, 1989a: 196–211; also Deleuze, 1988c, and Lyotard, 1989b). Yet it is possible to trace a differend which separates them, even if we only do so here in a language-game drawn from Deleuze and Guattari. In *Anti-Oedipus*, Deleuze and Guattari had criticized Lyotard's early work, *Discours, figure*, for introducing a lack or absence into desire preventing his thought from leaving the realm of signification which he had shown to be so inadequate (1984: 244). Desire is then seen in terms of disorder and transgression; it still has to be judged from the perspective which it leaves behind. Perhaps such an absence can also be seen to operate throughout Lyotard's later work: the absence of legitimation in narratives, the absence of the differend in a judgement, and the absence of the event in the sublime. As with Foucault, Lyotard's work focuses around a non-site, a non-relation, or a void: one then encounters the problem of thinking and constructing the social bond (Lyotard, 1989a: 193). The relation across differences within language and society is a state of 'civil war' (Lyotard, 1989a: 357). The absence or 'privation' becomes a black hole around which Lyotard's thought circulates; his way of dealing with it is to fragment it, to multiply it, and to make it visible and thinkable in the form of the sublime. Difference breaks up the social bond and is made to pass everywhere.

Such considerations are the source of the brief but vehement attack which Guattari made on 'postmodernism' in the form of the thought of Lyotard and Baudrillard: Guattari attacked the 'social abandonism' that makes collective political action impossible by multiplying differences (Guattari, 1989a:

55–7). There is no possibility of any desire arising here. The social bond remains perpetually absent and postponed. Lyotard does not have a philosophy of immanence: the categories he chooses to think about always refer to something transcendent. Narrative refers to missing objects, events, and persons; judgement refers to a missing subject; and the sublime refers to a missing meaning. Yet the site of each of these absences is a differend – where differing regimes of representation conflict and contradict over a space which they construct in different ways. By contrast, Deleuze and Guattari are less interested in overlap and competition between territories than the ways in which such different territories can interact, affect, and deterritorialize each other. The difference between Lyotard, on the one hand, and Deleuze and Guattari, on the other, is therefore a matter of strategic emphasis: difference as against synthesis. Since, for Deleuze and Guattari, the whole realm of desire belongs to synthesis and production, this difference will be regarded differently from each side.

In Lyotardian discourse, one could ask how Deleuze and Guattari attempt to legitimate their metanarrative of the philosophy of desire. One may even formulate the response of legitimation by paralogy. For Deleuze and Guattari, however, all questions of legitimation, judgement, and meta-discourse are put aside as implying a false transcendence. Deleuze says, 'Better to be a road-sweeper than a judge' (Deleuze, 1987: 8). Deleuze and Guattari's discourse is merely added to the world; it does not stand above or beyond it in order to encompass it (1988: 23). Its only legitimation is the fact that it exists. Its possible utility can only be assessed by those who are able to work and produce something alongside it, adding it as part of a thinking-machine, and creating plateaus of intensity of desire. Deleuze and Guattari's thought can only be measured by the degree of creativity, vitality, intensity, and life which it introduces into the world.

The thought of Jean Baudrillard emerged from applying semiotic analysis to Marxist political economy. In his thought, the medium of communication, the sign, gradually gains increasing emphasis over its referents, whether these are of the order institutions, classes, meanings, production, power, or desire. The result is that everything is ultimately laid out on an immanent plane of simulations and seductions; this plane forms a double of Deleuze and Guattari's plane of immanence of desire. The difference between them is a question of direction: Deleuze and Guattari aim to construct a plane which has a certain 'consistency', where things hang together according to the bonds of desire; Baudrillard's plane is a celebration of inconsistency, of the power of seduction to lead astray any possible meanings which one intends to build. This kind of celebration of simulation and perversion is not foreign to Deleuze's thought: he had been one of the first to explore the Platonic theory of simulacra as rivals to faithful copies, and to reverse Platonism by the celebrating the free play of simulacra and their capacity to pervert Platonic truth (Deleuze, 1990b: 253–79). *The Logic of Sense* constructed a philosophy of surfaces in the forms of phantasms and simulacra. Yet *Anti-Oedipus* celebrates a rediscovery of the body, its affects, intensities, and desires, and its capacity to produce simulations and hallucinations of its own. The thought produced by desire is a simulation, but a simulation flush with the real – there is nothing lacking to which it refers, nothing outside of thought by which it could be judged (1984: 87). Deleuze and Guattari's concepts are the product of phantasy.

The condition which Deleuze and Guattari impose upon phantasy is that it should be a 'group phantasy', a product of a collective assemblage of enunciation, something produced by a machinic assemblage linking heterogeneous desires, operating at one specific time and place. All thought is therefore rooted in its determining and conditioning factors, and is considered and given meaning in terms of such conditioning factors. It is this specificity which is not to be found in the work of Lyotard and Baudrillard. For Lyotard, the three positions of using language – who, about whom, and to whom – are produced by the narrative itself, and therefore become interchangeable (Lyotard, 1989a: 188). A narrative can be taken up and retold by others, substituting different names in the process (Lyotard, 1989a: 122–54). In order to inquire into the referents of the narrative, a metanarrative would be required to give rules as to who says what, about whom, and to whom. This metanarrative itself has interchangeable referents; therefore Lyotard turns to the problem of judgement to assess the claims of narratives to an absent specificity. The result of thinking in this way is a satirical discourse characterized by reversibility: the speaker, addressee, and referent can all exchange places. Yet such an arbitrary, satirical exchange has no relation to the real forces which cause someone to say something at a particular place and time: the collective assemblage of enunciation.

A similar reversibility characterizes the thought of Baudrillard. In mass-media culture, communication replaces the real with signs. Such signs have no relation to a specific real, because they can always be replaced by an equivalent reproduction (Baudrillard, 1983: 146). Initially for Baudrillard, simulations are produced by operational machinic processes (Baudrillard, 1983: 3). This process of simulation has now become so extensive that it intends to make the whole of the real coincide with simulation models (Baudrillard, 1983: 2). The turning point, however, is when one can no longer distinguish between simulation and reality: one can only think about the real by simulating it (Baudrillard, 1983: 41). It therefore becomes impossible to establish criteria for judging between the 'true' and the 'false', for the real is no longer available for comparison. As a consequence, all the referentials are lost: production, signification, affect, substance, history, etc. (Baudrillard, 1988: 125). Each can be replaced by a simulation. Moving to the plane of simulations, like moving to Lyotard's plane of narratives, removes any anchor of specificity. Baudrillard can no longer protest against our simulated society, therefore, for his protest is nothing more than a simulation itself, without having any access to a specificity of real value. No possible dialectical polarity can exist, and everything can be replaced by its inverse: in the realm of the hyperreal, everything is equivalent to its opposite, because it is simulated by the same distinction (Baudrillard, 1988: 120). Any kind of political action, either for or against the existing power structures, has an equivalent effect: it works in terms of simulacra, and therefore intensifies the dominant semiotic regime which functions by producing simulacra (Baudrillard, 1983: 28). Desire, capital, and the law become equivalent (Baudrillard, 1983: 35). Baudrillard pointed out this versatility and reversibility of desire in Deleuze: 'an enigmatic reversal which brings this desire that is "revolutionary by itself, and as if involuntarily, in wanting what it wants," to want its own repression and to invest paranoid and fascist systems' (Baudrillard, 1983: 35; 1988: 124).

Simulation works and seduces by constructing an image of the real: it gives the illusion of direction and value. One has to believe in it in order to play its games. Baudrillard hopes to find a liberative strategy by playing the game of simulation at a more intense level: by demonstrating the reversibility of simulations, one destroys their illusion of value (Baudrillard, 1988: 123–4). One allows oneself to be seduced by simulacra, only to seduce their power in turn. For Baudrillard, everything circulates around the absence of the real: death. Seduction does not take place through libidinal investment, but through gaming and bluffing: 'We seduce with our death, with our vulnerability, and with the void that haunts us' (Baudrillard, 1988: 162). Where simulation produces an illusion of reality, dissimulating the fact that there is no real, seduction reveals this meaninglessness as its charm. Everything eventually returns to the void (Baudrillard: 1988: 163).

The world of simulations and the world of narratives have something in common: the content of simulation and narrative is cut off from the specificity which produces it. These discourses do not speak in the name of someone's desire; they are only considered in terms of the effects which they produce. The meaning of this emphasis on death is clear: one only attains to simulation, seduction, or narrative by 'castration' of one's desire – the speaker is always missing in the speech. Lyotard and Baudrillard separate the subject of enunciation from the subject of the statement – but then castrate the subject of enunciation by looking for another statement in which it might appear. In a sense, they actually believe in and are seduced by their stories and simulacra: not in the sense that they follow the lure of real, metaphysical values, but insofar as they cannot conceive another regime of discourse outside of narrative and simulation. In practice, a certain kind of metaphysics of language is at work in their thought, encompassing all speakers in its totalizing embrace. Deleuze and Guattari, however, escape such a totalizing and castrating embrace by turning to the pragmatics of the subject of enunciation, as opposed to the meaning of the subject of the statement. While their thought can always be simulated, insofar as one can make statements about desire and production, it can only be produced by being enunciated. Statements made about desire by Deleuze and Guattari count for nothing; the desire which they produce, in all its intensity, expressed in the new concepts which they create, demonstrates in practice that they do not live in a world of simulacra.

Conclusion

Theoretical thought in France subsequent to the structural revolution has encountered an absence, an outside, void, displacement, or death at the heart of thought (1994: 55). This has led to the apocalyptic tones of the movement called 'postmodernism': all the projects of modernity are abandoned because they run up against this interior limit. Postmodernism tells us that we can no longer proclaim our own truth or speak in the name of our own desires: it effectively issues a castrating law. With a pose of cynical realism, it merely informs us that we can no longer desire, think, hope for, or project all that we have done previously. The seductiveness of this rhetoric, usually presented without evidence or argument, arises from its castrating power. One only attains to thought when one interiorizes the limit and displaces it; one thinks under an indefinite reprieve. Postmodern thought circulates around a black hole of subjectification; one thinks by following a segmented line from one displaced limit to another. Oedipus is alive and well, even among those thinkers who dismantle the subject and explicitly repudiate it. Oedipalized representation is not only confined to the simplistic thought of faciality; it is able to penetrate and produce some of the most sophisticated, ironic, and cynical theoretical viewpoints. Insofar as one castrates a state-ment of its collective assemblage of enunciation, disinvesting desire, then one's discourse may ultimately be manipulated by the dominant capitalist regime. Postmodern discourse expresses the repressive and antiproductive abstract machine of capital – it leads to an exponential growth in theoretical capital, convertible through the market in academic books into academic careers, fields of study, and even financial capital.[21] One can merely speculate as to the social productivity or efficaciousness of such a body of theory.

Deleuze and Guattari's thought also runs up against this limit of the unthinkable within thought. They even convert it into a body without organs, internalize it, and make it an essential component of their thought. Thinking no longer works except by breaking down and dismantling itself. For Deleuze and Guattari, however, 'absence', 'death', 'lack', or the 'void' are the illusions. These are merely shadows of the difference between the transcendental realm of abstract machines and the present realm of thought, the effect of chaos (Deleuze, 1994: 55; Guattari, 1992: 86, 109, 116). They have an entirely positive, affirmative ontology deriving from Spinoza. Behind all the masks of theoretical influences, their thought traces its line of flight to the pure plane of immanence described by him. The absolute limit, upon which all events are inscribed, is the body without organs of plane of consistency. This outside is not 'death', but desire.

Notes

1. Guattari emphasizes that his work is aimed at creating new kinds of subjectivity and authentic relations with others in all of his later publications (see, for example, Guattari, 1992: 18).

2. One may imagine that Deleuze and Guattari's discussion of 'faciality' has little relation to Lévinas's notion of the 'face-to-face' as an ethical encounter. In fact, Lévinas explicitly nominates the face as a transcendental signifier, a 'signification without context' (Lévinas, 1985: 86). Although Guattari appreciates Lévinas's move from an ontological to an ethical paradigm, the ethical relation of the face-to-face is oedipalized and castrated.

3. Bourdieu's notion of 'cultural capital' would be inappropriate here since we are concerned with the process of overcoding, rather than the filiative power of capital. Moreover, there are many different kinds of cultural codes, which are not in practice reduced to a single scale of equivalence.

4. The positive influences of these earlier movements on Deleuze and Guattari's thought would also be interesting to explore, but we do not have sufficient space here.

5. Deleuze and Guattari resist the move which Roy Bhaskar has called the 'linguistic fallacy' – defining being in terms of signification, by reintegrating the Marxist notion of 'production' into the meaning of human existence (Bhaskar, 1989: 181).

6. Guattari still regarded himself as a 'communist' in 1985, where communism is understood in the sense of the collective struggle for the liberation of work (Guattari and Negri, 1990: 8, 10).

7. Foucault's essay on this work, 'Theatrum Philosophicum', written shortly before the above essay on Nietzsche, provides evidence of this link (Foucault, 1977).

8. Foucault's critique (Foucault, 1980: 91, 139–41) seems to be directed at Deleuze and Guattari.

9. See Foucault (1979: 92) for power as a 'multiplicity of force relations'.

10. One suspects that this kind of Nietzschean pessimism, shockingly transgressive of all moral value and sympathetic feeling, provides a 'speaker's benefit' analogous to the one which Foucault detected in those who preach the revolution of desire (Foucault, 1979: 6).

11. In this reading of Foucault, Deleuze is not trying to speak for Foucault, but to trace 'a diagonal which runs forcibly' from Foucault to himself: Deleuze describes the acts of Foucault's thought which he is able to perceive (Deleuze, 1991b: 121).

12. 'Stratometers' and 'deleometers' (1988: 4). The concept of 'slowness' from *A Thousand Plateaus* is appropriate here as an absence of 'speed' or autoproductive becoming.

13. Such explorations have been carried out by others (see the essays by Braidotti and Grosz in Boundas and Olkowski, 1994; Braidotti, 1991: 108–32; and Irigaray, 1985: 140–1).

14. See Braidotti's summary of Irigaray's thought (Braidotti, 1991: 248–63).

15. Drawn from options presented by Braidotti in her genealogy of feminisms (Braidotti, 1991).

16. Irigaray's interpretation is also followed by Jardine and Braidotti.

17. In order to 'do the multiple', one must first subtract the 'one' – there is no 'subject' of a becoming (1988: 8–9).

18. This is not merely a phase exemplified in *Anti-Oedipus*, but is repeated in *A Thousand Plateaus* in the way in which all abstract machines are dated.

19. For example, Deleuze's wife, Fanny, and his daughter, are rarely mentioned in any of his writings; one can assume, however, that they formed a highly significant part of his social assemblage.

20. We are here concerned with French authors who identify their thought as 'postmodern', rather than the American reception of post-structuralism. Some readers also regard Deleuze as a postmodern philosopher, such as Ronald Bogue (Bogue, 1990). This is to sacrifice conceptual precision for a questionable historical periodization.

21. Indeed, this is the machinic assemblage into which this book is inserted.

6

Against the Strata

Deleuze and Guattari construct a theory of escape from the dominant powers operating within society. They aim to liberate desire by reinvesting it within the social formation that produced it. For the repression of desire had produced the illusion of desire wanting something outside of itself – a 'displaced representation'. Stratification works through this displacement, for when desire is invested in a representation, it no longer assembles operative components. Simulacra are signs produced by machinic formations other than those which have produced the desire. The conjugation of desire and a simulacrum, such as a face, does not build any intrinsic productive relation between the two – for desire is not able to change the face, nor itself, through such an investment. Consequently, extrinsic machinic assemblages can exercise power by repeating their productions of desire and face; the result is a sedimentation of desires and faces through which each is formed as a constant, appearing ready-made as a fiat, a judgement of God (1988: 40). Once such constants have formed layers of sedimentation, or strata, such strata can be folded, broken up, and placed in new extrinsic relations to each other. Society can be therefore considered as a texture of differing interwoven materials held together through the conjugations of desire. These relations of conjugation are antiproductive since a desire is never connected to another desire, but only to simulacra. The texture of society does not have its own fluid 'consistency', but only a fixed structure of the inter-relations between constants.

The operation of power through the process of stratification, which is the basis of *A Thousand Plateaus*, is the same as its operation through the self-repression of desire, the basis of *Anti-Oedipus*. In *A Thousand Plateaus*, Deleuze and Guattari prefer to write in dynamic terms of flows and breaks, lines and stoppages, rather than in terms of desire and its repression. The same process of conjugation links the two (1984: 90; 1988: 220): in conjugation, a flow is reterritorialized upon the flow which it encounters; in other words, it takes the expression of the encountered flow as the territory for its new mode of existence. Conjugation is contrasted with connection: although both relations are extrinsic and arbitrary, connection involves mutual deterritorialization. In conjugation, desire is repressed; in connection, desire is augmented (1988: 220). Connecting destratifies because, when deterritorialized, a desire leaves behind the constant nature given by its previous strata in order to cross a boundary and become something entirely different. The liberation of desire is at the same time a destratification with respect to the strata and a becoming with respect to the unconscious. Processes of destratification will be examined in this chapter, before turning to becomings in the following chapters.

The three main strata that function as geological components for humanity are biological organism, language, and subjectivity. For Deleuze and Guattari, these are constructed through social processes of organization, significance, and subjectification, respectively (1988: 159). Power is rarely a direct operation of force upon bodies, but operates through channels of communication and meaning through the construction of certain kinds of consciousness, through certain uses of language, and through the organization and distribution of bodies and organs. Deleuze and Guattari extend their analysis of power to the constitution of subjectivity, language, and organization as such. In each of these strata, desire is disinvested from the social assemblages that produce it, and reinvested in some extrinsic determination.

Problem 7: On materialism

Deleuze and Guattari replace genealogy with geology (1988: 40; 1994: 44). For desire will not be liberated by investment in some form of knowledge, whether of the truth or of simulations; nor will it be liberated by strategic resistance to dominant powers so long as it reproduces its own microdominations. It must be liberated at the level at which it is produced – the plane of abstract machines. There is a constant danger of falling back into simulation: one does not build an abstract machine simply by writing about it. Deleuze and Guattari need to build a new relation between thought and matter. In oedipalized representation this relation is modelled on hylomorphic dualism (1988: 408), where a pre-existing form that already shapes thought is applied to shape an inert matter, like Descartes moulding his ball of wax. By contrast, structuralism and many subsequent French theories abandoned belief in the possibility of an authentic correspondence between thought and matter, so as to explore the ways in which a mode of expression can govern the organization of matter. The consequence is the projection of some 'outside' to thought, language, or knowledge that shapes the organization of thought and society.

Such a projection can be obviated, at least in part, by a return from genealogy to geology. Deleuze and Guattari's turn to geology is an attempt to return to matter in the form of layers of stratification. At first sight, it may appear to be an attempt to historicize the grounds of the human condition in terms of an evolutionary history of the earth through successive layers of organization, including crystals, genes, and language. If this were the entire story, then making a body without organs through destratification would simply be a matter of vaporizing the entire planet. Instead, Deleuze and Guattari wish to retain the existing machinic processes of stratification, while adding further components, allowing the human organism to cross a threshold of deterritorialization to become a new, productive machine. The body without organs will retain all its organs as functioning parts of the new machine (1988: 158).

The appeal to geology is therefore problematic: Deleuze and Guattari pursue geology as itinerant metallurgists, passing through the human, linguistic, institutional, and biological matter of society, discovering the haecceities, singularities, and variable intensive affects of a metallic element that can be melted down into a body without organs and built into a weapon or machine, like the advanced robot of *Terminator 2*. The aim is to discover a machinic phylum or technological

lineage that is matter in movement, conveying singularities and traits of expression (1988: 406, 409). Instead of constructing a discourse that will govern or
resist the human matter of society, the turn to geology is an attempt to bring
matter into a collective assemblage of enunciation, to liberate its traits of
expression, to give a voice to the animals, plants, and rocks in humanity. It is an
attempt to gain the machinic phylum at work in society, so as to produce minor
forms of organization, signification, and subjectivity defined by variation, becoming, and deterritorialization.

Subjectification

Subjectification operates as follows (1988: 75–85, 119–34) a subject of
enunciation, or speaking subject, expresses itself in language in the form of
specific statements: 'I think . . . ; I believe . . . ; I want . . . ; I love . . . '
By contrast, the subject of the statement, or spoken subject, the 'I' present in
language, gains its meaning from the syntactical relations it has with the
other words in the statement. The kinds of relations into which it may enter
are governed by syntax; moreover, the kinds of terms which the subject of
the statement is able to think, believe, want, or love, etc., are given by
paradigmatic relations of substitutability for the object of the statement –
one may believe in God, romance, or subsidiarity, but not in a handspan. In
language, therefore, the subject of the statement surveys a predefined grid
that delineates its range of electoral choices; none of the allowable choices
will make a difference to the syntactical construction. Power operates
through grammar.

The process of subjectification takes place when a subject of enunciation,
the speaker, recoils into the subject of the statement (1988: 130). Its
dominant reality is given by the range of statements which are possible for
it. One learns the range of possible options that one is allowed to think,
believe, want, or love from those given within society: a subject of
enunciation forms its consciousness of itself out of the statements which it is
able to make as a subject of a statement. Descartes's *cogito*, often considered
the founding of modern subjectivity, is exemplary in this respect: 'I think
[subject of the statement, independent of its object] therefore [movement of
recoiling] I am [the subject of the statement now designates the subject of
enunciation].' The speaker then knows himself as a thinking substance. The
verb 'to be' always functions as a shifter that moves from an expressed
statement to give a 'reality'; this movement is mediated in modern thought
by the process of subjectification through which the speaker identifies a
given reality with the statement. In this way, reality comes to be constituted
by subjects acting as though their statements were true.

The self-consciousness of human subjects is a simulated product of
language. A person identifies himself or herself with the subject of the
statements which he or she is able to make. Yet the 'I' expressed in language
is merely a syntactical marker (1994: 17); it is a product of language, not
consciousness. The subject believes himself or herself to be the author of the
statements which are enunciated, without referring to the syntactical and

paradigmatic conditions under which these are produced. One appears to have a unique individual identity through possessing a self-consciousness which can be expressed in terms of its thoughts, beliefs, wants, and loves. This self-consciousness is derivative upon first being addressed as a 'You' (1988: 130). For the statements which we make are never our own; they have already been given to us. Deleuze and Guattari emphasize the role of education in this process (1988: 75–6). A teacher issues statements, whether of a personal or impersonal kind, which are then adopted and repeated by the pupils. Through this process, the teacher communicates a dominant reality which pupils then come to think of as their own. Positions of subjectivity have an equivalent position within a statement; consequently, statements can easily be translated from one person to another. For example, if a pupil hears a teacher say 'working hard is good', this can be translated through a series of statements: 'She thinks that working hard is good', is then conjugated with 'If I please her, she will like me', so as to become 'I want to think that working hard is good', 'I think that working hard is good', 'working hard is good'. Once the process becomes habitual, one can move straight from hearing the statement to repeating it. Belief in those who issue statements is not a precondition for subjectification, but a product. Similarly, disbelief can be produced by a similar process when the statement is conjugated with a negative attitude to the speaker.

Since the process of stratification is always a conjugation, it involves a double articulation of at least two statements. 'I think' is conjugated with 'I am'. The subject of enunciation is formed from overlaying the subject of one statement on top of another, so as to indicate an external identity lying outside of both statements. The condition for this conjugation is a kind of resonance, suggesting that the same 'I' is being spoken about: statements produce the effect of a transcendental subject of enunciation as a kind of black hole outside of language (1988: 79). Each subject of the statement resonates with this empty site or black hole, identifying its signified with such a site. The consciousness and desires of a subject produced in this way are cut off from their conditions of production. For the subject thinks and desires through the immediacy of self-certainty; it imagines that its thoughts and desires are produced by the black hole which it is. The result is that the 'desire' of such a subject is merely a simulation of desire; it is privatized, cut off from the social assemblage that produces it. It can have no productive relations with other desires for it is not a desire itself; it is effectively castrated. Consequently, when two such oedipalized subjects turn to each other and develop a passion for each other, they find each other unattainable (1988: 131). The object of desire appears to be for ever lost.

The stratum of subjectification appears to be relatively fluid and mobile. For each subject is a different centre, and can be produced by a different set of statements. All that is required is a point of subjectification to issue a kind of constant statement, and a new statement which will reterritorialize upon it. Different subjects are then led to have differing faces and opinions, even though these are marked out within a culture on the same kinds of grids. Yet this suppleness of subjectification does not prevent it from being a global operation of power through culture.

Deleuze and Guattari attempt to revitalize desire by exploring possibilities of desubjectification. One may expect schizoanalysis to dismantle the strata by examining their real conditions of production, so as to reinvest desire in the social field that produced it. This would involve a massive programme of regression in which each subject discovers the dominant realities it has accepted, and the points of subjectification which have led to the conjugation of statements. Such an analysis would bring the conditions of production to consciousness; in doing so, however, it would merely bring about a further subjectification through the production of a psychobiography. Discovering in consciousness which dominant forces have been acting upon one does not help one to reinvest desire in the social field. Schizoanalysis, unlike psychoanalysis, is not concerned with a regression to the past in order to construct a developmental history of an individual or a society. It only explores the strata in order to find lines of escape leading away from the present. Desire cannot be liberated by being subordinated to consciousness once more; schizoanalysis does not produce a plan of the past or of the future. By contrast, Deleuze and Guattari attempt to begin from the present. They aim to escape the strata, rather than undermine or overthrow them.

Deleuze and Guattari's simple technique is to replace conjugations with connections. An oedipalized subject is defined by a series of boundaries or prohibitions that limit the possible range of thought and desire; one is told what one is allowed to think and whom one is allowed to desire. Each conjugation reinforces the sense of identity. For Deleuze and Guattari, transgressing the boundary, adopting the daring stance of rebellion, has little importance in itself, for whether one accepts or rejects the prohibition, one's identity is still formed on its basis. Instead of directing desires towards either permissible or forbidden persons, Deleuze and Guattari encourage the connection of desires to determinations which are not signified by the range of statements at all. One enters pacts with non-humans – animals, molecules, bodies of knowledge, aesthetic products – the necessary condition is that such flows can never become the subjects of statements, even though they may be territorial and expressive. Desire no longer flows between subjects who to a greater or lesser degree express a normalized, majoritarian ideal; desire is no longer simulated by the resonance of subjects of statements. Instead, desire is territorial and machinic: one desires something together with which one can function in order to produce something. There is no need to dismantle the assemblage which has produced a subject; desubjectification works immediately on any kind of stratified assemblage. For as soon as one reterritorializes on a heterogeneous mode of life, then the machinic assemblage which had produced the strata is significantly changed by gaining another component with which it will function. Resonance and subjectification are blocked, and the new assemblage begins to produce statements escaping from dominant discourse. The subject of enunciation cannot be identified, for it is collective, resulting from the connection of various heterogeneous parts. New kinds of subjectivity are produced which are closer to the modes of existence of animals and rocks than humans (1994: 75). At this point, Deleuze and Guattari invoke modes of consciousness which are excluded from majoritarian reason: dreams, pathological processes, esoteric experiences, intoxication, rapture, or excess (1994: 44). The aim of desubjectification is not to deconstruct consciousness, but to discover other modes of consciousness beyond the confines of normalization.

Deleuze's work, like Foucault's, has often been thought of as a kind of anti-humanism that celebrates the 'death of the subject'. This should be understood as follows: the individual, majoritarian speaking subject cannot be taken to be the ultimate foundation of truth, meaning, or value; indeed, such a subject is merely a surface effect of resonance. As Guattari emphasizes, it is not a question of anti-humanism, but a question of whether subjectivity is produced solely by internal faculties of the soul, interpersonal relations, and intra-familial complexes, or whether non-human machines such as social, cultural, environmental, or technological assemblages enter into the very production of subjectivity itself (Guattari, 1992: 22–3). The emphasis upon subjectivity that one finds in the later work of Foucault, Deleuze, and Guattari is not the reversal of an earlier perspective, but an elaboration of their earlier work that seeks to produce new kinds of subjectivity and new states of consciousness. For Guattari, an ecology of subjectivity is inseparable from an ecology of society, and an ecology of the environment; these must be developed for specifically humane goals (Guattari, 1989b: 32–3). Subjectivity, in the mass-media era, suffers from as much ecological pollution as one finds in other domains, leading principally to an extinction of words of human solidarity (Guattari, 1989b: 35). An ecological revolution in subjectivity, based on aesthetic and existential criteria, begins by allowing the sectors of subjectivity that have been differentiated by their roles in the processes of production to connect and interact once more (Guattari and Negri, 1990: 122). New kinds of subjectivity are created by collective experimentation in domestic and working lives with relations between the subject and time, the body, phantasms, life and death, creating new systems of evaluation (Guattari, 1989b: 22, 65).

Signifiance

Subjectification depends upon language which functions as a kind of substratum out of which subjects can be built. The elementary unit of language that enables subjectification is the 'order-word' or slogan (1988: 75–110). Deleuze and Guattari derive the notion of an order-word from the illocutionary use of language: there are certain statements that accomplish acts by the very act of being spoken, such as asking a question, making a promise, or giving a command. Order-words function by conjugating a certain socially defined action with a statement that effectively accomplishes it. Order-words are entirely immanent to language, but they connect language to the outside through conjugation. An order-word is not made effective by the divine fiat of the author, but functions insofar as its meaning is socially accepted. Each order-word, therefore, encodes a presupposition or expectation of the social unconscious. Instead of such order-words being given by one subject to another, they depend primarily on a collective assemblage of enunciation which is immanent in language (1988: 80). Subjects are produced by order-words, the operation of power through language, and not the inverse.

For Deleuze and Guattari, any statement contains within it certain implicit commands which lay out structures of meaning. This is particularly evident in questions asked by people in authority – bosses, teachers, parents, police – for a question, however factual, always contains a set of presuppositions given by the social situation as a whole. It is also evident in statements issued by politicians which are so devoid of support in the form of analysis of evidence that they no longer pretend to inspire belief; instead, they merely tell us what to say (1988: 76). Instead of commands functioning as a minimal support for the communication of information through language, information functions as a minimal support for the issuing of commands. Order-words are not merely commands, however; they gain their power by effectively accomplishing speech-acts which change the social situation. The most obvious case is when the verdict of a jury transforms a defendant into a criminal; but speech-acts operate in all kinds of social situations. ('How could he have said such a thing? I'll never trust him again.') They always mark the limit of one situation and the beginning of another. In this way, all order-words are judgements or death-sentences: a certain arrangement of bodies will never be quite the same again. They are like the inscriptions on bodies of primitive regimes, producing meaning by the infliction of pain where language intervenes directly upon bodies. Yet a death-sentence is not an execution; there is a difference between an incorporeal transformation into the status of a condemned person, and the imminent physical act which accomplishes the execution. In this way, order-words are like the roar of a lion: they announce both a death-sentence and a warning to flee.

The second aspect of the order-word is the change in meaning which it produces in a situation. This level is immanent in language: every statement contains within itself a set of presuppositions given by the social situation. These can be expressed in the form of further statements which are virtual and participate alongside the expressed statement. ('Where were you last night?' may contain, 'Tell me!', 'Do not betray me!', 'Don't make me feel lonely!', 'Night is a time for enjoyment.') Where the expressed statement may be issued by a subject, the set of virtual statements which participate in its meaning remain unspoken by any subject; they have the status of indirect discourse, being reported or indicated rather than spoken (1988: 80). They are expressed by a collective assemblage of enunciation which comprises the social situation as a whole.

Deleuze and Guattari explore the stratification of collective assemblages of enunciation through the concepts of structural linguistics. One way in which a statement can refer to further statements is through signification, in which a sign always refers to another sign. This happens along two axes: syntagmatically, a sign can only enter into association in a sentence with a certain set of other signs in order to give a grammatically correct and meaningful statement; paradigmatically, a sign has a number of associated meanings which are given by the signs that can be substituted for it in a certain context. 'Signifiance' is the production of chains of signifiers; the signified is given by the chain as a whole, rather than being attached to specific signs. (For example, the signified of 'night' is given by its lengthy chain of associations.) For Deleuze and Guattari, the process of 'signifiance' is a form of stratification, for signifying chains become fixed and laid down. Clear communication is dependent upon sharing chains of signification, so that one gains a linguistic competence. Power, therefore, operates along both syntagmatic and paradigmatic axes: through grammar and association. A set of stratified signifying chains constitutes a regime of signs. Moreover, such regimes always try to extend themselves by carrying their signifying chains to new areas of operation: interpretation is the activity that consists of incorporating new signs into existing chains. Power may capture exterior elements for its own world of meaning through interpretation.

Signifiance is dependent upon a separation of language as an abstract entity (*langue*) from specific acts of speaking (*parole*). Deleuze and Guattari note that this distinction breaks down with the illocutionary use of language and the order-word (1988: 78). Signifiance does not tell us which specific chains of signification will be followed in specific social situations. ('Where were you last night?' has a different social significance when spoken by a boss, friend, or lover.) The relation between signs in signifiance is conjugation; signs are separated from their real social conditions of production. This is not to say that chains of signification do not operate through language, but rather that when they do operate, they stratify the set of presuppositions and speech-acts which are present in language. Signifiance determines the paths along which we are able to think; the order-words it contains tell us to conjugate signs in a certain way. For Deleuze and Guattari, speech-acts, the changes effected by language, are prior to the strata that are extracted as constants from them. Chains of signification, like subjects, are merely simulacra of constants extracted from language via a repetition of the same order-words. In order to destratify, Deleuze and Guattari do not follow a lengthy analysis of signifying chains, but begin by translating the strata back into the immanent collective assemblage of enunciation. Desire is reinvested in the social field when one begins to speak according to an immanent collective assemblage of enunciation. The next stage required to overcome the effects of power within language is a subtraction of the constant element, whether this is a speaking subject, a grammatical rule, or a paradigmatic metaphorical association.

Deleuze and Guattari do not attempt to eliminate order-words from language, even though power always operates through order-words. Instead,

they even deliberately write in slogans, in the hope of changing presuppositions and subjectivity (1988: 24). They adopt the indirect speech of implicit
presuppositions, often making the virtual explicit. At this level, however,
they can begin to build new associations and extend their collective
assemblage of enunciation. This operation is very simple, and depends on
the two meanings of the order-word. The propositional use of language,
based on the verb 'to be', uses the order-word as a death-sentence or verdict:
'He is guilty.' The verdict, recognition, or predication '*a* is *b*', defines limits
to the extent of '*a*'. As a warning to flee, the order-word has a different
linguistic operator, functioning by connection rather than conjugation: this is
the conjunction 'and'. Where the copula 'to be' stratifies chains of signification, the conjunction 'and' may make links to alternative routes. Flight is a
movement of deterritorialization in which one leaves one's present territory
in order to discover another. The set of virtual presuppositions that accompany any statement is like the territory or Bergsonian memory that coexists
immanently within it. The process of adding a further presupposition is a
movement of deterritorialization that changes the social assemblage or
territory presupposed within a statement.

In *A Thousand Plateaus*, Deleuze and Guattari only make a minimal
appeal to existing chains of signification in order to make their meaning
clear. Instead, each sentence adds a presupposition to the preceding one.
Each sentence changes the meaning of the whole preceding paragraph,
providing the presuppositions that were implicit. The sentences are conjugated together not via chains of signification, but by the way in which they act
upon each other in order to change each other's meaning. The work as a
whole can gain a consistency when the sentences function as implicit
presuppositions for each other. In this respect, one needs to have already
read *A Thousand Plateaus* before one is able to begin to understand it
properly, since any sentence only functions in relation to the whole. This is
not because it conceals its secrets; on the contrary, it makes a minimal
appeal to linguistic competence, a minimal allusion to the secrets of
interpretation that we all know and share. Reading, here, is an active process
of making connections between sentences so that one can add the virtual
presuppositions that coexist with each sentence. Now, instead of following
established paths of signification, Deleuze and Guattari make all manner of
unexpected associations and jumps. The text of *A Thousand Plateaus*
appears to be chaotic and spontaneous, but, through careful reading, it can
gain a consistency once each sentence can be linked up to others as an
implicit presupposition or component of the territorial assemblage. The
linkage made between sentences here is at the level of territory, or social
transformation; one sentence is linked to another by acting upon it in order
to change its meaning.

One can view a social territory, insofar as it acts on and through language,
as a set of implicit presuppositions which operate upon statements made at
specific times and specific places. A stratified society produces rules of
grammar and chains of signification, along with normative interpretations

and kinds of subjectivity – it becomes transparent so that everyone (apart from immigrants or incompetents) understands each other. Subjectivity is shaped around an ideal of linguistic competence, so that majoritarian subjects become uniform and interchangeable. It extracts constants from the variables of language. Deleuze and Guattari begin to think within such a context of French democratic capitalism; their speech expresses this society as its collective assemblage of enunciation. Yet once they begin to flee from these order-words and their normative power, and construct their own implicit presuppositions for their statements, they can begin to build a different kind of society with another use of language. Deleuze and Guattari call this a process of 'becoming a foreigner in one's own tongue' (1988: 98). One attains a level of linguistic and cultural incompetence where one no longer knows which implicit presuppositions accompany any statement. At this level, the presuppositions have to be made explicit: they are added, or created, by the process of establishing a new connection or using an atypical expression. Here, it is less important to break grammatical rules or create new metaphors than to operate at the level of social presuppositions. Once a text creates its own presuppositions and conditions as it proceeds, then it begins to have a revolutionary potential. For a social territory is maintained by repeated appeal to the same set of order-words; by contrast, the process of 'making language stammer' creates new order-words and presuppositions at the same time as it issues new statements. Society follows a line of deterritorialization by which all of its presuppositions can become transformed. In this respect, Deleuze and Guattari are able to create their own social territory in the form of the presuppositions expressed in their thought; a minor form of writing produces a new 'people' who are yet to come, in the sense of a new set of social and cultural presuppositions.

Deleuze and Guattari distinguish between two uses of language that correspond to differing kinds of social practices (1988: 101). A major language is defined not by cultural dominance, but by its tendency to extract constants from language. Such a usage of language is made by the science of linguistics, as well as political operations of homogenizing, centralizing, and standardizing language. Power operates through grammatical rules, dead metaphors, dominant interpretations and normative subjectivity. A minor use of language is defined not in terms of dialect or ethnicity, but in terms of a power of transformation of the variables of language. The essential point is that each sentence should act upon the social situation as a whole in order to change its implicit presuppositions. Both uses of language work with order-words, with their dual aspect of death and flight. A major use of language turns the warning to flee against itself, sheltering in the security of constants formed in flight from flight. A minor use of language turns the death-sentence against itself, so that each order-word acts to limit the previously issued orders within language. Language gains a power of transformation. Moreover, the different uses of language carry different kinds of implicit presuppositions and a different kind of social situation with them. A major language is based on a plane of stratification, formed through conjugation, where links between statements are formed by an exterior and fixed social assemblage that issues order-words as judgements. A minor language is based upon a plane of consistency, formed through connection, where links between statements are given by the way in which they act upon each other. All speech is indirect, coming from a collective assemblage of enunciation, but this assemblage acquires a kind of experimental autonomy in which it can determine its own conditions of production and meaning. Through such a minor use of language, Deleuze and Guattari are able to escape from the dominant presuppositions of their social milieu by constructing their own experimental but temporary presuppositions and assemblages of enunciation. Desire is able to transform itself by determining its own social and cultural conditions of production.

As with subjectivity, there is no attempt here to break with language or signification. Instead, the work of destratification or becoming takes place 'outside' of language, as the outside that coexists with signification and is modified through signification. This 'outside' is the unconscious, composed of intensities, codes, territories, and becomings.

Organization and Segmentarity

Beneath subjectivity and signification, we find a pre-linguistic layer of meaning at the level of bodies. The two strata of signifiance and subjectification depend upon the substratum of biological organism. A body is stratified by articulating separate organs with different functions. At the destratified level of the body without organs, there are no absolute distinctions but only various zones and intensities, with gradients of passage. Deleuze and Guattari point out, however, that the body without organs is less opposed to organs than to their organization – in fact, the body without organs depends upon organs as desiring-machines for its existence (1988: 158). They then explore ways in which one can make oneself a body without organs, and ways in which one can escape from the human stratum by strange becomings-animal. Their language seems to point to a programme of physiological disorganization of the human body as a socially liberative practice; this is where they attain their most humorous as well as incomprehensible level by transgressing the social presupposition of the stratified nature of the human body. We must issue a caution here: Deleuze and Guattari write about the way in which the body can be experienced, in intensity, in the schizophrenic unconscious; moreover, they also have a tendency to physicalize all the processes that take place in intensity. Dismantling the biological organism is not a question of dismembering one's own body; indeed, it involves no direct physical action on the body. Instead, removing organization is merely a question of changing the way in which the incorporeal dimension of meaning is produced from bodily processes so that a stratified order of meaning no longer falls back upon bodies in order to organize their arrangement and behaviour. Productive physical processes are able to govern themselves immanently, without interference from outside. In intensity, processes are considered as abstract machines, independently of their domain of concrete actualization. The organism that requires destratification, therefore, is not some private, individual body, but a stratum of abstract human biological material.

We have noted that the stratum of signifiance depends upon the prior organization of society. Incorporeal transformations that take place between bodies are the ground of language, and not the inverse. Organization is a process through which bodies are related to each other by means of some pre-linguistic meaning; for example, primitive societies can be organized into chains of filiation and bonds of alliance. Meaning does not only pertain to language; it also pertains to organic matter in the form of genetic codes and molecular structures. Similarly, it permeates society by dividing bodies into various strata or segments. In primitive societies, physical processes produced marks on bodies so as to constitute meaning in the form of codes; social meaning extended into bodies insofar as it was able to encode. In *A Thousand Plateaus*, however, Deleuze and Guattari isolate the element of expression which pertains to bodies as such, independently of any transformation into codes (1988: 43). This element of expression is the power that organizes bodies.

The process of stratification produces flows of expression and content relative to each other through a conjugation of flows, so that one takes the role of expression, the other, content. Expression and content are both composed of any kind of formed substances, and therefore take on their respective roles in relation to each other (1988: 45). For example, in a protein molecule, the content is given by amino acids which themselves imply the selection of certain atoms and their arrangement in a particular structure; the expression is given by the global molecule which implies the selection of amino acids and their arrangement in a particular polymeric chain. Yet we cannot say that expression depends on content, for the sequence of amino acids is arbitrary, determined from outside by an enzyme. A flow of amino acids, the content, is now conjugated with the order resulting from a flow of enzyme products, the expression. At this level, meaning is just as material as matter.

Deleuze and Guattari identify the kind of organization which is unique to the organic stratum through considering the genetic code: the linearity of the nucleic acid sequence allows expression to become entirely autonomous in relation to content – any nucleic acid can follow any other in the chain (1988: 59). This enables the organism to reproduce as well as evolve; the organic stratum is distinguished by being self-organizing, capable of becoming deterritorialized in relation to the conditions that allowed the production of amino acids as content. Genetic expression is a self-organizing system through which proteins and enzymes are reproduced by the sexuality of molecules. A further level of deterritorialization is attained when forms of expression become linguistic as opposed to genetic, gaining greater autonomy in the form of temporal linearity. This organization within language, however, is inseparable from the ability to organize the external environment through manual dexterity. There is an environmental machine for evolution: primitive humanity leaves the forest, stands upright on the plains in order to see, enabling hands to become free for increasing dexterity and the use of tools; at the same time, the voice is no longer required to shout through the forest, but can develop a more subtle range of quiet sounds (1988: 61–2). A change in environmental conditions has a knock-on effect in deterritorializing the whole assemblage.

The process of destratification is never a question of dismantling; it is merely a question of discovering the immanent processes of decoding and deterritorialization at work in the production of strata, and intensifying their effects. The aim is to introduce not chaos or disorder, but relations and conjunctions that cannot be contained within existing strata. Indeed, desire can be considered as 'more realistic, a better organizer and a more skilful engineer, than the raving rationalism of the present system' (Guattari, 1984: 86). Destratification is less a process of disorganization than a conjunction overcoming the segmentarity that prevents relations between strata. For Deleuze and Guattari, the machinic plane of consistency gives rise to the strata of biological organism as well as the movements of deterritorialization that carry it away. Constructing a plane of consistency, therefore, involves not dismantling organic assemblages, but transforming them into something else by adding new relations. Deleuze and Guattari seek progress by increasing deterritorialization, rather than regression to some ideal condition.

Whether organization occurs at biological or social levels, similar machinic processes may be at work. Social organization has effectively replaced biological organism as the machinic substratum for language; social relations are added to the organic stratum so as to give higher levels of deterritorialization. Such deterritorializations can be prevented, however, by the stratification of society into separate segments or layers. The autonomous line of expression is divided up into segments that mark the limits of arrangements of bodies (1988: 208–9). This happens in a binary fashion, following major dualist oppositions: gender difference, social classes, adults–children, rational–insane, etc. It also happens in a circular fashion, following geographical areas of locality: affairs relating to home, neighbourhood, town, country, the world. Segmentarity also happens in a linear fashion, relating to episodes in a life: family, school, college, work, unemployment, retirement. The substratum for language and subjectivity in our society is the institutional organization of socially defined segments, even if such segments have been formed in and through language and subjectivity. Statements that define and govern such segments do not appeal to any reasons or foundations for legitimation; they are axioms, distributing rights and duties (1988: 454, 462).

Deleuze and Guattari distinguish segmentarity into kinds that cut across boundaries of size and coexist in individuals as well as society. The first kind is molar and rigid, behaving like bricks of solid matter: distinctions are considered according to large statistical aggregates, where differences and exceptions are ironed out. Molar segmentation can take various forms. Binary distinctions, such as those between classes or sexes, are made in the same way by individuals and society as a whole. Circular segments resonate around a single centre, so that various authorities and places refer back to the same State, or perhaps even a global village. Linear segments are endowed with an equivalence and translatability between units; for example, the wage-regime establishes an equivalence between monetary segments, production segments, and consumable-goods segments (1988: 212). The common factor is that molar segmentation operates according to a machine that is exterior to the one generating the segments in the first place; it organizes by manipulating and reproducing pre-given segments of society as so many bricks of social material. Molecular segmentation, by contrast, operates according to the kinds of machinic processes one finds in biochemical interactions such as the construction of proteins. Although binarities, circularities, and linearities are produced here as well, they are constructed by other molecules such as enzymes and catalysts that lie alongside and interact with the amino acids. Molecular interaction has a very different character from the interaction of large-scale solids because it involves self-organizing systems. Expression and content are flexible and relative to each other; the same term, such as an enzyme, can be a product in one reaction before becoming a catalyst in another, switching between content and expression. Deleuze and Guattari's distinction of the molar from the molecular should be understood literally, not analogically: it concerns this style of machinic operation, rather than size. Molecular segments have distinct territorialities lying alongside them, other molecules that function as machinic components in their assemblage; molar segments, by contrast, are reterritorialized on transcendent or universal distinctions and boundaries.

Deleuze and Guattari use this distinction between the molar and the molecular to define qualitative differences between processes in society: molar segments are defined as subjugated groups in relation to an external authority, and molecular segments are defined as subject-groups in relation to productive processes that lie alongside them. In molecular production, the product can influence the process. Yet they emphasize the errors that must be avoided: the distinction cannot be equated with those between the good and the bad, the psychological and the social, the local and the global; moreover, they are not entirely independent of each other, nor always inversely proportional to each other (1988: 215). One does not liberate desire by proclaiming the rights of the local or psychological. Deleuze and Guattari take fascism as the counter-example to these errors: they regard this as a permeation of fascist desire through every cell and area of society, before these can resonate together to form a totalitarian State. Fascism is defined by micro-black holes that stand on their own and communicate with others before resonating in a generalized, central black hole (1988: 214). Postures, attitudes, perceptions, expectations, and semiotic systems are shaped by points of subjectification that turn desire towards black holes of love or death, passion or resentment. Establishing this subjectified structure of desire is the precondition for the black holes beginning to resonate, turning into a passion for the pure race, and revenge against others. Microfascist investments at a molecular level can then be combined with leftist political commitments at a molar level. When desire 'turns against itself to desire its own repression', this is never passive submission, masochistic hysteria, or deception by an ideological lure, but a positive and complex machinic formation at molecular levels (1988: 215).

At this stage, we can return to the immanent analysis of the operation of power. Power operates through machinic formations that produce certain strata of meaning in society: subjectification, signifiance, and organization. The former two depend on organization, and this itself depends on molar and molecular segmentarity. These two kinds of segmentarity are in reciprocal presupposition. Deleuze and Guattari note that the stronger the molar organization, the more it induces a molecularization of its elements and relations: capitalism induces a molecularization of work in the form of private enterprise and performance-related pay, and totalitarian states rely on a micropolitics of insecurity (1988: 215). Secondly, however, molecular movements tend to thwart or disrupt molar organizations: they always leak between the large-scale segments on a line of flight. For Deleuze and Guattari, a society is defined by its lines of flight, which are molecular; changes in society always derive from transformations that are imperceptible from a molar point of view, even if they ultimately result in a reshuffling of molar segments. Molar and molecular are therefore to be distinguished by the system of reference in which they operate.

Deleuze and Guattari also note that every well-defined segmented line continues in a different form as a quantum flow, having only poles, singularities, and quanta. They reconsider the fundamental capitalist exercise of power in the form of a monetary flow with segments. In a corporate budget, money is separated into clearly defined segments: real wages, net profit, management salaries, interest on assets, reserves, investments, purchase expenditure, etc. The flow of financing or credit money, however, has only poles, such as the creation and destruction of money; singularities, such as nominal liquid assets; and quanta of inflation, deflation, and stagflation, etc. Financing money is tied to belief and desire, rather than being conjugated with fixed segments. Power centres, in capitalist society, have a role analogous to that of central banks: their function is to regulate as much as possible the communication, conversion, and coadaptation of the two parts of the circuit. Banks cannot control the quantum flows of credit money, but they can ensure its conversion to a molar perspective. Power centres, therefore, are not defined by the possession of some kind of substantial essence of power, or even money; on the contrary, they are defined by their impotence, by the lines of flight that escape them. Power is a trial and error operation of ensuring the adaptation of segments to quanta (1988: 217).

For Deleuze and Guattari, therefore, power can only be understood at the micropolitical level of quantum flows of belief and desire. Yet it must be considered according to the way in which it relates segments and flows. A power centre is a molar resonance chamber that overcodes all the existing segments: it always ensures the prevalence of one binary segment over the other; it gives a centre a relative resonance over other circular segments; it underscores the dominant segment through which it passes itself (1988: 224). A power centre, however, is also molecular and exercises its power over a micrological fabric of society that it segments in detailed hierarchies in families, schools, factories, corporations, prisons, and psychiatric hospitals, etc. This microtexture is the level at which the oppressed can participate in the 'repression of desire' by their hierarchical prominence within microsegments. Power and impotence complement and reinforce each other; power is merely a capacity to adapt line segments to the quantum flows that escape them. Impotence is a third level of power, relating to the quantum flows that power can never control or define. Mutant flows always escape codes; their degrees of deterritorialization are measured by quanta. Such flows can only be considered in terms of their intensity. Power always aims to stop the mutant flows; it does so by extending its overcoding machine so as to segment all the dimensions of the assemblage, leaving no room for escape. A totalitarian state aims to gain a monopoly over the assembling of flows of belief and desire, so that flows of desire come to coincide with the operations of the segmenting machines. It does so by delimiting the range of assemblages and machines into which desire can be invested, and by which desire can be produced. It adapts its segmented lines to quantum flows, so that society is only envisioned from the perspective of segmentarity. Such a perspective is the precondition for the operation of power in capitalist society.

The liberation of desire does not attempt to 'overpower' the molar centres of power in some form of revolution that would aim to seize control of the State apparatus. Nor does it primarily function at the micropolitical level of local discursivities, genealogies, codes, and territories that are dispersed through the social fabric. Instead, the liberation of desire aims at the production of mutant flows and successive quanta of absolute deterritorialization that will make the whole system explode. The revolution of desire functions through impotence, tracing lines of escape. It constructs a positive line of absolute deterritorialization that carries its own perspective along it; this line is connected to the entire social assemblage, and may function as an agent of deterritorialization for the rest of society. The revolution of desire consists in attaining a series of becomings that transform society and the world.

PART III

LIBERATION OF DESIRE

7

The Revolution of Desire

> Nothing is more distressing than a thought that escapes itself, than ideas that fly off, that disappear hardly formed, already eroded by forgetfulness or precipitated into others that we no longer master. ... We receive sudden jolts that beat like arteries. We constantly lose our ideas. That is why we want to hang on to fixed opinions so much. (1994: 201)

Nothing? Happy life of the philosophers! What about, for example, the primary repression of the schizophrenic, the paranoiac machine with 'its tortures, its dark shadows, its ancient Law' (1984: 18)? What could be more terrible than when a 'harrowing, emotionally overwhelming experience, which brings the schizo as close as possible to matter, to a burning, living center of matter' (1984: 19) turns to annihilate the schizophrenic? But perhaps there is a little of such suffering even in books of philosophy. In any case, it is chaos that is at work, whether it escapes us or attacks us. We need a little solid ground beneath our feet, opinions and strata, to shelter us from dragons breathing fire. And this is the beginning of a whole set of more mundane forms of suffering.

One can become trapped on the other side of the protective mirror of reason, enmeshed in the fantasies of others: a face is constructed to mask one's body, so that one's movements are not seen, one's voice is not heard, one's products are not valued, except insofar as they trace the contours of the given face. It is distressing to be excluded from the socius – the suffering of women, children, immigrants, minorities, others. It is even more distressing not to have a face at all, so that one is entirely excluded from the means of production of subsistence or thought. Alternatively, one might find oneself included by the boundary of reason, but compartmentalized and trapped in a small segment, unable to project messages, gifts, or weapons towards those in other cells – dwelling in a prison, a classroom, a ward, a shop, a home, a sex, a class, a hierarchy, an age, a generation, a profession. Then again, it might be a question of machinic enslavement, being a component part, possibly alongside technical machines or animals, of a machine that constitutes a higher unity and determines one's function – feeding information into a word-processing machine, or becoming less of a user or consumer of television than an output generating feedback in terms of viewing ratings (1988: 457–8), or as a part of an electoral machine feeding back information at the polls. Alternatively, a technical machine may remain external to the human who functions as a worker or user, producing social subjection by defining the dominant reality available – a road system that determines the directions and speeds taken at every point of a car journey, or an education system that determines what should be studied at every stage of a course. Indeed, both machinic enslavement and social subjection can operate at the same time in relation to the same things (1988: 459). Finally, there is a third boundary in addition to that of representation within the socius and that of the productive composition of a machine: a line of pure terror. This is most evident when a military–industrial complex takes charge of capitalism to develop a war economy aiming at annihilation of both the enemy, and one's own population and economy, as in Nazism; or else when the military–industrial complex takes charge of politics, world-wide order, and peace, producing a condition of universal terror and deterrence (1988: 421). The worldwide war-machine becomes all the more extensive when terror and deterrence molecularize and spread throughout the social field, directed against an unspecified enemy, in a generalized paranoia and quest for security where each defends their rights against all (1988: 467). Such paranoia is most effective as a pure form with unspecified content, but frequently the phantasm of the enemy may crystallize a face onto a race, a religion, or a lifestyle, directing the full force of a war-machine against any who are judged to fall on the wrong side of the boundary.

Exclusion, compartmentalization, machinic enslavement, social subjection, paranoia, annihilation: all psychosocial disorders, and good reasons to proclaim a revolution of desire. The capitalist socius, whatever compensations it affords, does not merit the investment of our desire, as well as our labour, in its machines of production. The boundaries of representation, machinic functioning, or paranoid fantasy function as double binds: included or excluded, one will be oppressed by external powers. In this respect, it will not be sufficient to shift the boundaries, establishing new axioms and rights so as to include others within the socius, although minority struggles must necessarily take these paths (1988: 471). For any reform of the global or social order will be incomplete if subjectivity itself is polluted by micro-physical forms of exclusion, compartmentalization, machinic enslavement, social subjection, paranoia, and annihilation, for these pollutants exhibit excessive cruelty in everyday life, whether or not microfascisms resonate and suddenly reform into machines of destruction. After political revolutions, the same kinds of power-relations will re-emerge from the social unconscious. For example, the mass-mediatization of subjectivity means that speech, conversation, banter, and even conspiracy have been subjectified by the discourse of the mass-media that distributes possible issues, opinions, and modes of subjectivity (Guattari and Negri, 1990: 12). Similarly, the compartmentalization and privatization resulting from a molecularization of the division of labour means that interpersonal relations have spoiled, and are now often characterized by indifference, disingenuous disgust, and self-hatred – and here the exceptions, our productive relations, only prove the rule about the majority of interpersonal relations.

It may also be insufficient to purify subjectivity and interpersonal relations through therapeutic techniques for personal 'growth' and 'healing', if the earth itself is polluted – both the extensive earth or exterior milieu of the natural environment and the interior milieu containing the strata that ground humanity: subjectification, signifiance, and organism. Here again, purification will not be sufficient: moving to the privileged perspective of a purified subjectivity, claiming to hold a moral and truthful viewpoint onto the social field, will accomplish little if language itself is riddled with manifestations of power. Establishing a more precise interpretation of the socio-historical field through purifying signification, developing the perfect critical theory, will accomplish little if such a theory remains compartmentalized in an educational institution where it can only be bought, sold, taught, learned, debated, reformulated, and criticized without ever being acted upon. Furthermore, any redistribution of institutional order along new lines will be insufficient if these lines are boundaries of representation, machinic functioning, or paranoid fantasy.

The crises of the three ecologies, global, social and mental, cannot be solved independently (Guattari, 1992: 38). Each will re-emerge from the others unless they are engaged at the plane where global, social, and mental strata and boundaries are produced: the machinic plane of desire – ecology is machinic, concerned with productive relations of machinic heterogenesis between milieux, species, and assemblages (Guattari, 1989b: 68). If this machinic plane seems to be a cross-section of human subjectivity, so that the sole acceptable goal of human activity is the production of self-enriching subjectivities with their own systems of values in a continuous relation with the earth (Guattari, 1989b: 65; 1992: 38), then this is merely because *Homo sapiens* is the most deterritorialized creature that holds the global assemblage together. The machinic liberation of desire is coextensive with a liberation of work, because this is the one human activity that is simultaneously collective, rational, and interdependent. The collective work experience is the site where it is possible to create a revolutionary transformation of subjective consciousness and generate solidarity through micropolitical experimentation (Guattari and Negri, 1990: 14, 19). Deleuze and Guattari's own theoretical production is an example of such a collective production of subjectivity.

The Schizoanalytic Unconscious

If Deleuze and Guattari can be considered to have invented a new 'domain' of thought and 'field' of inquiry, alternately called schizoanalysis, rhizomatics, pragmatics, or nomadology, it is because they occupy and hold a smooth space (1988: 410) that is no longer striated by boundaries or strata. This smooth space of the machinic unconscious is the 'outside' that has an ultimate determining role in nature, history, society, and subjectivity. Desire is the power of machinic heterogenesis, the coordination of multiple causes, or the emergence of complexity that cannot be comprehended in terms of the organization of bodily or institutional components, nor in terms of linguistic structures of signification, nor through the interpretation of subjective intentions and choices. One cannot tell in advance which stratum is going to communicate with which – for example, when a technical phenomenon will provide a fertile environment for the development of certain insects or bacteria. On the machinic plane of consistency, there are relations between the most disparate things and signs: 'a semiotic fragment rubs shoulders with a chemical interaction, an electron crashes into a language, a black hole captures a genetic message, a crystallization produces a passion, the wasp and the orchid cross a letter . . . ' (1988: 69). Nature itself operates through category mistakes. How will a chemical interaction know how to follow the laws of chemistry without rubbing shoulders with semiotic fragments? Another example: perhaps the movement of a free electron may crash into a set of signifiers stored in electronic code, producing a mutation of language that is appealing, becomes fashionable, and is repeated. Nevertheless, this example is still too stratified; hylomorphic dualism, resulting from the double articulation of the strata, leaves an abyss between form and matter, meaning and behaviour, the laws of physics and the movement of particles, mind and brain. Consequently, any interaction between a multiplicity of causes or heterogeneous forces, especially those that might be reciprocally determining, remains unthinkable in science and history alike. An interaction between meaning and matter, such as an assemblage including a wind, a resentment, a signification, a rifle, a bite, a proper name, and an odour (how many stories could one invent with these elements?), escapes understanding and prediction. Of course, one can take a given stratum as essential and determinative, while all the other components of the assemblage remain circumstantial, so as to predict 'normal' behaviour as a repetitive ritual, a compulsion, a custom, a law, or striving to attain a moral ideal. On occasion, however, a combination of accidental elements may add up to produce a fortuituous event that could never have been predicted in advance. All it may take is for the South wind to blow, perhaps as a result of that famous butterfly in Japan whose wings determine global weather conditions, and an assemblage will be irrevocably changed so that a monster is produced. It is such events that function as thresholds for the emergence of new species and assemblages; they have a particular determining role as the singular points of history. What is most needed in our time, yet most difficult to think, is a genuine theory of complexity and machinic heterogenesis, even if such a theory will be unable to explain, predict, or control: a minor science of problematic thought that generates solutions through complexity and emergence (1988: 372).

Machinic heterogenesis is a universalized sexuality. One may distinguish between the oedipalized sexuality of matrimonial alliance that gives rise to evolution through filiation, and the perverse sexuality of a 'nuptial against nature', a symbiotic alliance such as that between wasp and orchid, where a creature incorporates an element from outside into its own mode of existence. In oedipalized sexuality, evolution occurs through a series of differences and displacements: the object of desire is always missing from its place in reality because it is symbolic – it is the transcendental signifier of the phallus that only appears as castrated or absent. A boy, to whom incest is prohibited, seeks to marry the woman who best embodies the phantasm of his mother – evolution takes place through filiation because the wife differs from the mother. But the phantasm of the mother is not the actual mother, being instead a recollected, idealized, reconstructed image. The phantasm is lacking in both wife and mother; yet it is also lacking in itself, being constituted by the castrating prohibition, since it can never become present. There is a hylomorphic relation in oedipalized desire between the phantasm as form of expression and the content of the actual person who partially embodies it, with the result that the phantasm is unchanged but intensified by the encounter, and interpersonal relations are governed by the form of the phantasm. Whether experienced by men or women, oedipalized sexuality has only one sex constituted by the missing symbolic phallus – the desire of the Other – leading to the absence of woman in psychoanalysis except as a figure of male discourse. The schizoanalytic unconscious, by contrast, is defined by perversion, having as many sexes as there are terms in symbiosis (1988: 242). 'Involution', to be contrasted with evolution, is the way in which change is produced by the involvement, enfolding, or invagination of heterogeneous elements – it may happen more suddenly than evolution and often with greater consequences. Hence Deleuze and Guattari's disregard for history and genealogy.

The schizoanalytic unconscious is concerned with multiple sexualities and relations that escape consideration in terms of the strata. If the 'outside' or unconscious appears to be imperceptible, this is not because it is so in essence, but because the categories of stratified thought are unable to comprehend it (1988: 281). The unconscious does not conceal any contents; it merely designates accidental features which have previously been regarded as too insignificant to bring out. Sometimes, however, they can make the difference between life and death. There are intensive quantities that mark the thresholds of assemblages (1988: 253): any hotter or cooler, and the bacteria would not have been able to breed; any sooner or later, and the explosion would have missed him; if that colour were brighter, I would have noticed it; if that whisper had been quieter, I would not have heard it. Physics is familiar with individuation in terms of quantities, for every material object can be considered as a specified combination of determined variables in a phase-space; in philosophy, an entity can also be considered in relation to a combination of certain thresholds of these variables beyond which the object would decompose or change phase, perhaps by fusing, melting, evaporating, or condensing. Yet such thresholds are always relative to another assemblage that counts them as significant. Intensive quantities, as thresholds or limits, define the contingent conditions necessary for effectuating a given event. Moreover, each assemblage has a certain speed of development by which it comes into being: if the bacteria breed too quickly, then she will not survive; if we can get her some antibiotics before the bacteria spread too far, then she may. Where the growth of bacteria and the rapidity of medical treatment designate rates of progress, the approach of thresholds designate intensive speeds of coming-into-being (becoming). If the doctor arrives in time, then she may live: the event of her continuing to live is actualized by the arrival of the doctor, determining that it happens; but the meaning of what happens is individuated as a possible event by the threshold that marks the speed of development of the illness. Libidinal, unconscious, molecular, intensive multiplicities are merely events individuated by the combination of such thresholds (1988: 33). If one adds a further threshold, then the whole multiplicity will change in nature.

There is a second aspect to the schizoanalytic unconscious. Every body composed of intensive quantities has a degree of power that corresponds to what it can do. For each relation between thresholds as extensive parts there is also a capacity. The horse who appears in Freud's analysis of Little Hans has active and passive affects: 'having eyes blocked by blinders, having a bit and bridle, being proud, having a big peepee-maker, pulling heavy loads, being whipped, falling, making a din with its legs, biting, etc.' (1988: 257). Little Hans himself also has an assemblage that composes this episode of his life: 'his mother's bed, the paternal element, the house, the café across the street, the nearby warehouse, the street, the right to go out onto the street, the pride of winning it, but also the dangers of winning it, the fall, shame . . .' (1988: 257–8). The problem of Little Hans' becoming-horse is whether he can play with it or form a symbiotic relation with it: 'an assemblage, for example, in which the horse would bare its teeth and Hans might show something else, his feet, his legs, his peepee-maker, whatever' (1988: 258). Each affect is a possible exterior relation: the machinic assemblage of the horse involves blinders, bit and bridle, heavy loads, a whip, a street, but also pride and a penis as exterior elements like the others. For each element of the assemblage, one asks what can be done with it. There is no resemblance here: if Hans succeeds in becoming-horse it will not be through imitating the horse, but by including the horse in this episode of his life, consequently changing the entire assemblage.

One may easily describe an episode or a life in terms of such intensive quantities and affects. Yet it is not entirely clear why the terms 'becoming' or 'desire' should be appropriate. Why should Hans wish to play with the horse? How has the horse become his desiring-machine? An affect is not merely a capacity but an exercise of power: it is the effectuation of a strange imperative that 'throws the self into upheaval and makes it reel' (1988: 240); it is not merely possible, but real (1988: 238). Hans has already been bitten by the horse before he runs out into the street, he cannot possibly resist, he is infected by contagion. There is a demonic, non-local transport of affects (1988: 253). The affect is an order-word, like the oedipal prohibition – yet it signifies nothing for it enacts the desire that it announces, like a performative statement. The becoming-whale of Captain Ahab in Melville's *Moby Dick* is a desire or imperative that takes over the entire voyage, leading the ship on a line of flight across the ocean in search of the monstrous white whale. Although the voyage is ostensibly based on an imperative to destroy this one particular whale, this order is only issued secondarily by Captain Ahab – Ahab has first received the order from his previous encounters with the whale itself. The becoming-whale of Ahab is therefore constituted by the collective assemblage of enunciation that issues the imperative. In this respect, the whale appears twice: as mode of expression and content of the imperative. It is this particular kind of reflexivity that constitutes the force of desire as a power of coming-into-being. Out in the ocean, Ahab has seen something that is too much for him, that he must destroy – the phantasm of the white whale. What Melville demonstrates through his writing is the pure being of the phantasm that determines an episode or life.

Becoming-Revolutionary

> We must believe in the body, but as in the germ of life, the seed which splits open paving stones, which has been preserved and lives on in the holy shroud or the mummy's bandages, and which bears witness to life, in this world as it is. (Deleuze, 1989: 173)

Beyond simulations and all the displaced representatives of desire, the liberation of desire requires a return to content in the form of the body. The desired body, however, is always a seed of desire, or a crystal: there is an unnatural participation or exchange of codes between expression or content. Whereas in oedipalized desire, the displaced representative of desire is either arbitrary or governed by some order of resemblance, the body as a seed of desire contributes something of itself to the emergent desire. Without the possibility of this contribution, there would be no affect: the great white whale would swim inertly, making no difference to Captain Ahab, even if it has bitten his leg off. This contribution is emergent, escaping prior representation: Ahab and the whale cannot be compared as potential rulers among sea-monsters leading to a simple rivalry; rather, the whale's mysterious line of flight through the oceans is repeated in the voyage that expresses Ahab's quest.

Becomings-animal, the desires and events of the schizoanalytic unconscious, are forces or imperatives that remain inconceivable to stratified thought, oedipalized representation, and psychoanalysis. They are the strange perversions and alliances that shape the unconscious – the manifestations of the real that respond to, surprise, and generate desire through deterritorialization. Deleuze and Guattari's theorems on deterritorialization (1988: 174–5, 306–7) are nothing other than the mechanics of perverse sexuality. Desire is revolutionary in its essence because lines of representation, machinic functioning, and paranoid fantasy are fractured by lines of escape: revolution is a process of decompartmentalization (Guattari and

Negri, 1990: 126). In perverse sexuality, boundaries that exclude, repress, and compartmentalize desire are neither erased nor displaced but dissipated in a smooth space, adsorbed onto a surface by being fractured, multiplied, and fractalized. Firstly, boundaries are regarded no longer as extensive coordinates that specify a previously individuated entity, but as intensive ordinates or thresholds that individuate an entity itself. The lines of representation that compartmentalize or exclude are dissipated in thresholds that distinguish the remarkable from the ordinary, crossing each other at singular points, allowing the return of affective and evaluative dimensions of thought. Becoming turns the boundaries into lines of escape insofar as it implicates intensive thresholds within the lines of representation. This minor mode of existence is imperceptible because unrepresentable, yet it is implicated in an affective evaluation of a line's significance. There is no possibility of dialectical recuperation of minority from a majoritarian standpoint because of the asymmetry between the two kinds of lines: the line of escape implicates force, affect, becoming, and it is these which give it a being that is no longer in simple dualistic contrast with majority.

Secondly, a threshold only has importance in relation to another entity: one never deterritorializes alone, and there is a displacement of desire from one entity to another, a series of perversions. The boundaries of machinic functioning are perpetually displaced because a machine only functions by breaking down, always adding a new threshold and component, changing the assemblages, allowing the return of constructive and creative dimensions in thought. Lines of flight escape from machinic functioning and social subjection by functioning as cutting edges of deterritorialization that continually change the nature of the entire machine.

Thirdly, the substituted entity expresses a territory or possible world and life. If this territory is mapped back onto a particular object, such as the great white whale Moby Dick, then the line of becoming turns to a paranoid line of abolition; but if this territory is itself deterritorialized in a process of double becoming (1988: 306), then paranoia is turned back against itself, and desire reaches a threshold of absolute deterritorialization, becoming immanent within the whole process, as a phantasm or event.

In becoming, desire disengages the components that can be included in a phantasm or event, those which are neither active nor passive, neither internal nor external, neither imaginary nor real, neither personal nor individual, neither said nor signified (Deleuze, 1990b: 210–14). There is neither resemblance, nor imitation, but an exchange of affects – the unconscious, which always lies outside the individual, is shaped by the affects that seize it. The phantasm is always composed of a territory or possible world, a multiplicity or population, and their affects or capacities. When Deleuze and Guattari write about becoming-woman, they refer to an event in the unconscious that could happen to men or women. It is not necessary to define 'a woman' according to a complete list of thresholds and affects, for a woman is always crossing a threshold and becoming something else. A woman has a capacity for sexual multiplicity including erogenous zones that are not centred on the phallus. In this respect, becoming-woman is always an escape from oedipalized and phallic sexuality – even if this is an escape which women need to discover just as much as men. If all becoming proceeds by way of a becoming-woman, then it involves the constitution of a multiplicity of phantasms as erogenous zones that are no longer localized on a specific organ. When Deleuze and Guattari write about becoming-woman, they mean that one learns to add the affects of a woman, which might include Irigaray's list of capacities for sexual multiplicity, for otherness, for living as a body, for laughing, touching, and caressing (this list is far from complete), to one's own collective assemblage, whether one is male or female. Similarly, becoming-child is learning to acquire the subjective apprehensions of a child, including sexual fascination with the surrounding world, and particularly with animals, their affects, smells, and expressions, following trajectories of subjectivity that exist in the milieu, rather than in a unique person. If all becoming proceeds by way of a becoming-girl (1988: 276), this is because the girl is the one whose desire is stolen from her first of all in order to impose a history or morality in the form of a specific social role or identity. A becoming-girl, however, involves entering the plane of desire completely, like Alice through the looking-glass (Deleuze, 1990b: 236). Nothing remains as a spectator outside the planes of thought, imagination, or desire: each moment or mode of existence through which the girl passes is an erogenous zone; everything can be affected.[1]

Becoming also proceeds by way of a becoming-animal. Unlike humans, animals do not participate in the strata of signifiance and subjectification. From a majoritarian perspective, becoming-animal would appear to entail a loss of language and subjectivity. For Deleuze and Guattari, however, becoming-animal is a process which can take place in a writer like Kafka through the act of writing itself (1986). Becoming-animal is therefore a process that only makes use of signification and subjectivity for the purposes of another mode of expression: the marking out of a territory. Animals are characterized by their capacity to express their territories, apart from signification, through rhythms, sounds, colours, and smells as various contents; there is a becoming-animal particular to modern art and literature which attempts to replicate this function where the mode of expression is inseparable from the content (1988: 310–50). When Deleuze and Guattari write about 'becoming-animal', therefore, they refer to this function of expressing territories. In language, however, such territories need not be conjugated with physical areas of land, but refer to a virtual domain of implicit presuppositions. Presuppositions can striate the space of the unconscious as a set of axioms, or else they can sketch a smooth space as lines of flight and experimentation, changing direction at every move.

Similarly, plants express and reproduce their genetic codes through their interactions with the milieux of sun, air, rain, and soil. 'Becoming-plant' is therefore a process of organizing and reproducing a certain intercalation of milieux on the basis of codes. Genetic codes are characterized by their capacities for random mutation, reproduction, auto-catalysis, and reciprocal exchange; plants provide a vehicle or content for the propagation of such successive forms. In language, however, codes need not express the 'selfish gene', but can refer to the socially defined or encoded speech-acts that perform incorporeal transformations within the order of society. Social codes grow, reproduce, and evolve like plants. If one is to follow current biological dogma and reject the Lamarckian inheritance of acquired characteristics, then the only question concerning codes is whether they are present in embryo at a particular place, and whether they can propagate in a given milieu.

Furthermore, biochemical molecules are distinguished by having their codes and territories expressed in other molecules, lying alongside them, that constitute the machine that synthesizes them in chemical interactions. Here an aparallel evolution, with the inheritance of acquired characteristics, becomes a possibility once more. Hence the use of explicit atypical expressions that deterritorialize the implicit presuppositions of other statements is a becoming-molecular of language. Moreover, the conjunction of deterritorialized quantum flows is a becoming-crystalline of language. Hence these becomings have no essential meaning in themselves, but only function in a particular context, such as an experimental use of language, by connecting up to heterogeneous contexts. Becoming-woman, -child, -animal, -plant, -molecular, or -crystalline are the imperceptible modes of existence constructed within the schizoanalytic unconscious.

The War-Machine

Deleuze and Guattari's revolution of desire is to be conducted by nomads – these are the people who occupy the smooth space of the social unconscious. Whenever there is insubordination, rioting, guerrilla warfare, or revolution then a nomadic mode of social existence is constituted (1988: 386). The imperceptibility of such a rhizomatic movement – the grass-roots of society – is simply due to its lack of organization, its exteriority to representation. Nomads are the social embodiment of the polymorphously perverse sexual unconscious – there is never a sufficient reason or moral law that governs their actions. Nomadic events are simply happenings.

Nomadic war-machines express three forms of exteriority: they have a spatio-geographic aspect, an arithmetic aspect, and an affective aspect. The smooth space of the nomads is exterior to the strata: it is not found within subjective interiority, nor within linguistic signification, nor within an objectively organized or segmented site. It escapes being represented as either interior or exterior since it follows the lines along which strata sediment, fold, segment, and are carried away. The emergence of new forms, in machinic heterogenesis, always comes from a pure space of exteriority that is no longer defined in relation to a boundary: '*They* come like fate, without reason, consideration, or pretext; they appear as lightning appears, too terrible, too convincing, too sudden, too *different* even to be hated' (1984: 191).[2] The consequence of such an emergence is the crossing of an intensive threshold, a singular or remarkable point: things have changed, but one cannot perceive the source of change. The territory occupied by the nomads is imperceptible because the nomad reterritorializes on deterritorialization itself: the earth deterritorializes itself, like the ever-shifting of dunes in the desert (1988: 381). Change no longer refers to an underlying genealogy, a history, or a transcendent principle, for it does not repeat an identity or law. Instead, change changes in relation to other changes: it has an absolute, intensive speed, which occupies a smooth space in the manner of a vortex, always repeating that which differs (1988: 381).

Nomadic thresholds are designated numerically. This is not a question of measuring quantities of space or counting a population. When a nomadic army is divided into tens, hundreds, and thousands, this is not for the purpose of assessing numerical strength, but for the strategic purpose of moving and coordinating separate parts (1988: 389). These are ordinal, not cardinal, numbers, defined in relation to a complex of other numbers (1988: 391). In this respect, thresholds are always demarcated in relation to other thresholds; they are not remarkable in themselves, but only become remarkable in an assemblage relating them to others. Power, in the war-machine, is defined by the number of relations that any special body might have; the site of this power is dynamic and provisional, depending on the maintenance of actual networks of exchange. If there is a power centre that actually ordains numbers, rhythms, directions, and movements, then this power centre is constituted by a special body that extracts its members numerically from all tribes of the nomadic band. When Moses composed the nomadic Hebrew people into a war-machine, the firstborn were extracted as a special body, whose role was substituted for by the Levites; the people then paid taxes to the Levites in order to redeem their firstborn (1988: 392). There is a perpetual exchange between bodies and numbers.

What is exchanged in nomad bands? What gives the group their consistency? A band of nomads maintains consistency, as against fragmenting into a chaotic multiplicity, from the internal relations that take place between parts. These might be constituted around an anomalous individual, the most deterritorialized in a multiplicity, who functions as a special body as well as a limit or threshold of the assemblage (1988: 243–5). The consistency of a band of nomads that defines its boundary is given by the affects that are exchanged with the anomalous individual, or the number of dimensions of the terms that exist in symbiosis. The affects exchanged within a nomadic war-machine are weapons – capacities for making war (1988: 394). One can distinguish between the kind of production that arises from the war-machine and the production of machinic assemblages subordinated to State or capitalist powers (1988: 395–402). Weapons are projected: they result from free action, discharge emotions, and produce an effect outside them. Tools, by contrast, are introjected in State production: they work against resistances, preparing a matter for use, producing feelings and an interiority in the subject of labour. Work is predetermined by codes and signs that govern how it should be carried out. Weapons are not defined, here, in terms of their capacity to cause destruction, but rather in terms of their capacity for projection, producing outside effects. The war-machine does not have war for its object, except in special circumstances when it raids centres of resistance, as in guerrilla warfare. Instead, Deleuze and Guattari deterritorialize the war-machine so that it becomes in its essence the constitutive element of a smooth space, occupying it and displacing people within it (1988: 417).

The nomadic war-machine requires its own relation to matter or content. The affects or weapons of nomads are contributed by itinerant metallurgists (1988; 404–15). Although metallurgy can operate according to a hylomorphic schema, imposing a given form on units such as ingots, it also proceeds by following lines of variation – mining the sites where ores are to be found, heating metal until it crosses a singularity and melts, producing alloys of varying proportions, and moulding weapons or tools. Metallurgy works experimentally by discovering spatio-temporal haecceities as locations, singularities such as points of fusion and decarbonation, and affects of metal such as hardness, weight, and colour (1988: 405–6). In this way, metallurgy treats matter according to its inherent properties, so the affects and energetic materiality of metal overspill its prepared forms (1988: 410). Metal is the body without organs of matter; the whole machinic phylum is metallurgical (1988: 411).

In this respect, the weapons of the nomadic war-machine are material seeds of desire insofar as the productive process of metallurgy utilizes haecceities, singularities, and affects that are indiscernible from the nature of the nomads themselves, although actualized in a very different material. The whole assemblage of nomads and metallurgists produces the war-machine that will effect the liberation of desire. Instead of regarding assemblages as being composed of statements and visibilities that are juxtaposed in arbitrary non-relations that constitute power, as Foucault does, all assemblages are assemblages of desire, the machinic conjunction of separate series of expression and content that become indiscernible on the plane of consistency (1988: 69, 397, 531).

Problem 8: On the revaluation of values

God makes the world by calculating, but his calculations never work out exactly [*juste*], and this inexactitude or injustice in the result, this irreducible inequality, forms the condition of the world. The world 'happens' while God calculates; if the calculation were exact, there would be no world. (Deleuze, 1994: 222)

There is always something which escapes that which is thinkable. If the world as a whole were infinitely thinkable and calculable, even from a divine perspective, then it would merely be a fantasy, an insubstantial simulacrum of itself. I know that the world exists insofar as it escapes both my control and my comprehension – it shocks me. There is an experience of difference that reveals the world insofar as it differs from my representations. For even an infinite power of representation, possessed by a Leibnizian or Hegelian God, is only able to approach comprehension of the world asymptotically, and there remains a qualitative difference between a tangent and the curve that approaches it (Deleuze, 1994: 42–50, 171–2). The material existence of the world is guaranteed by the being of the sensible (Deleuze, 1994: 236): when one considers matter as that which is perceived but not thought, a sensation apart from thought, then matter becomes that which is imperceptible in itself, but that which makes perception possible by the force it exerts upon me (Deleuze, 1994: 139–40). These conditions are often realized by modern art: it tends to free the work from representation in order to make it into a theatre that dramatizes the forces of sensation (1994: 56). 'Nature is contingent, excessive, and mystical essentially. . . . Nature is miracle all. She knows no laws; the same returns not, save to bring the different' (Deleuze, 1994: 57).[3]

Deleuze gave three examples of repetition in nature that imply a difference that escapes representation: the discrete, the alienated, and the repressed (Deleuze, 1994: 15). To illustrate the first example, the concept of an electron refers to an object that can exist at any point in space and time; if one designates a discrete electron existing at a particular space and time, however, then there are no conceptual characteristics that can distinguish this particular electron from any other. The result is a failure to individuate a discrete electron, and a pullulation of individuals sharing the same concept and space–time location (Deleuze, 1994: 12–13).[4] Even if this example of the discrete were to fail in respect of electrons or Epicurean atoms, it still succeeds in relation to the difference between words as elements of a language system and words actually used in speech (Deleuze, 1994: 13). Which meaning, among a multiplicity of signfieds, was present when you just spoke?

The second example is that for every representation one can always find at least two objects that correspond to it, even if these are simply mirror-images of each other, or the more and the less, or the positive and the negative, or the earlier and the later. Directional or truly differential determinations cannot be defined in terms of representations because they are reciprocally determined in relation to other indexicals: I can only designate the left or right, the more or less, the positive or negative, and the earlier or later in relation to me or my standard. In this respect, representation is always alienated from nature (Deleuze, 1994: 14).

The third example is when a representation lacks consciousness of itself, and there is memory without remembrance. In this case, the memory is played, enacted, or repeated, without being recognized – as knowledge, it presents itself to consciousness, determining the shape of subsequent thought, without representing itself within consciousness. It is a knowledge that is not known. This concealed role for knowledge belongs to knowledge by right; it does not only occur in dreams, slips of the tongue, jokes, or other conditions discovered by Freud. Repression, and the consequent compulsion to repetition, are properly transcendental, as opposed to natural, phenomena (Deleuze, 1994: 14). Like King Oedipus, one lives in a theatre, acting out roles, unaware of the ironic presence of a knowledge that shapes one's thoughts and deeds like fate.

Representations are always defined in relation to certain limits, boundaries, or thresholds. These limits mark certain *values* that are imposed upon experience in an exercise of power, like cutting codes into human flesh. Even if the limit is infinitely displaced towards the large or the small, in a kind of 'orgiastic representation' (Deleuze, 1994: 42) exceeding conventional values, allowing tumult, passion, restlessness, and monstrosity to surface, and converging towards a ground of experience, this still presupposes a certain evaluation. The principle of the identity of the ground and infinite representation, upon which convergence is based (Deleuze, 1994: 49), devalues the differences found in the discrete, the alienated, and the repressed, and hence excludes both matter and the unconscious.

There is a Nietzschean experiment corresponding to such crucial experiences of difference: 'every time we find ourselves confronted or bound by a limitation or an opposition, we should ask what such a situation presupposes' (Deleuze, 1994: 50). The question of the value of values or the limit of limits invokes an alternative means of constructing values. Deleuze and Guattari's treatise on nomadology is nothing other than a revaluation of all values. It constructs a social space apart from representation. One may differentiate between social relations mediated by representation, based on the model of recognition, where one either recognizes or fails to grasp the representations made by the other, from social relations mediated by affects or forces, based on the model of encounter, where one is moved or forced to think (Deleuze, 1994: 139). Each has a different relation to the limit as the source of values.

For representations to be understood by differing parties in the same sense, under the model of the Signifier, then the pre-existence of a common stockpile of meaning is already implied, as part of an abstract State that is already effectuated in thought, along with its universal currency of values. It is possible for differing parties to relate to each other apart from common meanings and values, however, according to a model of exchange. Two groups might exchange axe-heads for seeds, or vice versa, for example. Deleuze and Guattari show how the reciprocal values of commodities are established in such situations of pure exchange: value is determined numerically in relation to a limit of use-value, beyond which the appeal of the exchange is lost (1988: 437). This estimated limit must be simultaneously anticipated and prevented, for the limit marks a threshold beyond which the material would acquire a different use. By stockpiling axe-heads or seeds beyond a certain threshold, an increase in planting would be required that would change the whole social assemblage of the group, possibly leading to an agricultural and sedentary way of life (1988: 438). The threshold or limit, therefore, is presupposed in an ideal form, governing a way of life, being repeated identically in each transaction.

In this respect, limits or values are established by a certain quantifiable scale that operates in the context of a particular reciprocal relation. The question of that which is presupposed by such limits, therefore, ignores particular values as well as variables that are valued, in order to explore the pure element of 'quantitability' or evaluation (cf. Deleuze, 1994: 171). What counts, from a philosophical point of view, is the units of measure (1988: 4) rather than the variables evaluated. Values depend on qualities. Such units are constituted by the idea of the machinic assemblage, the abstract machine of the reciprocal relation of exchange between the two groups. In this way, lines of representation already presuppose lines of machinic functioning.

There is a further question of presupposition to be explored. If the quality of machinic functioning is defined in relation to a limit, then qualities imply a pure element of qualitability that is marked by the limit (Deleuze, 1994: 175). Such limits to the assemblages are singular points that mark the emergence of new relations and hence new affects. Beyond the limit new units of measure are required for new values. One can therefore differentiate between two kinds of evaluations: an evaluation based on fixed units of measure, which simultaneously anticipates and wards off the limit, as found in primitive exchange; and an evaluation that questions the value of values, and is prepared to cross beyond the limit to discover new units of measure, along with new assemblages, in a revaluation of all values. One can distinguish paranoid anticipation, displacing the outside, from schizophrenic affirmation of the outside, leading to breakdown of the current assemblage and a voyage in intensity in search of new values. In this way, lines of machinic functioning depend on lines of paranoid repression.

Evaluation based on exchange, therefore, excludes the discrete from representation, the alienated from machinic functioning or production, and the repressed from affective relation and consciousness. In the light of these presuppositions, one merely has to invoke Nietzsche's selective test of the eternal return to produce a revaluation of all values: how does paranoid repression evaluate paranoid repression? Paranoia can certainly affirm its own values and units of measure; indeed, it is constituted by the emergence of a self-positing assemblage that evaluates the actions of others always in relation to itself. But it is based on a repression of its own paranoid nature; the re-emergence of the repressed into consciousness produces a new assemblage with a new scale of values. In the eternal return, therefore, it is never the same values that return, but always the extreme or the excessive that has already crossed the threshold or limit (Deleuze, 1994: 41).

Paranoia and schizophrenia constitute pure expressive forms of the warmachine. The difference between them lies in their machinic relation to content. For values do not exist as abstract modes of expression unless they can crystallize in relation to a specific content. The material of value is a quantifiable element that stands in for the pure form of quantifiability. Historically, metal has played a privileged role as the material of content because of its capacity to be remoulded under the signs of various emperors as differing units of measure. The alliance between the State and metallurgists forms a paranoid machine of quantification, producing coins for taxes. This can be distinguished from a schizophrenic alliance between nomads and metallurgists, producing weapons for a warmachine (1988: 415).

Values must be constructed; they do not spring from nowhere. A nomadic currency is constructed in the form of jewellery (1988: 401): it is a currency of heterogeneous values, a minor art, expressing traits of pure speed and free activity. Values that escape representation – those of the discrete, the alienated, and the repressed – have all the singularity of handmade jewellery. The revaluation of all values exchanges the equalizing power of money for the inequalities of jewellery.

Notes

1. The reduction of the gender difference to a purely historical asymmetry, such as the difference oppressor/oppressed, misses the intensive difference that is latent within it. If the woman differs from the man insofar as she differs from herself, whereas he is identical to himself, then the gender difference is constituted by an intensive difference that is always annulled by representation. It emerges from this that the gender difference is founded upon an intensive power of self-differentiation belonging to the woman – a power of becoming, of overthrowing foundations. If this difference is desire, the pure element of exteriority, then while the woman has a privileged access to it, she does not possess it as her essence or identity; it simply happens to her. Her privilege derives from a greater ability to escape her represented identity because this identity has not been constructed by her; it bears little relevance to the lived experience of her body and imagination.

Feminist attempts to criticize Deleuze and Guattari's becoming-woman as effacing the gender difference are merely dialectical acts of recuperation within representation (for example, Braidotti, 1991, 1993). They castrate desire once more. It may appear to be the case that a multiplication of sexualities, losing a specific feminine identity, is historically dangerous for women – and, indeed, it certainly would be in the short term – but closing off the critical routes by which the dominant power structures in thought can be analysed and overthrown has more serious long-term historical consequences for women and minorities, who always bear the brunt of social ills. Deleuze and Guattari's revolutionary aim is to overthrow the most insidious, molecular, and imperceptible power-machines that insist within the social field.

2. Nietzsche's text, of course, refers to the founders of states. But Deleuze does cite it in relation to nomads in his essay on nomad thought (Deleuze, 1977).

3. Deleuze is quoting Benjamin Paul Blood, a nineteenth-century American poet.

4. In spite of the Pauli exclusion principle that already presupposes that particles, even if not identifiable, are sufficiently discrete as to be countable.

8

The Liberation of Work

Repression of Work

Everyone wants to know the truth. That is, if they are not distracted from thinking by extrinsic concerns. So the general presupposition has it (Deleuze, 1994: 131). In relation to work, however, the converse presupposition holds sway: nobody wants to work. People are generally lazy. If they do work, it is only so that they might improve the conditions of their rest (Nietzsche, 1961: 56–8). One might work because one desires a pleasure, or because one is anxious about satisfying a need. Pleasure and satisfaction are the end of work, and mark the end of work. In heaven, nobody works for a living. A phantasy of a universal condition of antiproduction existing by right, if not in fact, dominates the social field. Even the universe will finish working one day, and rest in entropic heat death. This fantasy of catatonia is the body without organs of the socius. Like a depressive who longs for immobility, the psychic investment in labour longs for rest.

The phenomenon of catatonia rarely expresses a lack of psychic activity. More frequently, it expresses a delicate balance of opposing forces and contradictory inclinations. This often takes the form of a cut-out mechanism, belonging to a finely balanced feedback loop that prevents excessive activity (Eigen, 1986: 102). Catatonia is a response to catastrophe: 'I am a shock going on and on in nowhere' (Eigen, 1986: 118). This leads one to suspect a repressive function for the phantasy of laziness – there is a work too terrible to be accomplished. In this respect, the general presupposition about work has an analogous function to the presupposition about truth. By supporting each opinion with an implicit presupposition of the form, 'and I believe that this opinion approximates to the truth', one excludes awareness of a knowledge that one does not know that one knows, or is perhaps too terrible to know, the kind of knowledge that might be uncovered by Socratic questioning or psychoanalysis. Similarly, the presupposition of a natural condition of rest allows work to be motivated by extrinsic factors, excluding the accomplishment of a work that one works upon work – a kind of working out or working through. The phantasy of laziness represses free action.

Economy, efficiency, minimal expenditure, minimal effort – a complete exclusion of moments of free labour. The accountancy model of management of labour involves reflection upon work as a secondary activity, a representation, before work is subjugated to representation in the form of legitimate goals, techniques, roles, long-term plans, fitness for purpose, and audits and appraisals that quantify performance. At every stage, it assumes that we know exactly what our work is for and where it is going. Segments of labour are overlaid with segments of represented activity; these again are overlaid with quantifiable segments, and conjugated with capital in the form of levels of funding and performance-related pay. Whether such codifications and stratifications of the processes of labour lead to machinic enslavement or machinic subjugation, explicitly motivated by the increase of wealth and capital, they capture the activities of workers by forming an alliance with anxiety. In free market competition in a global context, the prospect of 'winning' is less of a motivation for the majority, whose only prospect of winning is in the lottery, than the fear of 'losing', given the dire states of existing poverty that can be held up as examples and threats. Poverty, exclusion from the economic socius, is both real and artificially fabricated, for at the same time as molecularizing the quantification of labour throughout the economic socius, zones of unemployment, idleness, and antiproduction are also propagated, as well as economic short-circuits in the form of crime. Capital aims to reproduce capital, not production; it profits equally from legitimate and illegitimate activity. The artificial production of poverty and crime, however, is not sufficient by itself to motivate labour; poverty and crime must be widely represented in the media in a general culture of paranoia.

Paranoia suspects secrecy everywhere, but there is little need for secrecy in capitalism – except when one breaks the rules in order to make a quick profit. Even if this rule-breaking is the norm, the logical outcome of anxiety and opportunity, and even if capital profits from this, it is not essential to capital. In this respect, while investigative journalism may function as a social conscience by denouncing excesses, media representation as a whole attains the condition of a generalized paranoia where secrecy is elevated from a finite content to an infinite form (1988: 288). It does not require a Stalinist bureaucracy and secret police to create a culture of generalized suspicion, where each may be a class enemy or a police informer. For each of us has a secret, even if this relates to work rather than ideology: it is a fact of life, as is well known in the medical profession, that one may be denounced for either exceeding or falling short of one's role, either engaging in free activity that has not been officially sanctioned or failing to meet one's commitments. In a culture of general mass-media paranoia, one is guilty a priori, in any event; one works to constantly forestall the plots of those who would denounce our guilty secrets. The collective subject of mass-media representation is a paranoiac in relation to which we are all conspirators. In addition, this paranoid collective subjectivity judges every public figure as guilty a priori – each has a guilty secret or ambiguous motives that, even if they cannot be directly exposed, can be anticipated or magically foreseen (cf. 1988: 288).

This paranoia only takes root because each does indeed have a secret in relation to work. There is a 'division of labour' between production and consumption: what one consumes has little effect on what one produces.

One is effectively compelled to participate as a producer in society via the economic infrastructure, and as a consumer via cultural mediation. The practical bond between these two roles is the conversion of labour power into a power of consumption through an exchange of money. Oedipus is present in both work and leisure, struggling to accept the law of the economic father: Do only the work that is required of you, neither more nor less! You may only enjoy the pleasures which are bought – all others are worthless! Whatever the success and status of the individual within the economic infrastructure, the affective disappointment in the form of unrealized opportunities for production is felt as a transcendent obligation, law, or duty that represses desire – one must succeed at one's job and earn one's living before playing with one's desiring-machines – even if this is a duty to oneself in terms of becoming successful in the economic infrastructure. The elimination of an affective dimension to work, involving creative possibilities of subjectivity, is maintained by confining this to consumption, where labour itself is limited. The consumer is also a producer, but what the consumer produces is an affective response; such quantum flows of affectivity then have little opportunity to connect up to other affective flows due to the architectural privatization of families as nuclei of consumption, and little opportunity to connect up to other flows in general because they have no consistency with the productive machines into which the consumer's labour is incorporated in his or her capacity as a producer. A previous evening's television viewing has little productive impact on the following day in the workplace – except as a source of passwords allowing entry into conversation and sociability.

This predicament, a contemporary form of the repression of work, appears in fantasy in simplified form as a mythical attempt to resolve the conflict: it is dramatized as a conflict between duty and freedom, law and desire, society and individual, or a 'reality principle' and 'pleasure principle'. One of the major forms of cultural production, therefore, is a set of narratives and images that focus on this conflict between duty and freedom, and aim to shift the balance of power in the direction of the free, desiring individual. Hence the high cultural status of adolescent, youthful, rebellious autonomy, embodied in certain ideal body shapes and clothing, popular music, dance, and film characters. Such cultural representations are mythical, however, insofar as they do not conform to the behaviour of the individuals who imagine them. A more mature but similar range of cultural products are those that attempt to resolve the conflict by constructing and criticizing some image of repressive State culture, and aim to construct in opposition to that a transcendent duty of freedom, a higher law of desire, and a better society of more individualized and differentiated persons.

At any rate, counter-culturalism is a dominant motif of mass-media culture and its political commitments, both left and right. Paradigmatically, it fills a notable proportion of prime-time television, whether in the form of fiction or documentary. When social, cultural, and political criticism becomes a majoritarian culture, it becomes fashionable to speak as, on behalf of, or alongside some form of excluded, counter-cultural minority. Such 'minorities' are often identified from a majoritarian perspective according to some common trait, irrespective of their cultural coherence or homogeneity of role in the dominant culture. Cultural critique is then merely a matter of changing dominant codes and significations that separate minorities from the majoritarian ideal of the autonomous individual. This is extremely beneficial to some, but also extends the current power-assemblage through the social field.

When cultural critique itself becomes a majoritarian cultural product, the liberative value of cultural criticism as an academic discipline itself is called into question. Although not afflicted by the sensationalizing, infantilizing, and banalizing power of the media (Guattari, 1992: 165), cultural criticism may gain its popularity from its participation in the majoritarian-culture machine just described through the construction of counter-cultural social identities that oppose a higher justice to the dominant, repressive social system. Each liberation from a repressive presupposition discovered in cultural theory may bring an affective reward, but only on rare occasions does it have an opportunity to influence the productive assemblage of the academy in particular, and wider society in general.

Guattari has consistently attacked the 'human sciences' for aping a fashion of 'scientific rigour', drawing attention away from the political issues at stake (Guattari, 1984: 88, 106, 163). The human sciences constitute a vast doxology, an argument over anything we see that affects us (1994: 155). Its opinions propose a correspondence between perception of a quality common to several objects and an affection supposedly common to several subjects who experience it (1994: 144). Opinions, therefore, grasp a state of affairs inasmuch as the work that has produced it has finished, and grasp a subjective affection inasmuch as the force that distends it has finished acting: the human sciences are unable to grasp work in progress. The ideals of neutrality and objectivity, a dispassionate end to work, are still present in structural and systematic interpretations of society. Yet an engaged social and cultural critique, maintained in the name of higher values, springs from *ressentiment*, and lacks dimensions that are intrinsically evolutive, creative, and self-positing (Guattari, 1989b: 25). Guattari suggests that these scientific and moral paradigms should therefore be replaced by an ethico-aesthetic paradigm. By 'ethical', Guattari wishes to underline the responsibility for engagement, intervention, and production of forms of individual and collective subjectivity. By 'aesthetic', Guattari wishes to emphasize that the unconscious can be reconstructed from zero, without following pre-existing presuppositions (Guattari, 1989b: 29). Consequently, poetry can teach more about social liberation than the human sciences by means of its direct effects on subjectivity and the unconscious (Guattari, 1992: 39). The liberation of work follows from an aesthetic engagement of the unconscious.

Adopting sceptical, critical, or cynical outlooks, from Descartes to the present day, generates a neurotic, self-positing structure – having doubted the value of everything except for critique, one is compelled to criticize even if one also criticizes critique. The force of paranoid suspicion is not commensurate with the power of conviction of its strategies of suspicion; if anything, the converse is the case. As with paranoiacs, religious fanatics, or pseudo-Nietzscheans, the more improbable, outrageous, or transgressive the opinion expressed, the greater the affective reward and the more firmly held the conviction. The values and roles expressed within cultural production contrast with those of its consumers; it is this contrast that allows libidinal investment. In fact, the degree of libidinal investment in mythical representations of the destruction of dominant values, the power of affective compensation that they offer, is proportional to the extent to which the affective dimension of experience is excluded from production.

Work is not simply repressed. It is captured by a displaced representative of desire. In a paranoid culture, surplus labour is something that must be anticipated and prevented in one respect, while necessarily being produced and stockpiled in another. When anticipated and prevented, surplus labour is represented as lying beyond the threshold of economic viability – too many workers, too much time-wastage, excess production. But in order for this threshold to be produced, activities need to be valued by being compared, linked, and subordinated to a common and homogeneous quantity – abstract labour – that can be conjugated with flows of money through the wage relation (1988: 442). Labour value results from the monopolistic extraction of a surplus value from labour by the entrepreneur. The economic apparatus through which work is captured in labour is structurally homologous to the apparatus through which land is appropriated in the form of rent, and commodities are appropriated in the form of taxation – the monetary values of labour, rent, and taxes are fixed in relation to a limit, the least valuable, in a direct comparison of exchangeable productivities, territories, or commodities (1988: 441–4). Labour is quantified by being overcoded, through representation, by an abstract, quantifiable scale, always in relation to the limit of economic viability.

The fantasy of antiproduction, the breakdown of production at the end of its economic viability, is always the limit in relation to which abstract value is measured. The illusion of economic finitude is generated by a repetition of this fantasy of antiproduction: firstly, as a principle of intrinsic motivation, so that no one is willing to work unless that work can be exchanged for the bought soothing of anxieties, satisfaction of needs, and consumption of enjoyment; secondly, as the extrinsic source in relation to which value will be measured, so that excess labour lacks value insofar as no one is willing to pay for it. This repetition, within and without, closes off the world of labour from the infinite forces of the cosmos. The value of labour is measured in relation to a constructed site of subjectivity that does not itself work. Here, as elsewhere, the absurdity of evaluating human activity on a scale that is measured in relation to zero activity is the factor that gives authority to such a standard of evaluation. When it comes to faith, one is never persuaded to believe in the absurd, requiring no reasons; a practical leap is sufficient, driven by compulsion. The nihilism of capital, eliminating all scales of value with an ounce of subjectivity, is the source of its oedipalized attraction – nothing could be more transgressive, rebellious, or iconoclastic than capital. For if one is already guilty in relation to work, there are two extreme strategies for exorcizing the guilt: 'workaholism', the neurotic compulsion to perfectly fulfil one's oedipal role in the workplace, or entrepreneurship, the ultimate transgressive strategy for destruction of an oedipal role. The compatibility of such strategies allows a resolution of Oedipus at last. The fantasy of antiproduction generates a compulsion to work.

What really lies beyond the threshold? What is the paranoid secret of the abstract quantification of exchange? The comparison and abstract quantification of differing kinds of work are only possible through a relative evaluation of the exchange of their stockpiled products, alienated from their conditions of production (1988: 440). Work is evaluated in relation to its end product, the condition of inactivity when the day's work is over. Work itself, the activity of producing, is obscured in the quantification of labour. This material evaluation of the repetitive activity of work, capable of being conjugated with a material flow of money, takes entropic equalization as its paradigm – value in exchange aims at a condition of balance where debts are annulled. As with the transcendental illusion of the physical law of the increase in entropy (Deleuze, 1994: 228–9), this equality can only be maintained by implicating inequality elsewhere: flows of credit or finance capital only appear to be equalized with exchange capital, but in fact can be created as and when they are required (1984: 229); and the self-reproducing cultural production of myths of critique and rebellion expresses and reproduces an inequality of affective intensity, separated from social production. Credit and debt in relation to labour are produced in ever-increasing quantities. Drawing on the Marxist theory of alienation, one might say that the abstract representation and quantification of labour excludes the discrete, the alienated, and the repressed (cf. Deleuze, 1994: 13–15): the actual, discrete worker; the materiality of production and the product, including moments of change in the conditions of production; and the affective, intensive moments of the processes of production. The catatonic fantasy of idleness as the natural condition of the worker is therefore a repressing representation that obscures the vast inequalites, dynamisms, and energies that it also produces. We need inactivity, abstract quantification, and mythical rebellion as umbrellas to shelter us from chaos (cf. 1994: 202). The revolution of desire, by contrast, draws its vital energy from chaos; it opposes unitary evaluation by creating new systems of evaluation, and a gentle slide towards new 'banks' of heterogeneous values (Guattari, 1989b: 65–7).

Work and Art

Deleuze and Guattari's thought describes a world that is more and more artificially fabricated. Their 'Marx–Freud' synthesis affirms a world of machines, where capitalist technology is retrospectively projected to become coextensive with the fields of nature, history, and society. This appears to be a triumph for technological reason, even if not for mechanistic determinism. It is, moreover, a deliberate attempt to introduce machinic relations at every level; for example, unrestrained experimentation in genetic science, a further deterritorialization of the organic stratum and its reterritorialization on technology, are consequences of this way of thinking (Guattari, 1992: 17). Yet there is another sphere of activity which is just as artificial as technological production that draws on the most sophisticated technological innovations: art. The realization of abstract, deterritorialized processes does not find its fulfilment in technology so much as in art. For mechanical assembly and aesthetic composition can be distinguished according to whether they are governed by external or internal dynamisms. Technology is teleological: it is produced in order to serve extrinsic purposes. The plane of composition proper to art, by contrast, is a plane of immanence; it is capable of reabsorbing the technical plane (1994: 195). For where the product of technical machines is decided in advance, the product of the work of art is a psychic effect on the viewer that cannot be predicted in advance. Art has its own economics: it can create new values and finalities for human relations and productive activities (Guattari, 1992: 127). Deleuze and Guattari have an aesthetic rather than a technological vision of the world (Guattari, 1992: 137–64). Moreover, their thought becomes expressly oriented towards extending aesthetic relations throughout the fields of nature, history, and society. The ultimate goal of the revolution of desire is 'life as a work of art'.

Art is distinguished from technology by its different relation to matter: in art, matter becomes expressive, instead of purely functional, short-circuiting the division of labour between production and consumption. According to an aesthetic paradigm, the material of culture has a role to play in the processes of production. For the cultural world is territorial, composed of expressive signs; it is closer to an ecological environment, composed of various attractive or repellent expressions competing for the consumer's attention, than a factory in which all significant decisions are taken in an enclosed boardroom. Certainly, capital is able to profit from the fragmentation, plurality, and competition characteristic of such a culture, leading to an ever greater permeation of power-relations throughout the cultural field through machinic domination. Yet if capital depends upon quantum flows of creativity and desire that escape it, then there remains the possibility of these rejoining on an aesthetic plane of composition, apart from the wage-relation.

The molecular revolution is cultural, rather than political, even if it does result in the diminishment of political centres of power. For it pervades all kinds of relations of production – not only those between persons, but also those between any productive machinic processes and territories. The revolution is a multiplication of a kind of desire: instead of desire being reterritorialized on constants such as the coital act, hierarchical status, success, fame, consumption of wealth, accumulation of capital, religious transcendence, rebellion, or transgression, desire diversifies into all manner of becomings. This micropolitical revolution occurs in the domain of popular culture, and can only spread by contagion. Popular films, music, visual art, and fashion are all expressive media that permeate the social field with signs of various territories; they may express a becoming-animal of culture in general. Popular culture can encourage molecular sexualities attracted to rhythms, colours, styles, and mannerisms, even if these flows of desire are reterritorialized on capital through the culture industry. The revolution of public consciousness found in the past four decades, including presuppositions, values, significations, practices, and even humour, witnesses to the power of a cultural revolution, even if this revolution's main achievement so far is only a molecularization of consciousness and politics. As a result of such molecularization, social concern operates at the local level of the status accorded to various minorities or disadvantaged groups, while reactionary politics shifts from emphasizing public obligation and national pride towards private morality and ethnic pride. This molecularization of consciousness does not prevent dramatic, large-scale changes, as witnessed by the molecular revolutions of Eastern Europe. Nor does it prevent microfascisms from proliferating and resonating in such forms as the stereotyping of various supple social segments. Molecular desires may still resonate to form black holes, such as a desire for wealth or fame. The molecularization of culture may reinforce the spread of capital throughout the social field; but it also opens the possibility that culture may be carried away in a revolution of desire. For if it is now from popular culture that people derive their structures of meaning, then it is at this level that power operates, and through engagement at this site that micropolitical revolution can occur. Popular culture is the scene of the politics of desire.

The political valence of culture and art leads us to a familiar problem: is it possible, or even advisable, to distinguish between 'true art' and fashion? Would such a distinction coincide with one between 'high culture' and 'popular culture'? Or is it possible, on the contrary, for fashion and popular culture to overlap the immanent plane of aesthetic composition? Deleuze and Guattari do appear to make a somewhat elitist distinction between high modern art and popular culture; the frequency and distribution of their references corresponds moderately well to a modernist aesthetic canon. Moreover, the instance of aesthetic works that effectively function to resist the dominant socius is regarded as rare (Guattari, 1992: 128). This does seem strange considering their emphasis on collective subjects of enunciation, as opposed to the genius of individual authors, and the need for becoming-minoritarian. Yet the distinction that Deleuze and Guattari draw is not between molar high culture centred on a canon and molecular popular culture centred on diverse cults, trends, and fashions, nor is it one of the cultural status of the author, nor of whether the product has mainstream or 'cultic' popularity; by contrast, it is a question of whether a cultural product expresses a constant or a becoming. Within consumer culture, many products reterritorialize on the same few kinds of heroes, stories, stars, rhythms, forms, colours, fashions, etc. The territories expressed by many marketable products have a reassuring familiarity that is intended to guarantee their economic success and constitute a safe investment. Consequently, such constants reinforce the stratification and segmentation of society. For constant territories have nothing more that they can do; they can only be conjugated for extrinsic purposes, lending themselves to the operation of an economic base. Yet while the resonance of a multiplicity of micro-consumptions is necessary for the survival of large-scale, multinational industries, capitalism also requires the constant renewal of cultural products for its survival in order to renew the needs for consumption and production; it must allow the escape of quantum flows of deterritorialization (1988: 225). Cultural products that express becomings work directly upon desire, and can therefore cut across social boundaries. They effect a deterritorialization, a change in the current state of social presuppositions. They are the dynamisms of intensive difference, the work of desire upon desire.

Deleuze and Guattari explored this distinction in relation to the novel, for this is where many misunderstandings arise (1994: 170). Many novels are constructed in the manner of a diarist or journalist: one reports observations, feelings, opinions; one relates situations one has encountered and people one has met. Such novels express the significations and subjectivity of the author, especially when they are not explicitly biographical. For the leading character, or subject of the statement, is constructed as a constant subject even if this character is not a double of the author. The implicit presuppositions of such works become clearly stated constants. For a novel to become a 'work of art', however, the implicit presuppositions must be constructed at the same time as the text, and through the construction of the text. Art has to attain an immanent plane of composition, where the assemblage of components is determined not by some pre-established code or territory, or a set of implicit presuppositions, but by experimentations of desire in the form of becomings.

Every production of a work of art follows a line of flight, escaping dominant presuppositions. For the author has seen something 'intolerable' in life that shatters the security of a fixed subject of enunciation, whether this 'intolerable' is the banality of everyday life, some terrible evil or catastrophe (1994: 171), or the actual conditions and inequalites of capitalism. Unlike labour, art wishes to tear open the firmament and plunge into chaos, before returning as if from the land of the dead (1994: 202). Writing does not aim to report, observe, or imagine this intolerable vision; instead, like a character in a French New Wave film, the author seems to become incapable of reacting to or naming the atrocity. The vision expands to become coextensive with life, filling the immanent plane. Where labour constructs a closed and finite world, sheltering from chaos, art rediscovers the infinite through the finite object that it fashions, restoring the infinite as a principle of composition (1994: 197).

There is an economy to art: an economy of intensification with respect to change rather than an economy of production with respect to investment. For whereas labour mediates between distributions of commodities, products, and wealth as fixed states or end products of work, the work of art mediates between affective and dynamic excitations. Capital is a self-positing absolute that always displaces its own limits, conjuring away any excessive work or affection by means of an aversion sacrifice: because one works so hard, as labourer or entrepreneur, one need never encounter free activity; because one rebels so vociferously, as critic or cynic, one need never encounter an unknown passion. By contrast, art, like nature, affirms the excessive and wasteful in the form of free activity and unbearable affectivity. By working through matter, art makes visible the imperceptible forces that work upon matter, as well as rendering sensible the non-human forces that work upon us (1994: 182).

Deleuze and Guattari seek salvation through materialism. Instead of conjuring away the unequal and the infinite by representing costs, debts, and equalization in material exchange, art struggles with its own constitutive inequality. For that which is unequal is working and its product, sensation and the object consumed, representation and the forces that determine it, matter and the work of art itself. Moreover, there is a difference in kind between the materials that support a work of art, such as paint, canvas, film, stone, sound-waves, and the work itself. Art only attempts to fashion a material object, having a finite duration, so as to create a being of sensation', which is preserved in itself for an eternity that coexists with the short duration of the material (1994: 166–7). This bloc of sensations, standing up alone or positing itself, contains the working, sensation, and forces of the work.

A work of art can certainly acquire an exchange value. This, however, is of little importance. For the work is already redoubled in itself, repeated in itself, and excessive of itself, in an exchange between matter and sensation. There are three forms of this repetition – vibrations, clinches, and openings (1994: 168). Firstly, the work of art discloses its singularity and discrete existence, even if it is reproduced many times by technical means. It exceeds the combination of material variables from which it is composed. In this respect, the work of art resembles a traumatic encounter insofar as it raises a question: what happened (1988: 192)? A traumatic occurrence – perhaps a physical accident – may be quite explicable according to the laws of nature and chance, but exceeds such an order of law and generality by means of its impact: Why did it happen to me? What has happened? It reveals a fundamental inequality between general laws and discrete events. This resemblance is often noted when works of art are simulated by a work which has a shock value; but art exceeds trauma because it allows us to see and sense things differently. As a result of trauma, one may seek out a purpose for events, yet find none. When one questions a work of art, however, the 'meaning' is to be sought on another level. The technique for extracting a bloc of sensations from material is always the same: 'saturate every atom', 'eliminate all that is waste, deadness, superfluity' (1994: 172).[1] Both the perception and the object are subtracted in order to leave the pure being of sensation. Perceptions and affections that conform to the everyday organization of the world, through codes and presuppositions, must be subtracted in order to raise the problem of the principle of composition. Deleuze and Guattari's favourite example of a minor author is Kafka: his stories most clearly present the social conventions and expectations that are laid upon the characters. Personal episodes actualize the social forces, obligations, and desires that are at work in society as a whole. By removing extraneous content, Kafka's *The Castle* reveals a pure authority, independent of any specific persons or commands; Kafka's *The Trial* reveals the pure social form of the law and its charges, independent of specific prohibitions or actual crimes. Pure forms of authority and law are varieties of the social unconscious in person. In this respect, sensation is first of all a vibration: once the organization of the world in terms of law, generality, and expectation is broken, one is left with a simple 'matter of fact', a suchness, whose principle of composition vibrates in the matter it holds together, becoming indistinguishable from it (1994: 173).

Secondly, affections and feelings are subtracted or subordinated to affects. The work of art reveals the force of that which is 'repressed', that which we do not know that we know. Here, however, affects are passions that escape representation by right – they are emotions that exceed all feeling, constraints or compulsions that are enacted rather than being reflected upon. One does not bring the affect back to the security of representation in consciousness; by contrast, the affect must be sought where it is (Deleuze, 1994: 14). Deleuze and Guattari adopt a motto from Kierkegaard: 'I look only at the movements' (1988: 281). The affect is an internal dynamism that is too deep to be felt; it can only be observed through the actions that repeat it as a compulsion. In order to render the affect sensible, sensations or vibrations couple, without resemblance or identification, each dramatizing, repeating, and becoming the other until the two become indiscernible (1994: 173). Affects exceed liveable experience. Characters in a literary novel are too alive to be 'true to life' or experienced; instead, they incarnate possibilities of life or moments of the world (1994: 171, 177).

The role of the affect is to bring a force of deterritorialization to bear directly upon the recipient. It gives one a sensation that acts directly on the body, without needing to be processed by the significations available in the mind. Deleuze is fond of the paintings of Francis Bacon, which often show cuts of raw meat, contorted bodies, or flesh flowing off bodies onto the ground. The aim of this, according to Deleuze, is not to give one a sensation of horror so much as to allow the nervous system to attain a direct, unmediated sensation. For the sensing body can dramatize the cuts of meat or movements of flesh in the painting; its own movements of deterritorialization can be connected up to those in the painting. Sensations are then experienced directly as intensities on one's body without organs. For

Deleuze, one of the most important functions of art in our age of subjectivity, signification, and simulacra is to make us 'believe' in the body, to
restore a direct self-awareness to the body (Deleuze, 1989: 172). This can
only be done by showing the body in its limitations, along with its postures
and movements such as tiredness, sleep, and illness by which it interrupts
signifiance and subjectification: the body itself becomes expressive
(Deleuze, 1989: 189). Such an awareness of the body is a becoming-animal
that enhances rather than diminishes the possibilities of life, for it awakens
a sensitivity to intensities. All art is haunted by a becoming-animal because
it is capable of expressing codes and territories as intensive physical and
social presuppositions (1994: 175). Art, therefore, has a role analogous to
psychoanalysis: it aims to bring the social unconscious into consciousness
by making the recipient feel the implicit presuppositions that are at work in
various social situations. Where critique leads to the decision by autonomous individuals or societies to censure unacceptable presuppositions, art
acts directly upon such presuppositions in the unconscious in order to
deterritorialize them. Art affects us by showing us ourselves, by incarnating
our deepest presuppositions.

Thirdly, sensation is wrested from perception of the object and states of
the perceiving subject, to become a percept that belongs to matter itself.
Everything is vision, becoming – percepts are the moments of vision that
constitute the world. 'The landscape *sees*. . . . The percept is the landscape
before man, in the absence of man' (1994: 169). The work of art is matter
in a state of nature, alienated from humanity, no longer responding to human
needs or interests. The work of art pays homage to matter as it exists in
itself, apart from its use-value. For if matter itself is shaped by forces and
machinic processes, then it has its own Humean contractions, its own
passive synthesis of time, no longer shaped by human passions. The work of
art opens thought onto the body and landscape, so as to give a voice to the
body before all words (Deleuze, 1989: 172), discovering its postures,
capabilities, and the forces which work upon it. While the percepts of the
landscape cannot be given directly, a withdrawal, division, or distension of
sensation may open sensation onto that which lies outside it. Instead of
being simply shaped by the extrinsic machinic requirements of capital and
efficiency, the work of art opens onto all the forces at work in the
cosmos.

Art and Liberation

Deleuze's works on the cinema are concerned with percepts: the cinema's
ability to construct crystals of time, through the immanent linkage of
apparently unrelated fragments, means that it is particularly suited to
revealing percepts of invisible forces. The crystal is expression, an economy
or exchange of the unequal – matter and sensation, the actual and virtual, the
limpid and opaque, the seed and the environment become indiscernible
while yet distinct (Deleuze, 1989: 74). It is a question of finding a special

kind of balance between the actual and virtual, or the exterior and interior, as the precondition for their exchange. It is a question of fashioning a partial object or phantasm that compensates for the progress and failures of activity (Deleuze, 1994: 99). Whereas capital increases the inequality and disjunction between the material and the intensive, producing a dynamic system that perpetually reproduces and intensifies itself, the work of art is an attempt to become equal to forces, affects, and dynamisms so that they can be expressed and left behind. For the compensatory object of capital, the myth of progress, rebellion, and revolution, only feeds back to intensify the capitalist machine. Myth only constructs an oedipal law, and whether this is obeyed or transgressed, it is merely repeated as an imperative from without or a compulsion from within.

Each production of a work of art is an act of transference or substitutionary sacrifice, a masochistic dramatization of the conflict between law from without and compulsion from within. One escapes oedipal repression by repeating: one constructs a material monument that is adequate to the myth – a chiasmus or figure 8 may be formed that links and exchanges the dissimilar actual and virtual centres of object and sensation (see Deleuze, 1994: 100). By repeating the compulsion in such a way that one becomes equal to it, repetition becomes a condition of creation where the same ritual is no longer repeated (Deleuze, 1994: 19). 'Perhaps one day we will know that there wasn't any art but only medicine' (1994: 173).[2] Art is a question of extracting an irresistible little health from a vision that is too great, to liberate the life that is trapped in man and his organs (Deleuze, 1993: 14).

In cinema, montage, the discontinuous linkage of shots, opens out onto thought as much as it joins images together, for it raises the problem of the reason for each discontinuity. It is the cinematographic act *par excellence* for Orson Welles (Deleuze, 1989: 111), and a number of interesting points can be illustrated through *Citizen Kane*. Kane, entrepreneur and media tycoon, was a man of excess, a giant, a character too great to be real. The film tries to come to terms with the traumatic impact of this excessive figure by exploring his effect on those around him. In one scene, Kane passes before a pair of mirrors, and is infinitely redoubled in a virtual series of figures, into which the actual character is absorbed (Deleuze, 1989: 70). Among the various series of terms that dramatize Kane's life, the film seeks out the limit of the series, the force that constitutes Kane's person, giving meaning to his life and death. Beginning with the death of Kane, the film explores his previous life from the point of view of his death. What was it all about? Kane dies, bereft of friends, pronouncing a single last word: 'Rosebud'. An investigator, suspecting that the meaning of Kane's life, motivations, and desires is embodied in this cryptic word, sets out to discover this meaning by interviewing significant acquaintances of Kane, who each in turn recollect a portion of Kane's life. The camera and the plot of the film are guided by this investigating question: what is 'Rosebud'? Who was Kane? What happened? The subjective force of questioning is made perceptible by the structure of the film. Each portion of Kane's life is reported by the recollection of a witness – each constitutes a layer of the past that coexists with the present time of the investigation. Through each exploration, the film searches for the buried secret of 'Rosebud' in order to restore its vital power. Each recollection fails; 'Rosebud' remains elusive. The pastness of each layer is made perceptible by being recollected in relation to Kane's death. But although many of the recollections film the past as though it were an ancient present, as though it actually happened as such, Welles's technique of using depth of field enhances the perception of the past. Looking into the depth of the image is as though looking back upon the past, with Kane as a distant figure reflected entering the room at the time of his wife's suicide attempt (Deleuze, 1989: 106). The special quality of the depth of field is to show time for itself, defined by memory, as a sheet of the past (Deleuze, 1989: 109).

If Kane is therefore only encountered through the memory of others, it is not surprising that the vital principle which shaped his life is not embodied there. In each of the recollections, the investigator is presented with an account of Kane possessed by a will to power that eventually causes a break with each friend when they are unable to share in his quest. Since time is reconstituted in the film on the basis of the past and judged in relation to a present death, the vital principle has not been observed by others, except as an excess that caused Kane's path to diverge from theirs. The film shows the 'misadventures' of time itself: either past recollections are evoked, but are now useless, or evocation of the past is impossible (Deleuze, 1989: 110).

Once Kane had accumulated unparalleled wealth, he exercised his will to power by collecting a vast quantity of strange and largely worthless artefacts from around the world. After Kane's death, these are burned, and the investigator unwittingly leads the camera to the solution, seen only by the camera: 'Rosebud' is inscribed upon a wooden sledge that is being burnt in a furnace along with the other artefacts; the word is only revealed in a moment between the burning of the paint that had concealed it and the burning of the sledge itself. It is a pointless image, of interest to no one; as such, it raises questions about the truth and value of the other recollections encountered (Deleuze, 1989: 111). There is no longer a truth of Kane's life, only what the witnesses have seen (Deleuze, 1989: 148).

The sledge links back to the opening scene: when Kane had pronounced 'Rosebud' and died, he dropped a child's glass ball containing snow flakes and a winter scene; the ball breaks, and the snowflakes swirl up and engulf the camera until it is filming Kane, as a child, playing on the same sledge. The continuous shot breaks with chronology and a real course of events, only to film Kane's act of remembering; the crystal breaks only in order to give the environment of the film its act of recollection. The trivial nature of the sledge, as an answer to the investigation, would appear to show the vanity of the past, and the vanity of Kane's life as a whole as a failed quest for immortality, based upon accumulation of a memory that is destroyed at his death, along with his possessions. Yet Deleuze sees something beyond this nihilism: instead of referring to the vanity of recollection, the mean-

inglessness of Kane's death reacts back on his whole life to coexist with it
– life itself is a state of permanent crisis, founded upon the fixed point of
death (Deleuze, 1989: 112). Instead of remaining at the fixed point around
which the film is structured, Kane's death retroactively enters the past, now
separate from recollection, so as to coexist with every moment of his life –
time is in a state of permanent crisis or discontinuity; the very foundations
of existence are in crisis. The film, therefore, reveals percepts of three
existential forces through its structure: the force of questioning that
investigates the past; Kane's driving force as a will to power; and a death-
instinct that afflicts the whole of life. By raising the investigative question,
one enters the past; the compulsion that structures experience in the past is
a negative will to power, holding forces in conflict; but the principle or
imperative that structures existence as such is a death-instinct, a move
towards decay.

The aim of art, for Deleuze, however, is not to make moral or existential
judgements about our conditions of experience. Instead, it is a question of
wrestling with the vision that is too much for us, in order to disengage a
force of life. The negative will to power as a compulsion from within and the
death-instinct as an imperative from without are too much for us, too strong
to be lived, insofar as they constitute the being of the past in general.
Deleuze had criticized the Freudian death-instinct for deriving from a
conflictual model of the drives (that is, a negative will to power) and a
material concept of repetition (Deleuze, 1994: 111) – here actualized in the
form of anticipating a repetition of 'Rosebud' as it had previously existed.
Death, here, has only an extrinsic and objective definition (Deleuze, 1994:
111). The work of art, by contrast, can dramatize the experience of death so
as to rediscover its meaning in the unconscious (Deleuze, 1994: 114). When
'Rosebud' is finally presented in *Citizen Kane* it is through a time-image of
the passing present moment: the word is revealed momentarily in the
interval between the burning of the paint that conceals it and the burning of
the sledge on which it is inscribed. When repeated materially, therefore,
'Rosebud' is merely seen by no one, in a pure percept of matter, of no
interest to anyone and immediately being destroyed. At the same time,
however, the unconscious meaning of death is seen by the viewer. Now it is
no longer Kane who dies, and whose death constitutes the extreme limit of
his power, but death itself is an impersonal singularity – the meaning of
death is that 'one' dies who is without any relation to Kane, for in the fact
of Kane's death, Kane is no more (see Deleuze, 1994: 112). At the
beginning of the film, Kane's death was intensely personal, and his life,
which was too weak for his strong character, slipped away at a moment that
was becoming present; death was actualized. At this stage, 'Rosebud' must
be defined in relation to the character of Kane. At the end of the film,
however, Kane is no more – he is too weak for life, and life overwhelms
him, scattering its events in no relation to him; death is counter-actualized
(see Deleuze, 1991b: 151–2). Now, by pronouncing the word 'Rosebud',
Kane merely bears witness to a life that is independent of him and too strong

for him. This is actualized in the film itself, independent of the influence of the character of Kane.

The work accomplished by the film is therefore something much greater than a nihilistic presentation of vanity in the face of the predicament of impending death. Death is turned back against the excessive compulsions and imperatives of recollection. In a later film by Welles, *Mr Arkadin*, the problem is that of how to prevent one's own past from being recalled. The hero wards off an investigator by murdering all the witnesses who could recollect his past (Deleuze, 1989: 113). Freedom from the past is never gained by recollection, reconstituting an event as though it were present; it is gained by forgetting, so that the event may turn back upon itself and repeat itself in itself. *The Trial* takes this movement to its conclusion. The problem has changed again: in which layer of the past is the hero, now also an investigator, to look for the offence of which he is supposed to be guilty? The layers of the past now send forth hallucinatory presences instead of recollections: a series of women, books, little girls, homosexuality, and paintings in juxtaposition, where nothing is decidable any more (Deleuze, 1989: 114). The past breaks up into chaos. Death becomes a permanent present, and time, as perpetual crisis, becomes a primary matter, intense and terrifying (Deleuze, 1989: 115). Layers and discontinuities are ordered by a higher justice, but the most serious law-book is also a pornographic book (Deleuze, 1989: 114). The true name of law is desire.

Art passes through the finite and rediscovers the infinite (1994: 197): the infinite compulsion of desire and the infinite justice of chaos (1994: 203). It expresses this compulsion by repeating a refrain, a material object that is infinitely repeated in itself, in intensity. In each repetition, it appears as disguised and displaced: it can therefore acquire a double status, participating in both matter and sensation, rendering the two indiscernible (1994: 193; Deleuze, 1994: 123). Through a counterpoint of affect and percept, infinite forces can be framed in a house or territory, and rendered liveable (1994: 179, 186). For the work itself becomes a home, balancing the inequality of the infinite and finite in its material composition and framing – home economics, penetrated by the forces of the cosmos, replaces capitalist exchange. The unconscious itself, the home of the work of art, becomes a questioning and problematizing force (Deleuze, 1994: 108).

The artist longs for work, is compelled to work, but the work itself is produced by an other whom the artist becomes in the process of working. If the work itself remains discrete, alienated, and repressed, this no longer reflects an inadequacy or principle of death at work in the artist so much as an excess of life present in matter. For nature, like art, combines finite compounds and an infinite plane of composition (1994: 186). Nature is filled with internal dynamisms that escape representation on a scientific plane of reference. In the work of art, humanity ceases to be alienated from the plane of nature. There is no longer a distinction between nature and artifice, between the products of work and the products of nature. The percept made possible by art is always a revelation of the unity of nature and humanity

(Deleuze, 1989: 96). As affect or sensual revelation, this unity becomes intensely personal. If this revelation always comes too late, so that it is that which always escapes being shown, as in *Citizen Kane*, then it is because such a revelation belongs to the future as its mode of being: it is always revealed in eschatological terms as that which is yet to come. Art appeals to a future people who will grasp this grandiose revelation, and dwell in crystalline houses that open onto the infinite cosmos. In the utopia of immanence, the vibrations, clinches, and openings made possible for men and women (1994: 177) will constitute daily life according to an aesthetic paradigm.

Notes

1. Deleuze and Guattari quote Virginia Woolf (Woolf, 1980: 209–10).
2. Deleuze and Guattari quote Jean-Marie Le Clézio (Le Clézio, 1991: 7).

9

The Society of Desire

Collective Activity

Desire is collective: it is a quality of social relation that is actualized in collective production. It is a social plane that one constructs and a way of life within which one dwells, consisting of actual relations between people. Deleuze and Guattari's 'utopia', if one can use this concept at all, is neither an ideal society, nor the result of an anticipated historical development (1994: 99–100). Instead, it is immanent, 'here and now', present in the bonds that exist between people, even if such bonds quickly give way to betrayal (1994: 177). The aim of the politics of desire is to intensify these bonds between people.

The society of desire is not simply a loose, bohemian association of Parisian artists and thinkers. The revolution of desire does not aim to transform everyone into artists as such. Instead, the social domain itself becomes a collective field of aesthetic experimentation: one invents by establishing new kinds of relations and syntheses. Aesthetic experimentation is primarily directed to the micropolitical bonds between people, and between people and environment. Here, there is no individual mastery over a specific domain; all action is collective because a collective way of living is constructed. The aesthetic paradigm replaces current forms of art and social life by means of a collective production of subjectivity. In opposition to the current construction of subjectivity via the media, the revolution of desire involves the local development of the means of production of subjectivity. In line with his involvement in Radio Alice, a free radio station in Paris in the late 1970s, Guattari envisaged the arrival of a post-media era, characterized by a reappropriation of media by a multitude of collective subjects for the purpose of resingularization (Guattari, 1992: 17).

Collective activity is where the politics of desire meets its essential confrontation with capitalism. For capital regulates relations of production through its capacity to fragment, privatize, and segment the socio-economic field; it effectively dominates the bonds that exist between people by virtue of its segmentarity. Although capital itself exists within a broader aesthetic and ecological field, where anything might affect anything else, it prospers by segmentation, warding off its own limits. Invisible barriers are erected in the formation of individual subjects, with their own needs, thoughts, beliefs, and loves that are distinct from the conditions of experience. These barriers, constituted by lines of representation, are themselves dependent on the lines of machinic functioning, the invisible barriers erected in the production of technology along with the technologization of relations of production. Denial of ecological relation is inherent in the technological process, for the experimental scientific method depends on an isolation of the investigated process from unpredictable environmental influences in order to establish a functional dependence of certain selected variables. When the results of experimentation are applied in the production of technology, one constructs a machine that is similarly isolated from the unpredictable effects of the environment so that a given input will always be processed in a dependable way. The materials furnished for technical machines are often selected for their non-reactivity in appropriate contexts. Similarly, the organization of the means of production in a capitalist enterprise, whether it belongs to the industrial, commercial, or service sector of the economy, is designed to minimize the effect of environmental, social, and cultural influences in order to select a given input and process it with a maximal level of efficiency. Consequently, attention is turned internally to the process itself, along with its immediate input and output; more distant effects on the social, cultural, and ecological environment as a whole are irrelevant to the immediate growth of capital. In the activities of both production and consumption, capitalism requires minimal awareness and affectivity; hence its specialized knowledges are enveloped in an ignorance of the wider network of relations that constitutes the world. This refusal to examine the actual machinic relations that are produced outside and between economic units is the reason for capitalism's scandalous environmental incompetence.

Fragmentation of machinic functioning is itself dependent on the segmentation of desire. For technical machines, segmentation is simple and material: delicate machines are encased within walls of steel or plastic. At the organizational level, architectural segmentation reflects and augments pre-existing socio-economic segmentation. Yet for the repression of desire, the barriers preventing desire from being reinvested in the productive social field are incorporeal. Indeed, rather than repression working by enclosing a metaphysical energy or impulse within an imaginary box, repression operates through deterritorialization: desire is disinvested from its immediate socio-economic territory so as to be reinvested in something absolutely deterritorialized: a signifier or subject, a face. Segmentation is the facialization of the social field, where social events are now only simulated; every segment is interpreted by a regime of signification, and divided by black holes as points of subjectification. Such a deterritorialized desire wants something outside of the social field: a transcendental signified such as happiness, God, wealth, fame, or, if black holes are dominant, another subject. Desire that reterritorializes on a transcendental signifier is a negative will to power: it aims to encompass the whole world in its interpretations. Desire that circulates around a black hole becomes a death-instinct, a line of pure terror or abolition. The mastery of capital over desire then appears unshakeable, for desire will always turn towards absolute deterritorialization, even if this takes the negative form of a signifier or a subject.

This repression of desire finds its fulfilment in fascism. For Deleuze and Guattari, capital is haunted by fascism as the limit of the tendency of desire (1988: 230). Fascism arises at the micropolitical level, even if many microfascisms may later resonate and form a nationalist movement. For microfascism results when Oedipus becomes deterritorialized from a specific content of prohibition and a specific representation of desire, in order to attain an infinite form. Oedipus, deterritorialized from the family, may reterritorialize on a race, a nation, an ideal, a myth, a cause, a face, or capital itself; its failure to reconstitute such an ideal in reality gives strength to its repression of all that does not conform to the oedipal project. Having found the ideal, encountered through the infinite oedipal structure, Oedipus overthrows traditional forms of morality and humanistic concern in order to actualize its far superior ideal. The degree of terror it produces is commensurate with its level of paranoia.

In relation to this threat of absolute deterritorialization from wild and excessive destratification, conformity within the strata is far safer (1988: 160–6). The reason for Deleuze and Guattari's concern with fascist desire is that it also masquerades as a politics of desire, aping revolutionary moves at every turn. There is no end to the variety of ways in which desire may circulate around a signifier or black hole, engaging in paranoid repression, or exercising a will to annihilation of self and other. Indeed, caution, sobriety, and asceticism are required at every stage, for if a line of flight loses its power, finding no further terms with which to conjoin, then it may fall back into a line of pure abolition: the lines of flight 'emanate a strange despair, like an odour of death and immolation, a state of war from which one returns broken' (1988: 229). For lines of flight connect up to the infinite energies of chaos itself; if one fails to give chaos a consistency, a finite form, or a reference, then it turns to an unlimited force of primary repression – the hell encountered in psychosis.[1] The death-instinct is itself constituted by a specific arrrangement of desire that, having attained the infinite form, reterritorializes on the face of death itself (1988: 230–1).

Deleuze and Guattari's thought can be tested by the way in which it handles this resurgence of drives for terror and annihilation within desire. For there is no way of rationalizing moderation or caution in a purely active politics of desire, where forces always go to the limit, and the extreme form is always selected. This impasse, far from blocking the politics of desire in a 'post Holocaust neurosis' that fears the resurgence of fascism at any moment,[2] measures the profundity of Deleuze and Guattari's thought, and its difference from the marginals and drop-outs who might adopt similar slogans. For the dangers of despair, addiction, suicide, madness, and sociopathology that threaten all marginals who attempt to drop out of the productive economic socius are the direct result of being excluded from relations of production. Nomadic existence, by contrast, takes place in intensity, in the actual relations constructed between persons – within such a network of actual relations, there is no longer a danger of antiproduction. According to the politics of desire, one never makes a conscious decision to overthrow or escape from the strata – such marginal activity is largely fuelled by *ressentiment*. Instead, one can only be driven out by the creative impulses of desire that arise in unexpected encounters. Desirers are like Kierkegaard's knight of faith: they are imperceptible, even bourgeois – after a real rupture, one succeeds in being like everybody else. This requires much asceticism, sobriety, eliminating all complaint and grievance, all unsatisfied desire, defence or pleading (1988: 279). Desirers seek nothing, resent nothing, destroy nothing – they merely love and create, adsorbing transcendent illusions into their immanent plane. They advance like Japanese Sumo wrestlers: moments of inactivity, remaining within the strata, are interrupted by a movement and hold that is too fast to see (1988: 281). The politics of desire takes its voyages in intensity: one remains within the strata all the time, or at least on their surface, making the stratified world into a series of abstract lines and traits (1988: 280). There is no outside in liberated desire, and consequently no danger of paranoia; there is merely a surface that can be folded up topologically, rather like a Zen master who intersperses the everyday with nonsense and paradox.

The Illusion of Ends

Here we have arrived at capital's final dissimulation: the absolutely deterritorialized terms of a transcendental signifier or subject have no ontological status on a Spinozist plane of relations; similarly, a 'repressed' desire, whether in the form of a negative will to power, a desire to be repressed, or a death-instinct, has no ontological status. All we have are certain tendencies towards absolute deterritorialization produced by the faciality machine operated by capital. Given this limitation, the capitalist socio-economic machine cannot be regarded as having an absolute social status, even if it pretends to do so through its capacity to displace all relative internal limits. Fascism and death are not the end. Indeed, capital is merely an environment in which other kinds of power-formations can flourish. Guattari regarded the idea of a single, hegemonic global market as merely a myth; in fact, there are sectorial markets with independent power-formations and systems of values (Guattari, 1992: 170–1).

If capital is an illusory absolute, one can say that the revolution of desire is then simply a matter of forming alternative socio-economic assemblages; there are no real barriers to be overthrown. Indeed, the conjunction of deterritorialized quantum flows in order to produce new productive machines is happening all the time. Yet capital's real strength lies in its capacity to overlay such new flows of desire with its quantifying segments of capital, for every new creation can be fed back into the market, whether as production or as antiproduction. Capital will seduce desire with its promises of absolute deterritorialization. More rigorously, the revolution of desire can only succeed by pushing forward to a new threshold of deterritorialization. What is required, therefore, is not a dismantling of the capitalist socius so much as its superseding by a more advanced socio-economic machine. Capitalist segments must become the material for a new mode of expression: in the same way that nucleic acid molecules are merely building blocks for the genetic code, arranged in an arbitrary order that, not being determined by themselves, is imposed upon them by an external machinic arrangement, segments, faces, and simulations can become a form of content for an independent machine of expression. A cultural 'super-structure', composed of a new collective subjectivity, must seize the initiative from the economic base. Hence Deleuze and Guattari advocate an acceleration of the internal processes of capitalism towards its own demise, at the level of the machinic unconscious, rather than at the level of capital (1984: 321).

Capital is able to ward off an advancing socius by disempowering its own subjects and simulations: no immanent relations can form between these because they are not productive machines themselves. Simulations do not affect the social presuppositions that condition them because they do not act directly upon bodies. Capital destroys the bond between our thought, now in the form of simulation, and its productive action within the material world. In this regard, Deleuze's study of the cinema finds its full political significance in its discovery of a use of incorporeal images or simulations that is capable of directly affecting bodies through constructing a belief in this world, as it is (Deleuze, 1989: 172, 189). Instead of retreating to a pre-social mode of immanent relation, Deleuze affirms the separation, anti-production, or death that capital allows to suffuse everywhere, for this is the condition of our world as it is. When differing simulations, segments, or thought and the body confront each other, they do so across the void or non-relation that is death (Deleuze, 1989: 209). Segments and simulations cannot discover their own immanent interaction.

Deleuze turned to the later work of Foucault to simulate the discovery of a solution to this problem: 'folding the line of the outside' is a movement that will pull thought back from the void and snatch it away from death (Deleuze, 1988d: 96).[3] The plane of immanence does not belong to the simulations themselves; it belongs to an 'outside' or immanent surface that works on the bodies producing the images. The force of segmentation appears to be a force of the outside that works as a kind of death-instinct, destroying relation. Yet it can be 'counter-actualized' by applying itself back upon itself, so that segmentarity will itself become segmented from a smooth space of desire. The aim is not to do away with simulation and segmenta-tion, but to redouble them, exposing their illusory nature at the same time as constructing a machine to manipulate simulacra. The forces of death and separation can be neutralized by simulating them. For example, *Citizen Kane* simulates death, a negative will to power, and a death-instinct, but it does so by drawing on positive, creative forces from outside – not least of all, the question guiding the investigation that structures the whole film. The model or simulation of death can be worked upon in order to produce something. The creative thought that manipulates the images is more deterritorialized than the economic machine in which the film, is incorporated; it also has more enduring consequences in the form of its influence upon the range of expression available to later directors. Deleuze's work on the cinema, therefore, points towards a productive exercise of thought that is more deterritorialized than the productions of capital. For where the productions of capital are reterritorialized upon an abstract quantity, the productions of cinema images are reterritorialized upon a plane of 'thought' (Deleuze, 1989: 168). This is not simply the capacity of cinema to show our everyday processes of thinking, but a capacity to show the birth of thought, a thought alongside its own conditioning, or something 'unthinkable' at the heart of thought that gives rise to thought (Deleuze, 1989: 165–8). Then it is not the actual simulations themselves that interact and are placed in relation, but the unconscious bodies and desiring-machines that produce simulations: the plane operates by a machinic 'ecology of the virtual' (Guattari, 1989b: 68; 1992: 127).

In contrast to capitalist representation, Foucault's process of 'subjectiva-tion' is the production of a new kind of 'memory' or recording – even if it is no longer a territorial one (Deleuze, 1988d: 107). Instead of being a memory of former experiences, it becomes a resource-bank of technologies of the self. Real differences may be recorded once more. The techniques of production that one learns and discovers from elsewhere are folded back and applied to one's own life, so that life is produced as a work of art (Deleuze, 1991b: 137). When the line of the outside is folded, it encloses a small region of the forces from outside within the self that can act as a membrane across which our own plane of simulations and social forces can commu-nicate (Deleuze, 1988d: 122–3; 1989: 206–12). This 'memory' or 'mem-brane' is the plane of thought – the plane of immanence specific to thinking.

For Deleuze and Guattari, of course, the 'outside' is not a transcendent source of spontaneous forces, but a plane of consistency of desire that has to be constructed. There are no pre-existent 'forces of the outside'; indeed, the 'outside' is merely the plane of immanence. For prior to its construction, the immanent plane of desire takes the form of chaos. Deleuze and Guattari are also more interested in applying the notion of the fold at an immanent and collective level, as opposed to confining it within a self: in his work on Leibniz, Deleuze expanded the fold to become coextensive with life as a whole, giving an ontology and epistemology; in *What is Philosophy?*, Deleuze and Guattari discuss the fractalization or infinite folding of the plane of consistency (1994: 39).

The fold liberates desire from the capitalist socius. It fractalizes and reproduces itself by masquerading under the form of capital. For capital also includes a folding-machine within itself: if capital's first function is a generalized decoding and deterritorialization of all flows, followed by a reterritorialization of these on the abstract quantity of capital, its second function is folding this operation back upon itself, deterritorializing exchange capital so as to reterritorialize it upon a credit capital that measures anticipated rates of profit. The abstract machine of capital operates in an isolated, solipsist world where it only measures degrees of capital, and is only affected by other productive machines by translating their flows into its own terms of capital. Being able to overcome its contradictions, capital absolves itself from all other relations with the world.

There is one irresoluble contradiction that remains within the capitalist machine: it is inseparable from a reterritorialization. This occurs primarily as a reterritorialization of all flows on arbitrary, archaic signifiers, but it also occurs as a reterritorialization of credit capital onto exchange capital. Quantum flows are converted back into segments. This reconversion is only possible because the flows measured by exchange capital can be reterritorialized on signifiers. The insuperable contradiction of capital is that its quantum flows of belief and desire, inherent within credit, are more deterritorialized than its archaic signifiers. It is therefore theoretically possible to isolate the flows of belief and desire from their reterritorialization on credit capital, so as to fold them back upon themselves as specific styles and modes of existence. In practice, this process is already partially evident within capitalist culture: capital undermines its apparent ends and turns attention to the means. For example, in Integrated Global Capitalism, a particular style of believing in God or religious identity is more worthy of belief than the God believed in; a particular sexual identity is more attractive than sexual consummation; a particular social policy is less worthy of trust or mistrust than the politicians who carry it out; and the accumulation of a large quantity of wealth is less exciting than making a quick profit. Reterritorializations do not endure, for capital encourages a further reterritorialization on the process, as opposed to imaginary goals.

Revolution may occur through the intensification of this process within capital. Credit, folded back on itself, produces credit, not an exchangeable quantity. People are trusted who are capable of generating trust, and such trust becomes the precondition for collective activity. Such a refolded 'capital' no longer needs to be quantified; one discovers the liberation of autonomous and non-quantifiable flows of belief and desire. Trust, however, is inseparable from its own reterritorializations; while it may function as an unconscious presupposition, one only trusts another in regard to some particular purpose or end. As an a priori of social relation, trust is rather like the ethical principle of self-sacrificing altruism: one can only have compassion for another in relation to some particular end, such as health or wealth, that one renounces on one's own account. Trust merely needs to be folded back upon itself once more in order to open itself to a new threshold of deterritorialization: trust in trust, an immanent faith in this life as it is (Deleuze, 1989: 172), opens itself to be determined by the actual territorial relations existing in life: desire. Capital attains its own hidden plane of immanence, its own 'outside', which is desire. Such a liberated desire has a curious structure: it is deterritorialized from desire, and reterritorializes upon desire. There is a continuous exchange, a repeated, folded, fractalized movement, where the needle is also the pole: consistency replaces segmentation (1994: 38). Desire becomes a plane of 'thought' – the displacements of desire are directed by a 'thought of the outside' (Deleuze, 1990b: 220) which now constitutes the social field.

Virtual Utopia of Immanence

This liberated desiring-machine, like the abstract machine of capital, is only affected by the social field in such a way as to enhance desire. In a sense, it would appear to have a solipsist self-existence that bypasses the social field entirely.[4] The plane of desire is an experience of 'death', a body without organs consisting only of smooth flows (1988: 153). This socius of desire can only function, therefore, by incorporating the flows and segments of the social field into its own productive machine; the body without organs must be populated with intensities. Desire is the intense body without organs, the immanent plane of abstract machines that are interposed as becomings and mutations in the relations between assemblages, giving them a consistency (1988: 399–400, 506–8, 510–14). Desire operates by rhythmic intercalation: it joins non-reactive parts together (1988: 333). One does not begin in desire, or possess desire as a subjective drive; desire does not belong to an assemblage, for this, after all, is merely a phantasm or simulacrum. Instead, one is granted desire by being brought into a relation of consistency with another assemblage.

This socius of desire, the full body without organs, recalls Deleuze's empiricism: relations are external to their terms. The social field is like a set of film images, and desire is the director who constructs relations through montage. All the real action is taking place 'out of field' in the machinic unconscious; but the irrational cuts of desire have the capacity to reveal the forces that are out of field. The social field of desire now behaves with all the properties of the machinic unconscious: desire conducts its own politics. Desire escapes the field of simulacra and phantasms that constitute conscious and unconscious images. It has no substantial essence; the flows of desire only exist as movements of deterritorialization and reterritorialization on other flows – they are partial desiring-machines. When images are assembled, nothing happens; yet this moment of stoppage or antiproduction is the beginning of production. Desire dismantles the images, tracing lines of flight through new connections, in an attempt to produce the pure plane of desire, where everything stops once more. Life is contained between these two deaths, the model and the experience, but, between the two, life and creation take place (1984: 329–31; Deleuze, 1989: 209). In the same way that philosophical thought seeks an 'unthinkable' source of thought, desire seeks an 'undesiring' source of desire. Hence although the philosophy of desire begins with illusions and simulations, it constructs its own consistency and plane of existence.

The utopia of desire is no better than capital in giving an encyclopedic knowledge of the whole causal nexus of production that constitutes our world. Yet, having escaped from abstract quantification, it attempts to insert relations of desire and consistency throughout the socio-economic field. It therefore has a radical openness that is not shared by capital: it aims to construct relations of desire and consistency across all segments of the socio-economic field. It produces machinic heterogenesis. This means that instead of segments being isolated, or acting upon each other with a destructive force, interaction is always double deterritorialization. Mutual relationality is restored.

The revolution of desire is therefore a re-ecologization of the social field. Instead of processes being oblivious of their effects, they are immediately and directly affected and changed by their environment as a result of the way in which they change the environment. There is no preservation of particular parts, nor of some overall state of equilibrium. Instead, desire increases, as does the overall number and intensity of relations of consistency between heterogeneous processes of production. The ecological affectivity of each abstract machine is intensified. To achieve this aim, the range of relations available to each member of society or concrete machinic assemblage are increased; assemblages are produced that, unlike the blood-sucking tick, have the widest possible range of affects. These function as singular points in the social fabric, rather like clover-leaf highway interchanges (1984: 241). They are multiplicities with a vast number of dimensions, acting as points of exchange, transducers, or relays across a wide variety of segments. *Capitalism and Schizophrenia* as a work is a paradigm of such an intense, nodal interchange. Yet the multiplicity has to be produced at the level of the abstract machines, rather than the concrete assemblages; to this end, the concrete assemblages can even be isolated from the surrounding environment, like bodies without organs, so that they can build their own intense planes of consistency as memories of de-actualized affects. A book produces nothing unless its concepts are re-created in an intuition specific to them. Guattari called the mode of thought needed to work within the ecological field of desire 'ecosophy' (Guattari, 1989b: 70).

The revolution of desire is also an aestheticization of the social field: it takes the social field as its material that it will build into a monument of sensation, exceeding matter. The implicit presuppositions of social relations are sensed, not represented. Instead of desire being immediately present through territorial expression, as in societies of animals, it is withheld in order to be intensified (1988: 158). Then it is no longer simply a matter of popular culture – of signs, rhythms, images, colours, styles, and sounds being fused into an expressive territory. Instead, the territories become virtual, implicit, disguised, and displaced. Affects cannot be directly communicated; they can only be shown indirectly by the becomings-animal of artist-citizens. The real action takes place out of field: it is always aesthetic redemption from the illusory forces of death. The society of desire is therefore like an association of experimentally constructed subjects, each with their own memory or plane of consistency. Each communication between subjects points to the relations of desire that exist outside of the field of awareness. Such aesthetic communications, exemplified by *Capitalism and Schizophrenia*, entirely respect the autonomy of the recipient: all traces of force, power, and rhetoric are subordinated to an attempt to act at the level of desire alone.

This utopia of immanence is constructed as a kind of cultural super-structure, a way of thinking and living, within the socius of capital. In order for this seed to crystallize into a complete cultural revolution of desire, the seed has to be actually and historically present in a particular social relation. It may derive from an abstract machine that has never previously been actualized, but it can only spread once it has become historically present in a particular process of production, leaving a trace of itself that can deterritorialize the thought of others. The seed for the society of desire was in fact present in Deleuze and Guattari's intellectual relation. The co-authorship of Deleuze and Guattari, where each adopted the concepts and modes of thought created by the other, produces a kind of collective memory characterized by a high level of consistency. The processes of living and thinking that Deleuze and Guattari write about, the actual content of their work, express what they first of all practise in the virtual way in which they think. Far from the respective autonomies of their thought being compro-mised by co-authorship, with its constraints of signing one's name equally to the thought of another as to that of oneself, their capacities to explore their own independent intellectual projects and inquiries were enhanced by borrowing from each other's conceptual resources. Although Deleuze and Guattari may have had different fields of interest, the end product of the co-authorship, *Capitalism and Schizophrenia*, witnesses to consistency and indiscernibility where their concerns meet each other.

Desire, together with the way in which people think, is always produced by and within a particular social field. The social field that gave rise to Deleuze and Guattari's thought was their own collaborative intellectual relation. Not only is a collaborative project essential for a social theory of desire and relations, giving a real actualization of the abstract machines revealed in their thought, but Deleuze and Guattari's own social theory is both an adequate expression of the social relation that they constructed between them, and the means through which such a social relation could be constructed. The revolution of desire was created, in the form of a seed, in the life and thought of Deleuze and Guattari.

Problem 9: On ethics and becoming-Deleuzean

Whether or not Deleuze merited the extravagant praise accorded him by Michel Foucault, one thing seems to be clear: this century cannot simply be described as 'Deleuzean' (Foucault, 1977: 165). Indeed, few have even understood Deleuze's work, let alone count it as a determinative influence. Of course, it is probable that Foucault merely meant that Deleuze was able to conceptualize most successfully in *Difference and Repetition* the explorations and dynamics at work in French thought and culture. But perhaps one of the most appropriate acclamations from Foucault is to be found in the preface to the English edition of *Anti-Oedipus*: 'I would say that *Anti-Oedipus* (may its authors forgive me) is a book of ethics, the first book of ethics to be written in France in quite a long time' (1984: xiii). It is possible that the meaning and force of Deleuze and Guattari's concepts will always remain incomprehensible to the majority. If, one day, there may be some Deleuzeans, they will probably be those who add a specifically Deleuzean ethos or style of life to their mode of existence. Such an ethos can never be possessed or attained: one can merely enter and dwell in the middle of it, on a plane of immanence.

Deleuze admired, above all others, the ethics of Spinoza (1988: 153; 1994: 60). In many ways, both lived a contemplative, philosophical life, writing books, removed from some of the labours and cares of everyday life. For Spinoza, the philosophical beatitude of contemplating eternity acquired a strange twist: instead of the eternal being withdrawn from the temporal, in some Platonic realm of reminiscence, the eternal is a condition of being or power of existing, not simply an exercise of thought: it is an ethic, a way of living. A Deleuzean ethic, likewise, wishes to recapture the presence of the infinite (1994: 197). But the infinite must be torn from its representations in order to be rediscovered in life: Deleuze's vitalism struggles with an intense, unbearable, unliveable life surging in the chaos that lies between thoughts and things. A Deleuzean maintains struggles on two sides at once (1994: 203): against a death that is the completion of living, the grasping of which shelters us from access to vital forces – perhaps an opinion, a cliché, a product, a feeling, a perception; and against a too-vital life that overwhelms, scattering singularities and unbearable intensities all around – perhaps the chaos of science, with its unpredictable events, or else the chaos of thought encountered in psychosis. 'The philosopher is someone who believes he has returned from the dead, rightly or wrongly, and who returns to the dead in full consciousness. . . . This has been the living formulation of philosophy since Plato' (Deleuze, 1989: 209).

A Deleuzean lives in the world as though already dead. This is the condition of living a vital and full life, escaping repetitive movements of the death-instinct. Much can be dispensed with: morality, opinion, and judgement, for example. For all morality is based on a negative representation of death: everything will be judged in relation to whether it produces life or death for complete persons. To help is to restore to life; to harm is to destroy; but what kind of life is helped or destroyed? What opinion does one have of life? Unlike Guattari, who had much to say about everything, Deleuze expressed few opinions. A Deleuzean renounces life in opinion and representation in the hope of finding life in experience.

A Deleuzean is also one who is able to have done with judgement (Deleuze, 1993: 158–69). An ethic that lacks judgement would appear to mark the death of ethics, in the way that one used to announce the death of philosophy, or history, or reason, with a flourish of world-historical pathos. Perhaps one should say that this is a reduction of ethics to a condition of univocity, of single-mindedness, of simplicity: there is only one ethic of philosophy – *amor fati*, affirmation – the irresponsibility of necessity, the innocence of existence. How much complexity can be implicit in this simplicity. At any rate, the love of fate is necessary to have done with judgement, so that one no longer judges existence from a perspective that claims to be higher.

Deleuze extracted the condition that makes judgement possible from Nietzsche: conscience has a debt before God – the debt becomes infinite, and therefore unpayable (Deleuze, 1993: 158). Each time one judges, one claims sufficient knowledge of a particular case. Such an opinion appeals to an infinite knowledge of space, time, and experience: for each case of this kind, wherever it occurs, the same conditions apply. To judge is always to impose a boundary that will never be crossed: a case never transgresses what it is, never becomes something other. Moreover, judgement must appeal to ultimate criteria as absolute standards or grounds of legitimation. Such standards, if they are absolute, have absolved themselves from any kind of relation by which they could be affected and changed. Grounds themselves are unattainable – they merely ground themselves in a structure of turn and return: justice alone is just, the appropriate measure for itself. But what if justice turned out to be unjust, a pretender, a simulacrum (Deleuze, 1994: 60–2)? Justice justifies itself, in a structure of infinite regression. It is for this reason that any appeal to a standard of justice involves an appeal to the infinite – to the ground that grounds the ground. In each case, the ground is not self-present, but constitutes a problem.

This appeal to an infinite ground plays a specific micropolitical role: it absolves one from any genuine encounter. For the surprising, the painful, the over-whelming, the monstrous, the psychotic, and the sublime – while exceeding all representation – can reinforce the idea of the infinite, and the grounding of the ground, by making appeal to a ground that is not yet understood. Nothing can force one to renounce the idea of the infinite, for the greater the extent to which representation is exceeded, the greater the need for an infinite ground to ground representation. Judgement forms a white wall that reflects all encounter, or a black hole that absorbs all force, overlaying others with a potential face, even if it cannot be seen too clearly. By appealing to the infinite, one loses the finite – one is always cut off from others by fragmentation and segmentation. One defends one's territorial body with the walls of the infinite, constructing one's soul as a windowless monad.

It is extremely difficult to have done with judgement, with its infinite appeal, neurotic self-questioning, and compulsions. Deleuzean ethics counterpose affir-mation to judgement: they restore encounter. Ethics concern relations rather than representations – moral judgements are replaced with a micropolitical ethos, involving an exchange of forces, a contest, a struggle. Each encounter is a violent penetration of bodies or souls: one is wounded, changed, modified by an encounter, for one is struck by that which exceeds representation, affecting one's very constitution, including one's power of representing. Death no longer func-tions as the limit within representation, in relation to which all will be judged. Instead, it functions as a limit to representation, for one's continuing to live and think in the same way. Since a Deleuzean lives in the world as though already dead, the wounds that affect one have no effect in representation – there is no grievance, complaint, *ressentiment. Amor fati* – a Stoic and Nietzschean formula – does not complete Deleuzean ethics, but renders them possible.

How does one proceed? Once torn from the context of representation, ethical conduct becomes problematic. Particular cases can no longer be subsumed under general principles. Decisions must still be reached, but instead of these resulting from judgements, they resolve struggles between forces (Deleuze, 1993: 168). Conduct turns away from the infinite ideal of the Good, ceasing the pretence of participating in good conduct. Justice becomes impossible by right; all conduct exhibits a certain cruelty, even if this is only a cruelty exercised against oneself. For a force is not an action; there is a constitutive inequality in all action proceeding from force – one can never find precise compensation without causing further effects elsewhere. Force may dramatize and symbolize itself in action, disguising and displacing itself, but there is no action capable of 'resolving' a force.

An ethic of encounter has no concern with obligation or response, with placing either self or others first. All such questions may be directed to hypothetical situations, but an ethic of encounter explores the forces present in real situations. For one does not choose one's problems: they are given to one in the forces one encounters. This ethic begins with a tranquil atheism that finds no problem in the existence of God (Deleuze, 1988e: 7): the infinite in representation never acts as a force; it is a false problem. Ethics proceeds from a passivity or impotence at the heart of conduct: a power to be affected (Deleuze, 1988b: 123). If one is not affected by an encounter, one can enter no relation with the other encountered. The problem of ethical conduct is that of finding an appropriate response – in the sense of making life liveable once more – to express the forces acting in a specific encounter.

Ethical conduct is therefore problematic in several senses: all infinite grounds withdraw, so that one can no longer represent the 'just deed'; having renounced the infinite, there are no longer any guidelines or principles of good conduct except for local, provisional, and questionable ones; one cannot try to be moral – ethical conduct begins when one reaches the limits of one's power; one faces the problem of finding an appropriate response to a specific situation of encounter; and all responses are cruel, all action is beyond measure, for each act affects the discrete individual in a way that exceeds representation and cannot be anticipated. Ethical conduct can only begin with a modest acceptance of this problematic: we are not yet capable of ethical conduct.

Deleuzeans have little concern with the unjust strife between force and force. Impacts from others are received with a Deleuzean pathos that has its own values. Since destructive forces are always exchanged among people, it is much better to destroy oneself under agreeable conditions than to destroy others (Deleuze, 1988e: 12). There is a Deleuzean form of asceticism: one exercises a violence against oneself – the forces that react are turned back to modify one's own life. Consequently, one treats others with courtesy or politeness: one establishes a certain distance between people, neither too far nor near, so as to prevent an exchange of blows (Deleuze, 1988e: 13–14). If Deleuzeans exhibit philosophical detachment, seeming to be unaffected by the events, encounters, or wounds that constitute life, this is because they are affected too deeply to respond. This courtesy also expresses a disposition: one never knows in advance whether an other will be able to actualize the forces of life through their own processes and rationalizations (Deleuze, 1988e: 14). One does not establish distance for the sake of the other, but for the sake of the potential others who might come to life through the other. One acts, or refrains from acting, for the sake of the future, the people who are still to come. There is a specifically Deleuzean form of generosity: to allow others to work through their own processes, and to offer them resources for that end. One has faith in the other, in the possibilities of the other – one regards the identity of the other as mere simulation, the activities of the other as dramatization. One expects them to change. One shows generosity by not believing what the other says; instead, the speech of the other is merely necessary for them to have done with a specific opinion. One seeks an ethical intensity – the intensity of friendship – that always exceeds expression in speech and conduct.

In Deleuze's case, such ethical guidelines are an expression of a vitalist and optimistic philosophy. Each wound constitutes a problem for an affirmative ethos: one has to discover how to turn its sad passions into active joys. How does one turn excess into friendship? How does one rescue life from death? In Spinoza's ethics, all relations are mediated by the infinite, for every modification affects the monistic infinite substance. One affirms one's wound if one is able to relate to it from the perspective of eternity. In Deleuzean thought, the mediating infinite must also be rediscovered in the finite: one can regain the infinite if one is able to extract an event from states of affairs. Encounters become problems for thought. Self-destruction, detachment, and generosity are simply techniques for attaining an absolute threshold of deterritorialization, where a thought responds to an act.

There are events of friendship for which no one is responsible. Such events exceed all conduct – they happen if one affirms all chance. Unlike friendship conducted within representation, where one is attracted to others with whom one has something in common, a friendship of encounter relates the different to the different. When one is affected too deeply by this encounter with difference, conduct can no longer appeal to habits and memory in order to discover how to proceed – one has seen something in the other's life that one does not possess or understand. Perhaps it is something that exceeds the human; certainly, it is implicit, something of the order of a style of life, a force acting through the other that exceeds all representation. One becomes impassioned with the hope of learning such a style of living so as to make something with it. Passion motivates thought – the problem of ethics encounters something unthinkable that forces us to think. This passion disguises and displaces itself through the conduct that it selects: since that which is desired exceeds representation, then this passion does not know itself; it can only act through something else. It thinks by trying out roles and disguises, always adding something new to its way of life. It cannot speak on its own account, but requires a series of intercessors (Deleuze, 1991b: 171). Everything is performance, role, disguise; every act enfolds the intensity of the force. If such a passion is reciprocated, in a process of double deterritorialization, then asymmetrical evolution ensues: there is a mutual invagination of each other's processes, a sharing of intercessors.

There is also a plane of such events: the socius of desire. This plane is characterized by a fractalized, infinite movement of turn and return through which it builds consistency. In the course of history, events of friendship come and go: one remembers or anticipates them. On the geophilosophical plane, however, if passions affirm and enfold each other, then they constitute a single, abstract machine that acts through both. Great events of friendship affirm themselves: they are self-positing, the affirmation of force by force in an infinite movement of consistency. Unlike the infinite regression of the ground, they are the eternal repetition of an other, a force of differentiation or mutual passion, in the moment of encounter – an infinite progression of the future. A voice speaks in friendship that has never before been heard. It is the voice of a transcendental other, speaking in a foreign language of a possible world, showing its face through a series of intercessors, always singing a new modulation of its refrain. It joins expression and content, language and world, self and other. The finite bonds of friendship become an aesthetic form, a home in which one dwells, a mode of relationship that is affected by cosmic forces (1994: 177–97).

There is a body without organs specific to friendship.

> At any rate, you make one, you can't desire without making one. And it awaits you; it is an inevitable exercise or experimentation, already accomplished the moment you undertake it, unaccomplished as long as you don't. . . . On it we sleep, live our waking lives, fight – fight and are fought – seek our place, experience untold happiness and fabulous defeats; on it we penetrate and are penetrated; on it we love. (1988: 149–50)

This material of friendship is a 'first ontological fold' (see Guattari, 1992: 157) that detonates thought. What happened? What has become of us? What are we becoming? Intercessory modes that were formerly separate have been joined together. One creates a concept of their inseparability, intuitively grasping them as components all at once in the overflight of thought at infinite speed (1994: 21).

Thought embraces life in the concepts of friendship. The voice that thinks, a conceptual and ethical persona, is the other who inhabits the plane of immanence and animates the transcendental field. It has existential features, being a mode of existence or possibility of life (1994: 72): it creates a concept of friendship and creates friendship with the concept. It has juridical features, appealing to the absolute by right, positing an absolute immanent plane, while not excluding the multiplicity of other absolute planes (1994: 72). It has dynamic features, expressing itself through dramatization and movement, turning each intercessor into a symbol capable of affecting the mind outside of representation (1994: 71; Deleuze, 1994: 8). It has relational features, being itself a mode of relationship (1994: 71). Finally, it has pathic features (1994: 70): each ethical persona exceeds majoritarian social roles. One becomes ethical by dramatizing the thought of a nomad, a mimic, a schizophrenic, a believer, a masochist, a joker, an ascetic, a sorcerer, a singer, a lens-grinder, or an impassioned lover (Goodchild, 1996: 148–9). Earnestness is mere metaphysical presumption. Only humour, disguise, displacement, and passion can save friendship. Desire is a capacity to invert, laugh at, let go, forgive, transform, and express both self and other.

Notes

1. In *A Thousand Plateaus*, Deleuze and Guattari attempt to think as far as possible from a plane of consistency. This results in a minimization of the role of chaos (1988: 311–13), and the supplementation of abstract machines by forces of the Cosmos (1988: 326–7, 342–6). The abstract machines are in danger of becoming abstractions of thought, no longer invested by desire. There is a marked return to chaos in Deleuze and Guattari's latter work (1994; Guattari, 1989a, 1992).

2. As asserted by Nick Land, who argues for a return to the Freudian death-instinct as 'a hydraulic tendency to the dissipation of intensities' (Land, 1993: 74). Land does not address Deleuze's critique of the Freudian reasons for invoking a death instinct: a conflictual theory of drives, and a material model for repetition (Deleuze, 1994:111). Of course, such a hydraulic tendency is an illusory effect of desire (Deleuze, 1994: 240), but desire remains implicated in itself, intensifying itself, apart from its production of dissipation. By remaining attached to an transcendental principle, albeit a nihilistic and aesthetic one (Land, 1992), Land remains pious: there is no true immanence or libidinal materialism here. Indeed, attachment to such a principle prevents the emergence of desire, with its relations of consistency and positive ontology. The thirst for annihilation is merely the pure form of transcendental principle now self-consciously devoid of content; it is a transcendental form of fascism that destroys all joy in immanence and becoming.

3. Arguably, the use of 'folding' that Deleuze sees in Foucault's aesthetics of existence is derived from Deleuze's discussion of the 'narcissistic ego' (Deleuze, 1994: 110), and relates to esoteric understandings of the eternal return.

4. See my notion of 'spirit' in Goodchild (1996).

Conclusion

Supposing thought should function on an ecological plane ... There is no other conclusion that follows from pluralism, multiplicity. The modern rational ideal of a thought that seeks the truth is broken once more. Thoughts survive if they work, if they propagate, if they exchange fragments of code with other thoughts, if they mutate randomly, if they find an appropriate milieu, a welcoming territory. Thoughts are the genes of the spirit. They will only maintain their appeal if they can form some kind of alliance with what we do.

Thoughts are in competition for the scarce resources of our attention. To gain affective value, each thought has to make use of its intellectual milieu. There are thoughts that pass and fade. There are thoughts that conjugate with an experience that lends them validity. There are thoughts which repeat themselves over and over again, positing themselves as unquestionable absolutes. There are thoughts that attempt to ground themselves in other, successful thoughts, and share a little of their glory. There are rebellious thoughts that bring an affective reward. There are thoughts that organize human life so successfully that they manifest their own truth in their performance. There are thoughts that are merely tools of non-thinking powers. There are thoughts that evaporate, but become martyrs to their own evaporation: Evaporation is all! Non-thinking is all!

Perhaps thought has been admired too much. Gilles Deleuze, who has shown himself as one of the most intense thinkers of this century, has a formula of reversal: 'Life will no longer be made to appear before the categories of thought; thought will be plunged in to the categories of life' (Deleuze, 1989: 189). Theory can never be purified from its cultural, political, and psychological conditioning. Renunciation of an idolatrous worship of thought, and its pretensions to truth, involves many sacrifices. There will never be a thorough knowledge of society and culture. There will never be a perfect pragmatic or political strategy expressed in thought. There will never be utopian political progress heralded by theory. There will never be a perfect insight into unconscious conditioning. There will never be definitive rational moral guidance. The theories that have hitherto promised such possibilities have prospered largely through their success in gaining adherents, constructing partial visions of the world, functioning as a resource into which emotions can be invested. The time is coming when one will question the value of such pleasant activities.

Thought is a virtual environment, a plane in which we dwell. If we do not master thought, then thought may master us, and we will become its servants, or the servants of abstract machines that do not think, but govern thought. Each time we appeal to thought to solve our problems, we lend it an authority that it does not possess by itself. We allow it the pretension of participating in infinite comprehension as an angel of the rational God. If infinite comprehension becomes a prerogative or aspiration of man, so that thought speaks on behalf of man, then man becomes a form of imprisonment for humanity. We do not know what a thought can do. We do not know what each thought is up to, what it produces, what forces it serves – one only discovers these by experimentation and experience.

To have done with the judgement of thought: this is to strip thought of its infinite pretension. For a 'will to truth' is nothing more than a 'will to power': it is an act of metaphysical presumption, of vicarious conquest – even if I cannot grasp the whole world, at least I may participate in a thought that grasps the whole of experience, or fully grasps one tiny area of experience. By appealing to a potentially infinite power of comprehension, thought mediates relations between the thinker and the thought environment that leave both unaffected, yet fragmented. Under such conditions, autonomous, self-propagating ideas come to mediate relations within humanity, and between humanity and environment, that construct their own extrinsic, machinic purposes. The world becomes governed by impersonal abstract machines, the success of which depends purely on their ability to propagate themselves.

One will accomplish little in such an ecological context by struggling for the rights of man. For it is this very struggle that, appealing to the infinite, becomes a form of imprisonment for humanity. Instead, it is necessary to renounce the possibility of attaining the absolute in order to regain it actually, to find the absolute where it is. If knowledge is finite, then it is merely a modification amid a plane of modifications. The task of thought changes: one aims to increase in power rather than know the truth. One engages in a political and ecological struggle, motivated by a desire to create and become.

Political action itself has its own appeal to an infinite that is never evident: a will to dominate. One attempts to enclose the entire world within one's territories and representations so that one can predict and control each move, each gesture, each becoming. One wards off all unforeseeable relations, unnatural participations, becomings, and complex emergences. One stratifies and segments, fragments and compartmentalizes, decreeing opinions as though they were judgements of God. Nevertheless, there remains an 'outside' to the world that one does not control; failure to think about such an outside does not prevent it from acting. By expressing a will to dominate, one becomes subject to extrinsic machinic forces that make use of one's decrees for inhuman purposes. The appeal to the infinite, motivated by a paranoid fear of the future, judging life from the perspective of one's own death, enables one's own domination to be sealed.

To accept one's ecological finitude in respect of thought and action is to affirm the innocence of existence. It is the one ethical act, above all others, that is needed in our time. While masquerading as despair or nihilism, it rejoins one to the absolute. Identity and world-view become fragmented and partial. One identifies oneself as a complex adaptive system within a generalized ecology of body and mind: the only goals become repetition, random mutation, autocatalysis, exchange of codes, and heterogeneous emergence. A will to dominate is replaced by a will to power, where power is the capacity to affect and be affected. One relates to the other finite modes that constitute one's environment, milieu, and territory.

Deleuze and Guattari have constructed the first ethic appropriate to such an ecological vision of the world. The interest of their thought is determined not by its validity as knowledge, nor by its critical power, but by its capacity to form an immanent plane in which one may dwell: an ethos. Such an ethos constitutes a style, a way of living and relating, that is collectively constructed in the bonds between people. As a mode of relating, it is a politics of desire. Deleuze and Guattari offer a possibility for social and cultural revolution through a form of collective action. This operates on the social unconscious of desire by changing the way in which thought and meaning are produced. One enters this collective action not by following what Deleuze and Guattari have said, but by being infected by their desire. One gains little from reading *Capitalism and Schizophrenia* in order to critically assess expressed opinions; one gains much from reading it to experience its intensities, to build a memory of ideas, to put its ideas to work in various contexts, and to explore the paths that lead off in all directions. One gains even more from reconstructing its consistency: each movement of thought, wherever it is stolen from, is repeated in a different context to change implicit presuppositions and construct an unthinkable plane, a 'plateau of intensity', that gives birth to new ways of thinking, living, and relating. Deleuze and Guattari have no privileged position to speak on behalf of this unconscious of desire; yet their theory is able to show it in operation. Knowledge becomes a memory of techniques and resources for overcoming segmentation and returning to relation. Power becomes a capacity to produce new social relations between differentiated and fragmented terms. Desire becomes a drive to live a life of relation, creation, and intensity.

It is possible that such an ethos opens itself once more to an absolute: one that is no longer claimed by right, but discovered in experience, surging within immanent relations between people. It is possible that such an ethos opens the way to voyages in intensity, strange becomings, altered states of subjectivity and consciousness, disguises and displacements that dramatize the absolute amid everyday experience. Of such a possibility, little can be said – yet much can be done. Try it and see.

References

Deleuze and Guattari (Co-authored)

(1984). *Anti-Oedipus* (1972), trans. Robert Hurley, Mark Seem and Helen R. Lane. London: Athlone.
(1986). *Kafka: Towards a Minor Literature* (1975), trans. Dana Polan. Minneapolis: Minnesota University Press.
(1988). *A Thousand Plateaus* (1980), trans. Brian Massumi. London: Athlone.
(1994). *What is Philosophy?* (1991), trans. Graham Burchell and Hugh Tomlinson. London: Verso.

Other Works

Alliez, Éric (1993). *La signature du monde, ou qu'est-ce que la philosophie de Deleuze et Guattari?* Paris: Cerf.
Althusser, Louis (1969). *For Marx*. London: New Left Books.
Althusser, Louis (1971). *Lenin and Philosophy*. London: New Left Books.
Barthes, Roland (1972). *Mythologies*. London: Jonathan Cape.
Baudrillard, Jean (1983). *Simulations*. New York: Semiotext(e).
Baudrillard, Jean (1988). *Selected Writings*. Cambridge: Polity.
Baugh, Bruce (1993). 'Deleuze and Empiricism', *Journal of the British Society for Phenomenology* 24:1, pp. 15–31.
Bhaskar, Roy (1989). *Reclaiming Reality*. London: Verso.
Bogue, Ronald (1990). 'Gilles Deleuze: Postmodern Philosopher', *Criticism* 32:4, pp.401–18.
Boundas, Constantin V. and Dorothea Olkowski (eds) (1994). *Gilles Deleuze and the Theater of Philosophy*. London: Routledge.
Boyne, Roy (1990). *Foucault and Derrida: The Other Side of Reason*. London: Unwin & Hyman.
Braidotti, Rosi (1991). *Patterns of Dissonance*. Cambridge: Polity.
Braidotti, Rosi (1993). 'Discontinuous Becomings: Deleuze in the Becoming-Woman of Philosophy', *Journal of the British Society for Phenomenology* 24:1.
Caputo, John D. (1993). *Against Ethics*. Indianapolis: Indiana University Press.
Colombat, André (1990). *Deleuze et la littérature*. New York: Peter Lang.
Deleuze, Gilles (1971). *Masochism: An Interpretation of Coldness and Cruelty* (1967), trans. Jean McNeil. New York: George Braziller.
Deleuze, Gilles (1972). 'A quoi reconnait-on le structuralisme?' in François Châtelet (ed.), *Histoire de la philosophie 8*. Paris: Hachette.
Deleuze, Gilles (1977). 'Nomad Thought' in David B. Allison (ed.), *The New Nietzsche: Contemporary Styles of Interpretation*. New York: Dell.
Deleuze, Gilles (1981). *Francis Bacon: Logique de la sensation*. Paris: Différence.
Deleuze, Gilles (1983). *Nietzsche and Philosophy* (1962), trans. Hugh Tomlinson. London: Athlone.

Deleuze, Gilles (1984). *Kant's Critical Philosophy* (1963), trans. Hugh Tomlinson and Barbara Habberjam. London: Athlone.

Deleuze, Gilles (1986). *Proust et des signes*. Paris: Presses Universitaires de France.

Deleuze, Gilles (with Claire Parnet) (1987). *Dialogues* (1977), trans. Hugh Tomlinson and Barbara Habberjam. London: Athlone.

Deleuze, Gilles (1988a). *Bergsonism* (1966), trans. Hugh Tomlinson and Barbara Habberjam. New York: Zone.

Deleuze, Gilles (1988b). *Spinoza: Practical Philosophy* (1970), trans. Robert Hurley. San Francisco: City Lights.

Deleuze, Gilles (1988c). *Le Pli: Leibniz et le Baroque*. Paris: Minuit.

Deleuze, Gilles (1988d). *Foucault* (1986), trans. Sean Hand. Minneapolis: Minnesota University Press.

Deleuze, Gilles (1988e). *Périclès et Verdi*. Paris: Minuit.

Deleuze, Gilles (1989). *Cinema 2: The Time-Image* (1985), trans. Hugh Tomlinson and Robert Galeta. London: Athlone.

Deleuze, Gilles (1990a). *Expressionism in Philosophy: Spinoza* (1968), trans. Martin Joughin. New York: Zone.

Deleuze, Gilles (1990b). *The Logic of Sense* (1969), trans. Mark Lester and Charles Stivale. London: Athlone.

Deleuze, Gilles (1991a). *Empiricism and Subjectivity* (1953), trans. Constantin V. Boundas. New York: Columbia University Press.

Deleuze, Gilles (1991b). *Pourparlers*. Paris: Minuit.

Deleuze, Gilles (1992). 'What is a dispositif?' in Timothy Armstrong (ed.), *Michel Foucault Philosopher*. Brighton: Harvester Wheatsheaf.

Deleuze, Gilles (1993). *Critique et clinique*. Paris: Minuit.

Deleuze, Gilles (1994). *Difference and Repetition* (1968), trans. Paul Patton. London: Athlone.

Derrida, Jacques (1976). *Of Grammatology*. Baltimore: Johns Hopkins.

Derrida, Jacques (1978). 'Plato's Pharmacy' in *Writing and Difference*. Chicago: University of Chicago Press.

Derrida, Jacques (1979). *Spurs: Nietzsche's Styles*. Chicago: University of Chicago Press.

Derrida, Jacques (1981). 'Force and Signification' in *Dissemination*. London: Athlone.

Derrida, Jacques (1982). 'Différance' in *Margins of Philosophy*. Brighton: Harvester.

Eigen, Michael (1986). *The Psychotic Core*. London: Jason Aronson.

Erebon, Didier (1992). *Michel Foucault*. London: Faber and Faber.

Foucault, Michel (1966). *The Order of Things*. London: Routledge & Kegan Paul.

Foucault, Michel (1977). 'Theatrum Philosophicum' in *Language, Counter-Memory, Practice*. Oxford: Blackwell.

Foucault, Michel (1979). *History of Sexuality Volume I: The Will to Knowledge*. London: Allen Lane.

Foucault, Michel (1980). *Power/Knowledge*. Brighton: Harvester.

Foucault, Michel (1986a). 'Nietzsche, Genealogy, History' in Paul Rabinow (ed.), *The Foucault Reader*. London: Penguin.

Foucault, Michel (1986b). 'What is an Author?' in Paul Rabinow (ed.), *The Foucault Reader*. London: Penguin.

Foucault, Michel (1987). *History of Sexuality Volume II: The Use of Pleasure*. London: Penguin.

Foucault, Michel (1988). *History of Sexuality Volume III: The Care of the Self*. London: Penguin.

Foucault, Michel (1989). 'Maurice Blanchot: The Thought from Outside' in Michel Foucault and Maurice Blanchot, *Foucault/Blanchot*. New York: Zone.

Freud, Sigmund (1950). *Totem and Taboo*. London: Routledge & Kegan Paul.

Freud, Sigmund (1955). 'Beyond the Pleasure Principle' in *The Complete Psychological Works of Sigmund Freud Volume XVIII*. London: Hogarth.

Goodchild, Philip (1996). *Gilles Deleuze and the Question of Philosophy*. Cranbury: Associated University Presses.

Guattari, Félix (1984). *Molecular Revolution* (1977), trans. Rosemary Sheed. London: Penguin.

Guattari, Félix (1989a). *Cartographies schizoanalytiques*. Paris: Galilée.

Guattari, Félix (1989b). *Les trois écologies*. Paris: Galilée.

Guattari, Félix (with Antonio Negri) (1990). *Communists Like Us* (1985), trans. Michael Ryan. New York: Semiotext(e).

Guattari, Félix (1992). *Chaosmose*. Paris: Galilée.

Hardt, Michael (1993). *Gilles Deleuze*. London: UCL Press.

Heidegger, Martin (1979). *Nietzsche Volume I*. San Francisco: Harper & Row.

Heidegger, Martin (1993). *Basic Writings*. Basingstoke: Macmillan.

Irigaray, Luce (1985). *This Sex Which Is Not One*. Ithaca: Cornell University Press.

Jardine, Alice (1984). 'Woman in Limbo: Deleuze and His (Br)others', *Sub-Stance* 44/45.

Jardine, Alice (1985). *Gynesis: Configurations of Woman and Modernity*. Ithaca: Cornell University Press.

Kafka, Franz (1988). 'Josephine the Singer, or the Mouse Folk' in *The Collected Short Stories of Franz Kafka*. London: Penguin.

Kant, Immanuel (1929). *Critique of Pure Reason*. Basingstoke: Macmillan.

Kierkegaard, Søren (1983). *Fear and Trembling & Repetition*. Princeton: Princeton University Press.

Klein, Melanie (1969). *The Psychoanalysis of Children*. London: Hogarth.

Lacan, Jacques (1980). *Écrits: A Selection*. London: Tavistock/Routledge.

Land, Nick (1992). *The Thirst for Annihilation*. London: Routledge.

Land, Nick (1993). 'Making it with Death', *Journal of the British Society for Phenomenology* 24:1, pp. 66–76.

Le Clézio, Jean-Marie (1991). *HAI*. Paris: Flammarion.

Lévinas, Emmanuel (1985). *Ethics and Infinity*. Pittsburgh: Duquesne University Press.

Lyotard, Jean-François (1971). *Discours, figure*. Paris: Klincksieck.

Lyotard, Jean-François (1977). 'Energumen Capitalism', *Semiotext(e)* 2:3.

Lyotard, Jean-François (1989a). *The Lyotard Reader*, edited by Andrew Benjamin. Oxford: Blackwell.

Lyotard, Jean-François (1989b). *The Differend*. Minneapolis: University of Minnesota Press.

Lyotard, Jean-François (1993). *Libidinal Economy*. London: Athlone.

Mattéi, Jean François (1983). *L'Étranger et le simulacre*. Paris: Presses Universitaires de France.

May, Todd G. (1993). 'The System and its Fractures: Gilles Deleuze on Otherness', *Journal of the British Society for Phenomenology* 24:1, pp. 1–14.

Nietzsche, Friedrich (1956). *The Genealogy of Morals*. New York: Doubleday Anchor.

Nietzsche, Friedrich (1961). *Thus Spoke Zarathustra*. Harmondsworth: Penguin.

Nietzsche, Friedrich (1968). *The Will to Power*. New York: Vintage.

Nietzsche, Friedrich (1973). *Beyond Good and Evil*. Harmondsworth: Penguin.

Nietzsche, Friedrich (1979). *Ecce Homo*. Harmondsworth: Penguin.

Plato (1973). *Phaedrus*. Harmondsworth: Penguin.

Prigogine, Ilya and Isabelle Stengers (1985). *Order Out of Chaos*. London: Fontana.

Reich, Wilhelm (1961). *Selected Writings*. New York: Farrar, Strauss & Cudahy.

Reich, Wilhelm (1969). *The Sexual Revolution*. London: Vision.

Saussure, Ferdinand de (1974). *Course in General Linguistics*. London: Fontana.

Spinoza, Baruch (1989). *Ethics*. London: J.M. Dent.

Spivak, Gayatri Chakravorti (1988). 'Can the Subaltern Speak?' in Cary Nelson and Lawrence Grossberg (eds), *Marxism and the Interpretation of Culture*. Basingstoke: Macmillan.

Wheelwright, Philip (1959). *Heraclitus*. London: Oxford University Press.

Woolf, Virginia (1980). *The Diary of Virginia Woolf*, ed. Anne Olivier Bell. London: Hogarth.

Žižek, Slavoj (1991). *Looking Awry*. Cambridge, Mass.: MIT Press.

Žižek, Slavoj (1994). *The Metastases of Enjoyment*. London: Verso.

Glossary

NOTE: This non-technical glossary is intended to be neither exhaustive nor definitive. It is merely provided for readers as a reminder of the approximate meanings of words that often slip the mind. Its intention is to produce glosses rather than strict definitions of concepts.

absolute deterritorialization	crossing a threshold where produced elements begin to constitute their own worlds according to autonomous, machinic processes
abstract machine	the immanent relations that constitute a particular machine, process or assemblage
actuality	concrete presence
affect	a feeling or emotion that exerts a force; a pure, pre-personal state of emotion that is not defined in relation to a consciousness that experiences it; a capacity to affect or be affected
asignifying sign	a sign that has become a pure event, and no longer signifies anything outside of that which it is
assemblage	a collection of connected parts that has a consistency
becoming	a process, lacking subject or goal, undergone by a multiplicity when it is deterritorialized by another multiplicity; a production that identifies composition and function
biunivocal	two words that refer to the same distinction
black hole	a focus for meaning that is itself an asignifying sign
body without organs	an unproductive duration; a site where intensities are distributed; a desiring machine that does not function; the totality of all unconscious processes
chaos	the absence of consistency; 'primal' matter and/or thought
chaosmosis	the process by which chaos gives rise to consistency, and influences the course of events
codes	marks or signs that are taken to signify certain habits or conventions
collective assemblage of enunciation	the grouping of a number of factors that influence and produce a certain statement
conceptual persona	a style of thinking; a way of creating concepts and tracing a plane
conjugation	the joining of a pair of processes in such a way that production ceases
conjunctive synthesis	holding together diverse elements so as to produce an effect of identification
connective synthesis	assembling; the stringing together of intensities or desiring-machines with productive effect

consistency	the binding together of ingredients in a recipe so as to produce a single taste
content	the body or idea designated by speech
crystal	an exchange between actual and virtual terms that reveals their source
desire	a spontaneous attraction and emergence of relation
desiring-machines	the working components of the unconscious
desiring-production	the process by which desire and production increase each other
deterritorialization	leaving home and travelling in foreign parts
disjunctive synthesis	the separation of series; grasping syntheses as separate
duration	the passage of time grasped as a whole; the time that passes during a lived experience
earth	the whole of matter or content
existentializing function	a crystallization whereby the same entity appears in both expression and content
expression	style, manner, language
fractalization	infinite repetition of a process that can be grasped algorithmically all at once; the production of a complex entity through repetition of a simple process
genealogy	the study of the forces that produce particular symptoms
haecceity	thisness; an occurrence or happening
immanence	entering entirely into a produced plane, like a computer programmer becoming a variable in her own programme
immanent relations	relations that constitute the space in which they exist
imperial formation	a State society, organized around a transcendental signifier
incorporeal	an event or effect on the surface of bodies
intensity	degree of sensation or feeling; vibrancy or vitality
intensive difference	a difference that differentiates itself from itself, such as a change in intensity of light
machine	an assemblage of parts that works and produces
machinic heterogenesis	the complex emergence of an entity from an encounter between various differing formations that collaborate to give a single result
majoritarian	of the perspective belonging to the majority, the norm
majority	the constant features of a population against which all variations can be measured
micropolitics	the power relations that operate at an interpersonal level
minoritarian	expressing a process of becoming or transformation
minority	a part of the population that escapes the interpretive categories of the majority
molar	rigid sedimentations which function according to laws of statistics, so that the effects of precise details, differences and singularities are cancelled out
molecular	flexible processes, whose nature may be affected by the process or its constituents; working according to specific interactions; often occurring in local or small-scale situations
multiplicity	variety, diversity
oedipalization	the removal or repression of desire, by focusing attention on an ideal world or structure that is never affected by real processes
order-word	a command or slogan implicit in speech
overcoding	the encoding of a set of codes by another set of marks

partial objects	organs that are encountered in unconscious phantasy
percept	a vision or insight that is not defined in relation to an observer that sees it; a revelation of another mode of being
phantasm	an image, usually unconscious, into which libido is invested
phantasy	unconscious fantasy that motivates a certain conduct
plane of consistency	a level where all relations are immanent; same as plane of immanence
plane of immanence	an absolute level at which all things are grasped according to the immanent relations that constitute them; a presupposition about the nature of thought and being
postsignifying regime	a regime of signs where signs are punctuated by black holes, or a multiplicity of transcendental signifiers; often encountered in capitalism
primitive, territorial regime	a regime of signs that operates through marking bodies
refrain	the content proper to music; through its repetition, it can form a territory or else be deterritorializing
reterritorialization	making a new dwelling place
rhizome	a multiplicity that wanders like the roots of certain plants
segmentarity	the breaking up of a continuous process into discrete stages
signifiance	the production of chains of signifiers; a tendency to signify, or to interpret all meaning in terms of signification
signifying regime	a regime of signs where each sign refers back to another, and ultimately to a transcendental signifier; the regime of signs that operates in a State
simulacrum	an image that simulates an identity or essence
singularity	a remarkable, unrepeatable turning point in a process
socius	phantasm of social space; presupposition as to what 'being-with others' means
statements	components of discourse that make a difference to relations between bodies
subject of enunciation	the speaker
subject of statement	the speaker as represented in language as 'I'
subjectification	the process of formation of a particular, fixed subjectivity
subjectivation	a process of self-construction of a subject
synthesis of time	a formal process of grasping a multiplicity
territory	a group of objects, ideas, and persons that constitute one's dwelling place, to whom one relates and with which one functions; a territory is often grasped as a whole
transcendental signifier	an asignifying sign to which all other signs refer
univocal	having one meaning
virtuality	real, yet imperceptible potential, often stored in the past
white wall	a limit to meaning imposed by signification

Index